Exploring Vocabu

Routledge Introductions to Applied Linguistics is a series of introductory level textbooks covering the core topics in Applied Linguistics, primarily designed for those beginning postgraduate studies, or taking an introductory MA course as well as advanced undergraduates. Titles in the series are also ideal for language professionals returning to academic study.

The books take an innovative "practice to theory" approach, with a "back-to-front" structure. This leads the reader from real-world problems and issues, through a discussion of intervention and how to engage with these concerns, before finally relating these practical issues to theoretical foundations. Additional features include tasks with commentaries, a glossary of key terms, and an annotated further reading section.

Vocabulary is the foundation of language and language learning and as such, knowledge of how to facilitate learners' vocabulary growth is an indispensable teaching skill and curricular component.

Exploring Vocabulary is designed to raise teachers' and students' awareness of the interplay between the linguistic, psychological, and instructional aspects of vocabulary acquisition. It focuses on meeting the specific vocabulary needs of English language learners in whatever instructional contexts they may be in, with a special emphasis on addressing the high-stakes needs of learners in academic settings and the workplace.

Dee Gardner also introduces a new Common Core List, constructed from two of the most well-known and contemporary corpora of English – the British National Corpus and the Corpus of Contemporary American English.

Exploring Vocabulary is an essential book for undergraduate and postgraduate students studying Applied Linguistics, TESOL, or Teacher Education, as well as any teacher working with English language learners.

Dee Gardner is an Associate Professor of Applied Linguistics and TESOL at Brigham Young University. He is the co-author of *A Frequency Dictionary of Contemporary American English* (Routledge, 2010).

Routledge Introductions to Applied Linguistics

Series editors:

Ronald Carter, *Professor of Modern English Language, University of Nottingham, UK*

Guy Cook, *Chair of Language in Education, King's College London, UK*

Routledge Introductions to Applied Linguistics is a series of introductory level textbooks covering the core topics in Applied Linguistics, primarily designed for those entering postgraduate studies and language professionals returning to academic study. The books take an innovative 'practice to theory' approach, with a 'back-to-front' structure. This leads the reader from real-world problems and issues, through a discussion of intervention and how to engage with these concerns, before finally relating these practical issues to theoretical foundations. Additional features include tasks with commentaries, a glossary of key terms and an annotated further reading section.

Exploring English Language Teaching
Language in Action
Graham Hall

Exploring Classroom Discourse
Language in Action
Steve Walsh

Exploring Corpus Linguistics
Language in Action
Winnie Cheng

Exploring World Englishes
Language in a Global Context
Philip Seargeant

Exploring Health Communication
Language in Action
Kevin Harvey and Nelya Koteyko

Exploring Professional Communication
Language in Action
Stephanie Schnurr

Exploring Language Pedagogy through Second Language Acquisition Research
Rod Ellis and Natsuko Shintani

Exploring Vocabulary
Language in Action
Dee Gardner

Exploring Intercultural Communication
Language in Action
Zhu Hua

Exploring Language Assessment and Testing
Language in Action
Anthony Green

Exploring Vocabulary

Language in Action

Dee Gardner

Routledge
Taylor & Francis Group

LONDON AND NEW YORK

First published 2013
by Routledge
2 Park Square, Milton Park, Abingdon, Oxon OX14 4RN

Simultaneously published in the USA and Canada
by Routledge
711 Third Avenue, New York, NY 10017

Routledge is an imprint of the Taylor & Francis Group, an informa business

British Library Cataloguing in Publication Data
A catalogue record for this book is available from the British Library

Library of Congress Cataloging in Publication Data
Gardner, Dee.
Exploring vocabulary: language in action / Dee Gardner.
pages cm. – (Routledge Introductions to Applied Linguistics)
Includes bibliographical references.
1. Vocabulary. 2. English language–Rhetoric. I. Title.
PE1449.G3297 2013
428.1–dc23
2013006474

ISBN: 978-0-415-58544-6 (hbk)
ISBN: 978-0-415-58545-3 (pbk)
ISBN: 978-0-203-79868-3 (ebk)

Typeset in Sabon
by Saxon Graphics Ltd, Derby

Printed in Great Britain
by Bell & Bain Ltd, Glasgow

Contents

Illustrations

Figures

Tables

Series editors' preface

The Introductions to Applied Linguistics series

This series provides clear, authoritative, up-to-date overviews of the major areas of applied linguistics. The books are designed particularly for students embarking on masters-level or teacher-education courses, as well as students in the closing stages of undergraduate study. The practical focus will make the books particularly useful and relevant to those returning to academic study after a period of professional practice, and also to those about to leave the academic world for the challenges of language-related work. For students who have not previously studied applied linguistics, including those who are unfamiliar with current academic study in English speaking universities, the books can act as one-step introductions. For those with more academic experience, they can also provide a way of surveying, updating and organising existing knowledge.

The view of applied linguistics in this series follows a famous definition of the field by Christopher Brumfit as:

> The theoretical and empirical investigation of real-world problems in which language is a central issue.
>
> (Brumfit 1995: 27)

In keeping with this broad problem-oriented view, the series will cover a range of topics of relevance to a variety of language-related professions. While language teaching and learning rightly remain prominent and will be the central preoccupation of many readers, our conception of the discipline is by no means limited to these areas. Our view is that while each reader of the series will have their own needs, specialities and interests, there is also much to be gained from a broader view of the discipline as a whole. We believe there is much in common between all enquiries into language-related problems in the real world, and much to be gained from a comparison of the insights from one area of applied linguistics with another. Our hope therefore is that readers and course designers will not choose only those volumes relating to their own particular interests, but use this series to construct a wider knowledge and understanding of the field, and the many crossovers and resonances between its various areas. Thus the topics to be covered are wide in range, embracing an exciting mixture of established and new areas of applied linguistic enquiry.

The perspective on applied linguistics in this series

In line with this problem-oriented definition of the field, and to address the concerns of readers who are interested in how academic study can inform their own professional practice, each book follows a structure in marked contrast to the usual movement *from* theory *to* practice. In this series, this usual progression is presented back to front. The argument moves *from* Problems, *through* Intervention, and *only* finally to Theory. Thus each topic begins with a survey of everyday professional problems in the area under consideration, ones which the reader is likely to have encountered. From there it proceeds to a discussion of intervention and engagement with these problems. Only in a final section (either of the chapter or the book as a whole) does the author reflect upon the implications of this engagement for a general understanding of language, drawing out the theoretical implications. We believe this to be a truly *applied* linguistics perspective, in line with the definition given above, and one in which engagement with real-world problems is the distinctive feature, and in which professional practice can both inform and draw upon academic understanding.

Support to the Reader

Although it is not the intention that the text should be in any way activity-driven, the pedagogic process is supported by measured guidance to the reader in the form of suggested activities and tasks that raise questions, prompt reflection and seek to integrate theory and practice. Each book also contains a helpful glossary of key terms.

The series complements and reflects the *Routledge Handbook of Applied Linguistics*, edited by James Simpson, which conceives and categorises the scope of applied linguistics in a broadly similar way.

Ronald Carter
Guy Cook

Reference

Brumfit, C. J. (1995). 'Teacher Professionalism and Research', in G. Cook and B. Seidlhofer (eds) *Principle and Practice in Applied Linguistics*. Oxford, UK: Oxford University Press, pp. 27–42.

Acknowledgements

I wish to acknowledge the dedicated learners and teachers of English everywhere, for giving me the reason to write this book.

My special thanks to:

Series editors Ron Carter and Guy Cook, for their guidance and encouragement.

Bill Grabe, for teaching me the art of rigorous synthesis, and encouraging me in my career.

The many vocabulary and technology experts, whose scholarly work has informed my thinking and advanced vocabulary research and education.

I dedicate this book to my wife, Terri, our children and grandchildren, and to my parents, Allen and Melba Gardner.

1 Introduction

Setting the stage

In recent years, many books and articles have been written about the role of vocabulary in English language education, particularly as it applies to academic settings, where the stakes are high in terms of both educational success and its natural corollary – occupational opportunity. You might be asking then, "why another book on vocabulary?" The short answer is simple – we know more now than we did a few years ago about many aspects of vocabulary acquisition and teaching, and the impact of high-powered technology has not only changed our understanding of what to teach, but it has also given us many more tools for accomplishing the task. For the longer, more detailed answer to the question, I invite you to study the chapters of this book, as we discuss together the vocabulary issues we face in our various language classrooms, the most useful interventions for dealing with these issues, and the current research and theories that support these conclusions.

This book is more than a review of literature on topics involving English vocabulary; it is an interactive book, designed to build knowledge through examples and experiences, as well as through traditional references to important and current research on the topics addressed. I ask you now to "buckle up" and "dig in," because this is how true learning takes place, and it emphasizes the fact that the task of teaching English language learners (ELLs) is not simple and straightforward. My goal is to build your awareness of the vocabulary tasks facing our ELLs and to provide foundational concepts for dealing with these tasks in your various classrooms and tutoring experiences. I am not interested in presenting another easy-to-follow curriculum or a list of fun activities to build vocabulary, as there are plenty of resources available in these areas. Instead, I want you to know why these work or don't work, what makes certain vocabulary issues simple or complex, how to analyze specific learner needs from a variety of perspectives, and how you can adapt or create resources and curricula to meet those specific needs.

In the beginning, I want to make my position about English vocabulary education very clear, so that we have a mutual understanding of where we are headed together and why. My stance is informed by my many years of actual classroom experience with ELLs, my own experiences as a language learner, and my extensive study of vocabulary research from multiple disciplines, including Applied Linguistics, Second Language Acquisition (SLA), Teaching English to Speakers of Other Languages (TESOL), Reading Research, Cognitive Science, Educational and Classroom-Based Research, Educational Psychology, Teacher Education, Corpus Linguistics, Neurolinguistics, Language Assessment, Technology Enhanced Language Learning (TELL), Computer Assisted Language Learning (CALL), Computational Linguistics, English for Specific and Academic Purposes (ESP, EAP), and Content-Based Instruction (CBI).

I feel that this multiple-perspective approach adds strength to my conclusions and suggestions, and allows me to give you as ELL teachers the most complete picture possible as I currently understand it, rather than the all-too-frequent narrow perspectives that often appear to be motivated by ideological, political, or personal preferences. While I draw on research and theory in every chapter, I promise not to load you down with heavy statistics or unnecessary jargon, but to synthesize and paraphrase for you what the fields are saying about a particular issue (my job) so that you can actually implement this into your teaching efforts (your job).

My basic philosophy about vocabulary

I view grammar as the engine of language, giving it order and structure, and vocabulary as the fuel of language, without which nothing meaningful can be understood or communicated. Both are crucial, and there is actually a great deal of overlap between the two as we will see in later chapters. My specific attention to vocabulary in this book stems from the simple fact that words and phrases of English present such a formidable challenge in English language education because of their sheer numbers (estimates now in the millions – Crystal, 1995), their multiple and context-dependent meanings, the difficulties associated with determining which ones to emphasize in which instructional settings, and how to actually teach them. The four foundational tenets of my approach to vocabulary education that will guide the remaining chapters are:

1 "All vocabulary is not created equal"– i.e. some words show up everywhere in English and perform mainly grammatical functions (*the, a, and, of, to,* etc.); some are more technical and lower frequency, but carry most of the meaning of a given communication (*reciprocal, photosynthesis, mitosis, sarcophagus,* etc.); some are composed of multiple words (*in order to, in addition to, on the*

other hand, pop the question, kick the bucket, chew out, etc.); some have multiple meanings (*run, break, chip*, etc.). Additionally, vocabulary is acquired by each learner on a word-by-word basis, not as whole frequency levels, bands, or tiers of words, although such groupings are often useful in describing the relative frequency of vocabulary input.

2 "We must take our ELLs from what they know to where they need to go" – vocabulary learning does not take place in some sort of mental vacuum; rather, it is a constant interaction between existing knowledge and new knowledge. To assume otherwise is a logical fallacy. It is therefore crucial to understand what learners already know and what they need to know in order to be effective vocabulary teachers.

3 "Vocabulary instruction should focus on both forms and meanings" – the best methods for connecting word forms with their meanings must be known by teachers, taught to students, and practiced by both. I emphasize here that without knowledge of word forms (oral and/or written) there can be no access to meaning, and, conversely, without meaning to attach to, knowledge of word forms is essentially useless. Vocabulary instruction must therefore support both. I simply do not believe in a form-meaning dichotomy, or that one should be emphasized over the other.

4 "Time is of the essence" – ELLs generally do not have the luxury of becoming exposed to essential target-language vocabulary through natural encounters over long periods of immersion the way they did in their native languages. Therefore, it is crucial that language professionals find ways to expedite the vocabulary learning process for their learners, especially in high-stakes settings, such as in school and the workplace. I also assert that the issues surrounding English vocabulary knowledge are not trivial; in fact, they often have profound consequences for many learners of English who must attain high levels of proficiency in the language in order to compete in academic and occupational settings. As their teachers and prospective teachers, I hope you will find this textbook current, illuminating, and practical, as we explore together how we can effectively and efficiently manage our ELLs' acquisition of English vocabulary in whatever instructional contexts we may find ourselves.

Guiding questions

These philosophical positions also have practical corollaries. I offer these here in the form of fundamental guiding questions that I believe all teachers of English vocabulary should be asking on a regular basis:

1 "What English?" – we must determine which of all the possible registers (genres) of the English language our learners most need to be familiar with, and the specific themes and topics within those registers. Do they need social English or science English, business English or medical English? Do they need to read novels or textbooks or safety signs? Do they need speaking and listening skills or reading and writing skills, or both?

2 "What Texts or Tasks?" – based on (1) above, we must find (or produce ourselves if necessary) relevant texts or tasks (written and/ or spoken) that can be used as (a) the actual contexts for aiding in the vocabulary acquisition process; (b) the sources for determining important vocabulary to teach and learn; and (c) the means for assessing learners' vocabulary acquisition.

3 "What Vocabulary?" – we must analyze the actual vocabulary in the texts and tasks chosen in (2) above. In other words, we must engage in the art of linguistic investigation in order to know which words to emphasize and their particular characteristics, thus avoiding the all-too-frequent problem of teaching English as a general language, rather than as a specific, needs-based language.

4 "What Background Knowledge?" – we must determine what vocabulary knowledge (spoken and/or written) our ELLs already possess in both their first language (e.g. Spanish, Chinese, Korean), the target language (e.g. English), and any other language (e.g. French, Dutch, German).

5 "What Curriculum?" – we must determine the most efficient and effective instructional methods for bringing learners' vocabulary knowledge (4 above) to at least the minimum threshold levels necessary for negotiating the vocabulary (3) in the texts and tasks (2) that they need to comprehend and/or produce (1).

6 "What Strategies?" – in this whole process, we must always teach ELLs strategies for dealing with additional unknown words not covered in (5), and for becoming autonomous, life-long learners of vocabulary, no longer dependent on the classroom or the teacher for their future vocabulary learning.

The Three Realities of Vocabulary

In my experience, I have found that most approaches to vocabulary training and research tend to emphasize one of three main aspects of the vocabulary equation. I refer to these as the "Three Realities of Vocabulary":

1 The **Psychological Reality**, or *what is happening in the minds of actual learners* – i.e. what vocabulary ELLs already understand, how they learn new vocabulary, how they mentally deal with and

store vocabulary in more than one language (e.g. mental processes, strategies, memory constraints), and so forth.

2 The **Linguistic Reality**, or *what vocabulary actually exists in the communication events* that ELLs are expected to participate in (in the texts, in the tasks, etc.) – i.e. how many words there are for ELLs to negotiate, the characteristics of those words (e.g. meanings, morphology, phraseology, neighboring words), and so forth.

3 The **Pedagogical Reality**, or *how vocabulary is actually taught* in both informal settings (caregivers with children, playground talk, etc.) and formal settings (language classrooms, mainstream academic classrooms, etc.), or, in other words, how vocabulary is dealt with in a particular curriculum, how much attention is given to formal vocabulary instruction, which explicit vocabulary-building strategies are used by teachers and taught to learners, and so forth.

The problem, as I see it, is that an emphasis on one of these Three Realities at the exclusion of the other two can lead to less than favorable outcomes in terms of effective vocabulary education and the research that supports it. For instance, linguists are famous for coming up with lists of high frequency English words to teach ELLs (*Linguistic Reality*), especially with the help of modern computer technology which has taken away the tedium of counting words by hand. As informative as such lists may be, however, they are rarely accompanied by a "how to" explanation for actually teaching the words (*Pedagogical Reality*), and even more rarely with an explanation of the language skills and mental strategies that ELLs would need to possess in order to take advantage of such lists (*Psychological Reality*) – i.e. knowledge of inflectional and derivational relationships between words (e.g. *run, runs, running, ran, runner, runny*), knowledge of the context-specific meanings of words (e.g. *running*, as in *running a race* vs. *running*, as in *my nose is running*), knowledge of how individual word forms combine to form multiword expressions such as idioms (e.g. *run of bad luck, run for the hills, run up the score*) and phrasal verbs (e.g. *run out, run over, run through, run off*, and so forth). Do ELLs and their teachers have the skills and resources necessary to deal with these issues? If not, how useful are the frequency lists, and for which learners, and in which contexts of learning? Is there a mismatch between the way the vocabulary lists were conceived of and calculated by the expert linguists and the way they can be used by actual learners and their teachers? What has to be done to utilize such lists in an effective manner?

To take another example of the incongruities between the Three Realities, consider how often language teachers use a certain approach to vocabulary instruction because of tradition or intuitive appeal, without investigating what research has reported on that approach. For instance, it has long been assumed by many language educators that teaching new vocabulary in semantic sets is good practice (*Pedagogical Reality* – e.g. all the color words – *red, yellow, green, brown*; all the shape words – *circle, triangle, square, hexagon*; all the emotion words, *sad, happy, glad, ecstatic*, etc.). After all, it makes sense to do so, doesn't it? However, a body of research (see Folse, 2004, for review) suggests that such instruction may actually slow down and even confuse the vocabulary acquisition process (*Psychological Reality*), and that teachers should instead consider using thematic sets of words related to topics they are teaching (*Pedagogical Reality* – e.g. words related to travel – *tourist, customs, passport*; words related to mummies – *mummy, pharaoh, tomb, sarcophagus, pyramid*; words related to football/soccer – *net, goalie, offsides, free-kick*). Such thematic sets are readily identifiable (*Linguistic Reality*), thanks to modern computer technology and electronic texts.

Because such mismatches are common place, I propose a new approach to vocabulary education in this book that considers all three realities, so that language professionals like you can have a clearer picture and make more informed decisions. Figure 1.1 provides a graphic representation of the *Three Realities of Vocabulary*, and their interrelatedness. For clarification purposes, I have also provided common descriptions for each reality: *In the mind of the learner* (psychological reality), *In the texts and tasks* (linguistic reality), and *In the teaching practices* (pedagogical reality). I will use this framework to stay focused in the following chapters, and I encourage you to refer back to this diagram and the accompanying explanation above as often as needed in order to firmly grasp these concepts. I also hope you will find it useful in planning your own approaches to vocabulary instruction.

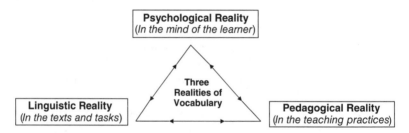

Figure 1.1 The Three Realities of Vocabulary.

The Vocabulary Project (choosing an instructional setting)

In addition to addressing the vocabulary issues that face all of us in the language classroom, I will also involve you in an ongoing Vocabulary Project that will eventually culminate in a portfolio of actual vocabulary resources, approaches, methods, and tools to meet a real-world need – one that is directly tied to your current situation if you are already teaching, or one that would likely be encountered if you are a teacher in training. While the Vocabulary Project is an optional component of this book, I strongly recommend that you do it, whether it is a formal classroom assignment or not. I am sure that it will cause you to see vocabulary in ways that are not possible through reading and classroom discussion alone.

Identifying an instructional setting and texts

If your instructor assigns the Vocabulary Project connected with this book, or if you choose to do the project on your own, it is essential that you identify early the instructional setting that you will address with the project, as well as a text or texts that ELLs will be required to read in that setting. The following are examples of instructional settings you might consider:

1 your own classroom (if you are an existing ELL instructor)
2 a classroom where you will be training to be a teacher (if you are a student teacher)
3 a classroom of a teaching colleague
4 a classroom you are particularly concerned with (if you are a school administrator)
5 a literacy training center in your area
6 a particular course at a secondary school, university, or vocational training institution
7 an ELL tutoring opportunity (formal or informal)
8 other (anywhere where English language learners are receiving English instruction, or where English is the language of instruction)

2 The vocabulary of vocabulary

Problem

If your experience is similar to mine, you have probably been frustrated at times by the many vocabulary terms that do not seem to be consistent from one article or book to the next. Even more disconcerting is the fact that claims and recommendations by experts often seem to draw on evidence from studies that use similar terms with quite different meanings. There is a sense of irony in the fact that the vocabulary of vocabulary is not always stable itself, attesting to the challenge we face in trying to help our English language learners (ELLs) with target-language words.

For example, what constitutes a "word" varies greatly in the literature (Gardner, 2007a). Is a word just a unique spelling like *hit* versus *hitting*, or are these two forms actually the same word but used in different ways? What about *hitter*? Is it a separate word, or just another form of *hit*? What about *hit up, hit off, heavy hitter* and *hit me with your best shot*? More importantly, how do we sort all of this out for analysis, teaching, and testing purposes – and why do we care? What difference does it make for the ELLs in our classrooms and how we teach them? The aim of this chapter is to come to some clearer understandings of the issues surrounding vocabulary terminology, not only to provide us with a foundation for discussions in future chapters, but also to help us be more informed readers of vocabulary research, and to allow us to better assess the claims and recommendations about vocabulary and vocabulary teaching that seem to be pouring in from a variety of different fields.

In one regard, your personal study of the vocabulary of vocabulary closely mirrors what your ELLs will be required to do, especially in academic settings. I highly encourage you to put in the necessary study time and practice to master the terminology discussed in this chapter. I also suggest that you use the internet and other resources to explore additional definitions and/or examples of the terms addressed here. Again, my primary purpose in this chapter is to build a foundation of linguistic knowledge about vocabulary in preparation for our more practical discussions regarding actual vocabulary instruction, and so that your future study of vocabulary can be more informed.

Intervention and theory

Vocabulary terminology

The terms *word, vocabulary item*, and *lexical item* are often used interchangeably in the literature when referring to individual words, and their counterparts, *words, vocabulary*, and *lexis*, are generally used when referring to groups of words. Related to the terms lexical and lexis is the term lexicon, which has many meanings, two of which are particularly pertinent to our discussions in this book:

1 The collection of all words and phrases (including idioms) of a particular language, partially recorded in dictionaries of that language (*Linguistic Reality*).
2 The mental system of an actual language user that contains all words and phrases known by that user (*Psychological Reality*). This is also known as the *mental lexicon* or the *mental dictionary*.

Applied linguists have also established a fairly stable set of terms to discuss more technical aspects of vocabulary. In general, these terms can be grouped by their emphases on three primary aspects of vocabulary: form (including both spelling and pronunciation), meaning, and relationships between words and their neighbors. As we will see, these three aspects form a complex and dynamic relationship that all teachers should be familiar with in order to better meet the instructional needs of their ELLs.

Terms to discuss the form-based concepts of vocabulary

The most basic form-based concept of vocabulary is the type, which, in the case of English, is usually defined as one or more contiguous letters of the Roman alphabet that form a distinct word. Types are separated by spaces or punctuation in written materials, or stress boundaries (in many cases) in continuous speech. For example, the sentence *I love ice cream* contains four different types (*I, love, ice, cream*) separated by spaces, despite the fact that *ice cream* is actually a compound noun consisting of two words. Each type in the sentence is spelled differently than the other types. Traditionally, a manual or computer-based count of types in *I love ice cream* would record four types, each with a count of one token. Thus, token is simply the frequency (number of occurrences) of types or other word units within a text, set of data, conversation, and so forth. The sentence *I love ice cream and whipped cream* contains six types, but seven tokens, because the type *cream* is repeated.

To illustrate further, the data set [*run run run runs ran ran*] contains three distinct types (*run, runs*, and *ran*), each with a different number of tokens: *run* (three tokens), *runs* (one token), and *ran* (two tokens). On a larger scale, the word *the* happens to be the most frequent type in English, accounting for approximately 6 percent of all tokens (notice how many times it occurs on this page alone). In a corpus (body of texts) of one million running words (tokens), this would mean that the single type *the* would have roughly 60,000 occurrences (tokens) in the corpus (6 percent of 1,000,000).

The importance of the type–token distinction for you as teachers and for your language learners cannot be overstated. For instance, a reading text containing fewer types with higher individual token counts is generally easier to read than a text containing many different types with lower individual token counts. Table 2.1 contains the type–token differences between the first 10,000 tokens of the popular science fiction novel *A Wrinkle in Time* (L'Engle, 1962) and the first 10,000 tokens of the high-interest informational science book, *The Bone Detectives* (Jackson, 1996), both of which are written for approximately the same grade level in school.

The difference in the total number of distinct words (types) between these two samples is 440 (2,362 minus 1,922) in the same number of running words (10,000 tokens). In other words, in roughly 40 comparable pages of reading, an ELL will encounter 440 more different types (approximately 11 types per page = 440 ÷ 40) when reading *The Bone Detectives* than *A Wrinkle in Time*. Also, each type repeats one less time on average in *The Bone Detectives* (4.2) than *A Wrinkle in Time* (5.2). Thus, the lexical density (number of different types ÷ number of total tokens) of *The Bone Detectives* (0.24) appears to be much higher than *A Wrinkle in Time* (0.19), and is therefore more likely to cause reading problems relating to vocabulary than its fictional counterpart. Keep in mind that I can only make this "difficulty" assumption based on sheer numbers of types at this point, because I have not analyzed the actual words to determine their individual and relative difficulty. I also do not know how many of the vocabulary items in the two texts are already known by the learners who will actually read them (*Psychological Reality*), and therefore cannot assess how difficult these texts would actually be on that basis either.

Table 2.1 Type–token comparison between two novels

Text	No. of types	No. of tokens	Lexical density[1]	Average type repetitions[2]
A Wrinkle in Time	1,922	10,000	0.19	5.2
The Bone Detectives	2,362	10,000	0.24	4.2

Notes:

1 Lexical density = number of types ÷ number of tokens.
2 Average type repetitions = number of tokens ÷ number of types.

Another form-based concept of "word" is the lemma (plural lemmas), which essentially assumes that different types are considered the same word if they have the same base form, if they are from the same part of speech (all are nouns, all are verbs, etc.), and if they vary only in their spelling for grammatical purposes. This relationship is considered to be one of inflection. Thus, the inflectionally-related verbs *crack, cracks, cracking,* and *cracked* are considered to be one lemma instead of four different types for counting, analysis, teaching, testing, and other purposes. The words *cracker, crackers, cracker's and crackers'*, while containing the same base (*crack*), are considered to be a different lemma, because they belong to a different part of speech (nouns instead of verbs). To distinguish between actual types and lemmas, I will use small capital letters when referring to lemmas (e.g. CRACK) – a distinction often used by corpus linguists (Biber, *et al.*, 1999; Stubbs, 2002).

To the extent that they are identifiable as frozen or fixed lexical units, phrasal lemmas are also a reality in the English language. A phrasal lemma such as RUN THE RISK would include the lemma members (*run the risk, runs the risk, running the risk, ran the risk*). More examples include DRY RUN (*dry run, dry runs*), FRONT RUNNER (*front runner, front runners, front runner's, front runners'*), and GET THE RUN-AROUND (*get the run-around, gets the run-around, getting the run-around, got the run-around*). Later in this chapter we will revisit the complex topic of multiword items in English.

It is crucial to point out that the term *lemma*, as it is used in much of the vocabulary research, does not assume that similar base forms have similar meanings. Thus, despite their different meanings, the various *run* forms in *a run in baseball, a run in the nylons,* and *a run in the park* would all be counted as the same lemma RUN, because they are all nouns. Likewise, the inflectionally-related *run* forms in *run the numbers, runs the risk, running the race,* and *ran for office* would be counted together as a different RUN lemma (all verbs), even though their individual meanings are also quite different from each other. In short, the concept of lemma-as-word often overlooks the multiple meanings of word forms. This dilemma is even more pronounced with the more liberal form-based concept of word family, which expands the definition of "word" to include not only types related by inflection (as in lemmas), but also types related by derivation – i.e. same base forms, but with suffixes or prefixes added that change parts of speech and/or meaning (e.g. *climb*, the verb, to *climber,* the noun; *logical* to its opposite, *illogical*). Using our *run* example, the types *run, runs, running, ran, runner, runner's, runners', runny, runnier,* and *runniest* could be considered one word family, with no distinctions for grammatical parts of speech (verb vs. noun vs. adjective) and no distinctions for meaning. For example, the verb *running* in *running the race*, and the noun *run* in *a run in the nylons* would be counted in the same word family. Complex word families like *constitute*, *stable*, and *vary* could conceivably contain all of the respective types displayed in Table 2.2, and their individual frequencies would be added together for each word family to determine the total tokens for that family.

Table 2.2 Examples of word families

CONSTITUTE (base form/headword)	STABLE (base form/headword)		VARY (base form/headword)
CONSTITUTE	STABLE		VARY
CONSTITUTES	STABILIZE	(U.S.)	VARIES
CONSTITUTING	STABILIZES	(U.S.)	VARIED
CONSTITUTED	STABILIZED	(U.S.)	VARYING
CONSTITUTION	STABILIZING	(U.S.)	VARIATION
CONSTITUTIONS	STABILISE	(British)	VARIATIONS
CONSTITUENCY	STABILISED	(British)	VARIANT
CONSTITUENCIES	STABILISES	(British)	VARIANTS
CONSTITUENT	STABILISING	(British)	VARIABLE
CONSTITUENTS	STABILIZATION	(U.S.)	VARIABLES
CONSTITUTIONAL	STABILISATION	(British)	VARIABILITY
CONSTITUTIONALLY	STABILITY		VARIANCE
CONSTITUTIVE	INSTABILITY		VARIABLY
UNCONSTITUTIONAL	UNSTABLE		INVARIABLE
			INVARIABLY

Adapted from Baselist 3 of the *Range* Program (Heatley, *et al.*, 2002).

Reading through these word-family lists, it becomes apparent that issues of spelling, pronunciation, and overall word meaning have a bearing on the relative ease or difficulty of recognizing and understanding the common base forms within the types of such word families. It is also obvious that the way "word" is defined will affect (1) how and what computers and humans count when they generate word-frequency lists (*Linguistic Reality*), (2) how and what we assess with regard to learners' existing vocabulary knowledge (*Psychological Reality*), (3) which word-learning strategies we will need to teach our learners (*Pedagogical Reality*), and so forth.

Terms to discuss vocabulary levels of form-based word families

A major point I wish to emphasize in this book is that all vocabulary is not created equal. One characteristic that distinguishes words, for example, is relative frequency and range (coverage in various types of English). Using Nation's (2001) scheme, English word families can be described in terms of four major groups or levels:

1 **High Frequency Word Families:** function words that provide the grammatical to the language (*the, and, of, in, to, that, for, it, she, he,* etc.) as well as high frequency nouns (*time, year, people,* etc.), verbs (*say, go, make,* etc.), adjectives (*other, new, good,* etc.), and adverbs (*now, more, here,* etc.). These are words that tend to be high frequency in all types of communication. If we use "word family" (see above) as our definition for what constitutes a word for counting purposes, Nation suggests that 2,000 such high frequency word families cover approximately 78–91 percent of the word tokens of the language, depending on the major register of English (Academic, Newspapers, Fiction, Conversation). In other words, they repeat very often.

2 **Academic Word Families:** words not in the high frequency list that tend to be found across many different academic disciplines and content areas (*data, research, variables, method, source,* etc.). These words are also less likely to be found in fiction, casual conversation, and other less-formal registers. Based on Coxhead's (2000) "academic word list," Nation indicates that 570 academic word families cover an additional 8.5 percent of academic texts, 3.9 percent of newspapers, 1.7 percent of fiction, and 1.9 percent of conversation. Keep in mind that these academic word families added to the high frequency word families described above account for only 2,570 of the total different word families of English, which may actually number in the millions (Crystal, 1995).

3 **Technical (Specialized) Word Families:** words that tend to be specific to a certain book, academic discipline, or specialized theme (*membrane, mitosis; granite, igneous; pulsar, asteroid; mummy, pharaoh; Churchill, Roosevelt,* etc.). In narrative fiction (novels, short stories, etc.) these words tend to be primarily names of characters and places. It is important to note that words at this level can repeat often in certain contexts, and infrequently, or not at all, in others.

4 **Low Frequency Word Families:** words that make up the rest of a particular communication event or text. These consist of (a) words that are just outside of a particular frequency list, (b) many proper nouns, (c) words that may be technical or specialized in one context but not in another, and (d) words that are simply not used very often in the language. Words at this level, along with words at the technical (specialized) level discussed above, constitute the bulk of the English lexicon in terms of different words, although, according to Nation, they generally account for only 7.8 percent of the total tokens of conversation, 10.9 percent of fiction, 15.7 percent of newspapers and 13.3 percent of academic text. This means that they do not repeat very often in general, and that some registers of the language have a greater proportion of these words than others.

It is important to emphasize here the difference between high and low frequency in English as a general language versus English for specific purposes. What may be low frequency in general English may actually be high frequency in a specific text, task, or theme. For instance, it is highly unlikely that *telophase* and *sarcophagus* will make any general high frequency lists of English, but they are sure to be high frequency technical terms in the themes of *cell division* and *mummies* respectively.

Because it is my aim in this book to focus on the specific language needs of our ELLs, I favor an approach that also looks at frequency in terms of specific contexts, not just English as a general language. Of course, many of the general high frequency function and content words will be in nearly all contexts of communication (*the, of, and, to, time, other, new*, etc.) and should therefore be learned early on. However, I emphasize that there will also be technical or specialized words in a given context that reach high levels of frequency in that particular context, such as *telophase* in cell-division literature and *sarcophagus* in mummy literature. These also deserve our immediate attention in language teaching, as they are absolutely essential for ELLs to know in order for them to understand crucial topics in school, the workplace, and many other settings.

Figure 2.1 provides a graphic representation of the vocabulary levels of the English lexicon. The solid white background shared by the low frequency and technical words emphasizes that these come from the same extremely large pool of words constituting the bulk of the English lexicon. To reiterate, words that are low frequency in general English may become emphasized and frequent in specific contexts. This context-dependent phenomenon is represented by the broken line surrounding *Technical Words* in the diagram. In other words, the set of words inside this circle changes very often – a linguistic reality of vocabulary that poses perhaps the greatest challenge for both learners and teachers, in terms of identifying such words and determining the most appropriate ways to help learners acquire them.

Terms to discuss spelling, pronunciation, and word-meaning issues

The English lexicon is full of examples of vocabulary items that are not pronounced the way they are spelled (*the, were, though, night*, etc.). Additionally, many of these are high frequency words of the language, resulting in the infamous "Great Debate" or "Reading Wars" in early English literacy education (Stanovich, 2000). Essentially, the debate is whether learners should be taught to sound out (decode) words phonetically (c-a-t, r-a-t, b-a-t, etc.), or whether they should simply study whole words because of the spelling-sound inconsistencies with many English words (*enough, comb, depot*, etc.). Alphabetic

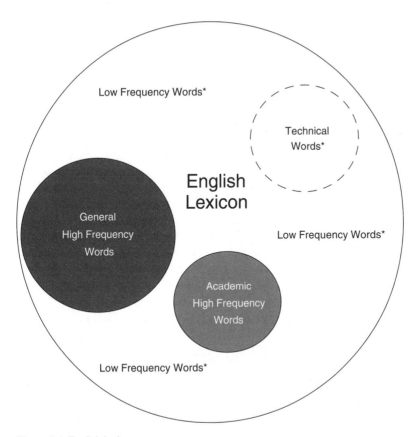

Figure 2.1 English lexicon.

Note:

Low Frequency Words become *Technical Words* in specific texts, themes, or tasks (e.g. *mummy, pyramid, pharaoh*).

languages such as English and French with many such spelling–sound inconsistencies are known as deep or opaque orthographies, whereas languages such as Finnish, Italian, and Spanish with few such inconsistencies are known as shallow or transparent orthographies. Thus, the orthographic depth hypothesis (Katz and Frost, 1992) assumes that beginning readers of shallow orthographies such as Finnish, Italian, and Spanish will have an easier time acquiring alphabetic reading strategies and general reading skills than beginning readers of deep orthographies such as English and French. Additionally, languages such as Chinese and Japanese have writing systems that rely on symbols to represent entire ideas (e.g. Chinese characters and Japanese kanji), making them the extremes in terms of orthographic depth.

At the crossroads of frequency and orthographic-depth issues is the concept of sight words. These are words of very high general frequency that many experts feel should be memorized by sight to speed learners' access to English reading (Grabe, 2009). The most famous lists of sight words are the Dolch (1948) and Fry (1996) lists. It is important to note, however, that these lists were constructed primarily with word frequency in mind, although many professionals have falsely assumed that they were constructed for reasons of poor spelling–sound correspondences among the words. While this is true of some of the words on the lists (*the, there, done, people*, etc.), it is not true of others (*at, fat, hat, sat; get, let, set; an, can, ran, man; it, sit*, etc.). Many words on these lists also follow consistent spelling–sound patterns, such as a final "e" makes the first vowel long (*ate, came, five, gave, like, made, make, ride, take, home, same*, etc.), or double consonants generally make a preceding vowel short (*better, funny, yellow, dress, happy, letter*, etc.). Using the lists as ammunition in the "Reading Wars" is therefore not justified. Appendix A contains a combined list of Dolch and Fry high frequency sight words.

Task 2.1

Study the list in Appendix A while answering the following questions:

1   How many of the words are opaque (do not sound the way they are spelled)?
2   How many are transparent (sound the way they are spelled)?
3   What does this tell us about the possibilities and the problems associated with English high frequency words?

Another issue facing ELLs with regard to spelling–sound issues is the presence in English of many heterophones (words with the same spelling, but different pronunciations and usually quite different meanings) such as *bass* (the fish) versus *bass* (a music term), *desert* (to leave) versus *desert* (a dry region), and *bow* (bending at the waist, or the front of a ship) versus *bow* (a stringed weapon, or an interlacing of material). Notice how your mind adjusts to the different pronunciations of these words as you try to connect to their various meanings. If you are struggling to make these distinctions, you might want to ask someone else for help, or look the words up in a dictionary and use the pronunciation guides next to the various entries for the words. I also encourage all teachers to search the internet for sites containing examples of heterophones and other types of words discussed in this chapter. Example sites include:

Heterophones: http://en.wikipedia.org/wiki/Heteronym_(linguistics)
Homophones: www.bifroest.demon.co.uk/misc/homophones-list.html

Homophones (words with the same pronunciation, but different meanings) are also problematic for ELLs. There are two types of homophones:

1 Words with the same pronunciation, different meanings, and *different* spellings (also called heterographs), such as *two/too/to*, *there/their/they're*, and *seas/sees/seize*. Notorious for causing spelling problems in English, they are also a chief source of puns (e.g. *the doctor lost his patients* vs. *the doctor lost his patience*; *non-profit organization* vs. *non-prophet organization*; *I scream* vs. *ice cream*; *resisting arrest* vs. *resisting a rest*). Native speakers generally sigh or chuckle at such "plays on words" – that is, when they finally "get" them – but most ELLs are simply mystified by them.
2 Words with the same pronunciations, different meanings, and *same* spellings, such as *roll* (document for keeping attendance), *roll* (a small rounded piece of bread), and *roll* (an airplane maneuver), or *class* (a group of students), *class* (a social level) and *class* (a characteristic of good behavior). This type of homophone is also a rich source of English puns (e.g. *teachers have **class***; ***swipe** the credit card*).

Because homophones are so frequent in English, they represent one more obstacle to native-like fluency. Homophones with similar spellings (*roll, class, swipe* above) are also considered to be homographs (same spelling, different meanings) in their written form. The reason for the different terms is that one emphasizes the similarity in pronunciation (homo*phones*) and other emphasizes the similarity in writing (homo*graphs*). The overarching term for both is homonym, meaning "same name." The derived terms homonymous and homonymy are often used in the literature to describe this condition.

Likewise, you may have already surmised that heterophones (same spelling, different pronunciation, different meaning – e.g. *bass*, the fish vs. *bass*, the musical term) are also considered to be homographs in their written form. Distinctions between words based on various combinations of pronunciation (phones), spelling (graphs), and meaning become very important for our ELL instructional purposes, particularly as we consider the mode of communication (listening, speaking, reading, writing) in which such words will be encountered and eventually acquired by our learners, and the unique challenges that these types of words will present to them. If this were a simple matter of rare exceptions in English, I would certainly not waste your time discussing it in such detail, but the fact is that many of the highest frequency words of English are also the most homonymous (have completely different meanings) and polysemous (have varying degrees of meaning differences – see Ravin and Leacock, 2000). For instance, *WordNet* (2010), an electronic database of English words with their various meaning senses, reports the number of different meaning senses in Table 2.3 for the high frequency word forms *go, move, run, break, firm,* and *hard*, some of which represent distinct meanings (homonyms) – such as a run in baseball versus a run in the fabric versus a ***run*** of bad luck – and some of which share varying degrees of common underlying meanings (polysemes) – such as the idea of "moving away from something" in ***run** from the dog* and ***run** from the truth*, or the idea of "changing the state of something" in *she **moved** to London* and *she **moved** to a more conservative political position.*

Table 2.3 Number of different senses for six sample words

Word	Senses as noun	Senses as verb	Senses as adjective	Senses as adverb	Total senses
go	4	30	1	–	35
move	5	16	–	–	21
run	16	41	–	–	57
break	16	59	–	–	75
firm	1	2	10	1	14
hard	–	–	12	10	22

To illustrate the extent of homonymy and polysemy in such words, consider briefly the 16 noun senses of *break* in Table 2.4 below. Many of the senses are quite distinct (homonyms – 1 vs. 2; 2 vs. 3; 1 vs. 3, etc.), whereas several share a more common underlying meaning (polysemes – 3 and 9; 1 and 5, etc.). Of course, the questions for us as teachers of ELLs are (1) how well can our learners distinguish between these various senses? and (2) can they find the common underlying meaning between those that are related?

Table 2.4 Noun senses of "break"

Sense	Noun senses of break
1	• S: (n) interruption, break (some abrupt occurrence that interrupts an ongoing activity) "the telephone is an annoying interruption"; "there was a break in the action when a player was hurt"
2	• S: (n) break, good luck, happy chance (an unexpected piece of good luck) "he finally got his big break"
3	• S: (n) fault, faulting, geological fault, shift, fracture, break ([geology] a crack in the earth's crust resulting from the displacement of one side with respect to the other) "they built it right over a geological fault"; "he studied the faulting of the earth's crust"
4	• S: (n) rupture, breach, break, severance, rift, falling out (a personal or social separation [as between opposing factions]) "they hoped to avoid a break in relations"

Sense	Noun senses of break
5	• S: (n) respite, recess, break, time out (a pause from doing something [as work]) "we took a 10-minute break"; "he took time out to recuperate"
6	• S: (n) breakage, break, breaking (the act of breaking something) "the breakage was unavoidable"
7	• S: (n) pause, intermission, break, interruption, suspension (a time interval during which there is a temporary cessation of something)
8	• S: (n) fracture, break (breaking of hard tissue such as bone) "it was a nasty fracture"; "the break seems to have been caused by a fall"
9	• S: (n) break (the occurrence of breaking) "the break in the dam threatened the valley"
10	• S: (n) break (an abrupt change in the tone or register of the voice [as at puberty or due to emotion]) "then there was a break in her voice"
11	• S: (n) break (the opening shot that scatters the balls in billiards or pool)
12	• S: (n) break, break of serve ([tennis] a score consisting of winning a game when your opponent was serving) "he was up two breaks in the second set"
13	• S: (n) break, interruption, disruption, gap (an act of delaying or interrupting the continuity) "it was presented without commercial breaks"; "there was a gap in his account"
14	• S: (n) break (a sudden dash) "he made a break for the open door"
15	• S: (n) open frame, break (any frame in which a bowler fails to make a strike or spare) "the break in the eighth frame cost him the match"
16	• S: (n) break, breakout, jailbreak, gaolbreak, prisonbreak, prison-breaking (an escape from jail) "the breakout was carefully planned"

Source: retrieved and reformatted from *WordNet* 3.0 online.

Task 2.2

Take a moment to look up *go, move, run, break, firm* and *hard* in the online version of *WordNet* 3.0 (or the latest version available), accessible at: http://wordnetweb.princeton.edu/perl/webwn. Which of the senses for each word are homonyms? Which are polysemes? Try this for other words you are interested in.

In this book, I will refer to individual word lemmas with unique senses and phrasal lemmas with unique senses as lexemes and phrasal lexemes, respectively. In many ways this choice is one of convenience – i.e. we simply do not have better terms to describe these phenomena. The following formal definition of "lexeme" most closely matches my own:

the smallest unit in the meaning system of a language that can be distinguished from other similar units. A lexeme is an abstract unit. It can occur in many different forms in actual spoken or written sentences, and is regarded as the same lexeme even when inflected... For example, in English, all inflected forms such as *give, gives, given, giving, gave* would belong to the one lexeme *give*. Similarly, such expressions as *bury the hatchet, hammer and tongs, give up,* and *white paper* would each be considered a single lexeme. In a dictionary, each lexeme merits a separate entry or sub-entry.

(Richards, *et al.*, 1992, p. 210)

Again, I wish to emphasize here the distinction between lemmas and lexemes. Even though some experts consider meaning issues in their formal definition of "lemma" (e.g. Stubbs, 2002), it has been my experience that, in practice, most computer-based vocabulary studies and applications using "lemma" have not dealt with variant meanings of similar word forms. Of course, some of this problem is due to the practical limitations of modern computer applications in terms of accurately distinguishing between the variant meanings of homographs and polysemes (cf. Landes, *et al.*, 1998; Ravin and Leacock, 2000; Sinclair, 2004a). What is important here for us as teachers and researchers is that we recognize such limitations and adjust our practices accordingly.

Task 2.3

Now test your knowledge of basic vocabulary terminology by correctly matching terms with definitions.

Terms	Definitions
1. Types = ___	A. A set of words sharing the same base form and part of speech, but containing different inflectional suffixes (e.g. the verbs *climb, climbs, climbing, climbing*).
2. Lemmas = ___	B. Words that have different, but related senses (e.g. *He **broke** his leg; The cup **broke**; She **broke** his heart*).
3. Word Families = ___	C. Words that are spelled the same, but have different pronunciations and different meanings (e.g. *bow* – bending the body to show respect vs. *bow* – a weapon with a string).
4. Lexemes = ___	D. Lemmas with unique senses (e.g. *roll* and *rolls* – noun lemma meaning "small round piece/s of bread" vs. *roll* and *rolls* – noun lemma meaning "document/s for taking attendance").
5. Heterophones = ___	E. Distinct series of letters bordered by spaces or punctuation (e.g. *car cat chair mitosis lunar*).
6. Homophones = ___	F. A set of words sharing the same base form, but containing different inflectional and derivational suffixes, and possibly coming from different parts of speech (e.g. *climb, climbs, climbing, climbed, climber, climbers*).
7. Polysemes = ___	G. Words with the same pronunciations, different meanings, and *same* spellings (e.g. *roll* – a document for keeping attendance vs. *roll* – a small rounded piece of bread), or words with the same pronunciation, different meanings, and *different* spellings (e.g. *two, too, to*).

Terms to describe relationships between words and their neighbors

You have probably already noted that the meanings of lexemes in real language use are determined by the neighboring words or collocates that surround them. Whereas the meaning of *break* by itself is ambiguous, in *break a bone* and *break a record* its meanings become specific. Thus, the collocates *bone* and *record* supply the additional help we need to understand the more precise meanings of *break*. The following is the entry for the verb *break* with its highest frequency collocates in a recently published frequency dictionary of contemporary American English (Davies and Gardner, 2010, p. 34):

501 break *v*

noun •law, heart, news, •rule, silence, story, •ground, •barrier, leg, bone, •piece, •neck, arm, •cycle, voice•

misc •into, •away, •free, •apart, •loose

up marriage, •fight, boyfriend, meeting•, girlfriend, union, band, pass, •demonstration, •monotony

down •into, •barrier, car•, •cry, •door, •tear, talk•, enzyme•, completely, negotiation• **out** war•, fight•, fire•, sweat, fighting•, riot•, violence•, •laugh, •hive

off piece, talk, •engagement, negotiation, branch, abruptly, •relation
72917 I 0.97

Note: the [•] preceding or following a collocate indicates (respectively) that the entry word occurs 80 percent or more of the time before or after that collocate. The collocates listed are the highest frequency examples for a particular word based on the 400 million token corpus.

This entry is informative in many ways: (1) the noun collocates of the verb *break* provide a clear indication that the high frequency lemma BREAK (consisting of *break, breaks, breaking, broke*, and *broken* – right?) actually represents many different lexemes (*break the law, break her heart, break the news, break the rule, break the silence, break ground, break his neck, break the cycle, his voice broke*, etc.); (2) the lemma BREAK is not only a stand-alone word, but it is often part of phrasal-verb structures that act as units of their own (*break up, break down, break out, break off*); and (3) even the phrases containing the lemma BREAK have their own multiple meanings that become apparent when their collocates are considered (*break up the marriage, break up the fight, break up the pass, break up the monotony; break down the barriers, break down the door, broke down in tears, the negotiations broke down*, etc.). Of course, the space constraints in the frequency dictionary did not allow all phrasal verbs containing *break* to be noted (*break over, break down*, etc.), nor all of the associated collocates for the entries that are recorded, attesting to the complexity of this issue.

> ### Task 2.4
>
> Using the collocate information from the *break* entry above, try to produce partial or complete sentences with *break out* and *break off* and their respective noun collocates (e.g. *the war broke out; break off relations*). Notice the similar and different meanings that the verb–collocate combinations create.

Older native speakers of English should have little trouble distinguishing between the different senses of these and other phrasal verbs, but the same is not true for younger native learners, and especially for ELLs at most levels of proficiency. Some of the problem stems from the fact that many phrasal verbs have both literal and figurative meanings, as evidenced in the 19 senses of the phrasal verb *break up* listed in Table 2.5.

> ### Task 2.5
>
> Carefully read through the senses in Table 2.5 and determine which ones have figurative meanings (e.g. no. 19) and which ones have more literal meanings (e.g. no. 8). The various senses also offer you another opportunity to distinguish between polysemes (find those with similar meanings) and homographs (find those with distinct meanings).

Multiword Items

Phrasal verbs are one of the major classes of multiword items in the English lexicon. Others include:

- idioms (e.g. *pop the question, beat around the bush, chip off the old block*);
- open compounds (*carbon dioxide, Education Reform Act, sleeping bag*);
- complex discourse markers (*in addition to, on the other hand, as a result of*);
- names (*George Washington Carver, Henry David Thoreau, William Shakespeare*);
- hyphenations (*action-packed, age-specific, mother-in-law*);
- stock phrases (*good morning, have a great day, see you later*);
- pre-fabricated strings (*the fact that …, the point is…, do you think…*).

This last group has also been widely studied under the terms lexical clusters, lexical bundles, and lexical chunks (Hyland, 2008).

Table 2.5 Phrasal verb senses of "break up"

Sense	Phrasal verb senses of "break up"
1	S: (v) disperse, dissipate, dispel, break up, scatter (to cause to separate and go in different directions) "She waved her hand and scattered the crowds"
2	S: (v) separate, part, split up, split, break, break up (discontinue an association or relation; go different ways) "The business partners broke over a tax question"; "The couple separated after 25 years of marriage"; "My friend and I split up"
3	S: (v) break up (come apart) "the group broke up"
4	S: (v) crash, break up, break apart (break violently or noisily; smash)
5	S: (v) interrupt, disrupt, break up, cut off (make a break in) "We interrupt the program for the following messages"
6	S: (v) dissolve, resolve, break up (cause to go into a solution) "The recipe says that we should dissolve a cup of sugar in two cups of water"
7	S: (v) crack up, crack, crock up, break up, collapse (suffer a nervous breakdown)
8	S: (v) disassemble, dismantle, take apart, break up, break apart (take apart into its constituent pieces)
9	S: (v) break, break up (destroy the completeness of a set of related items) "The book dealer would not break the set"
10	S: (v) sever, break up (set or keep apart) "sever a relationship"
11	S: (v) pick, break up (attack with or as if with a pickaxe of ice or rocky ground, for example) "Pick open the ice"
12	S: (v) calve, break up (release ice) "The icebergs and glaciers calve"
13	S: (v) adjourn, recess, break up (close at the end of a session) "The court adjourned"
14	S: (v) dissolve, break up (bring the association of to an end or cause to break up) "The decree officially dissolved the marriage"; "the judge dissolved the tobacco company"
15	S: (v) dissolve, break up (come to an end) "Their marriage dissolved"; "The tobacco monopoly broke up"
16	S: (v) break up, fragment, fragmentize, fragmentise (break or cause to break into pieces) "The plate fragmented"
17	S: (v) break up, disperse, scatter (cause to separate) "break up kidney stones"; "disperse particles"
18	S: (v) decompose, break up, break down (separate [substances] into constituent elements or parts)
19	S: (v) break up, crack up (laugh unrestrainedly)

Retrieved and reformatted from *WordNet* 3.0 online.

The point is that English vocabulary is often realized in multiple, rather than single, words. In fact, researchers remind us that mathematically there may be more different phrases in English than individual words (Jackendoff, 1995; Mel'čuk, 1995; Pawley and Syder, 1983), simply because individual words can combine in many unique ways to form novel phrases, whose meanings may be quite different than the sum of their word parts. We have already seen this with the phrasal verbs containing *break*. Additionally, words like *break* may combine with still other words to form idioms that most adult native speakers of English understand and even produce from time to time. Consider the following for example:

all hell broke loose	break out into a cold	can't make an
back-breaking	sweat	omelet without
make or break	break into song	breaking eggs
make a break for	break new ground	clean break
straw that broke the	break out in a rash	fever breaks
camel's back	break ranks	flat broke
big break	break the bank	get an even break
break [someone's] fall	break the ice	gimme a break
break [someone's] heart	break the law	give [someone] a
break [someone's] back	break the mold	break
break [someone's] neck	break the record	give [someone]
break a habit	break the rules	an even break
break a leg	break the silence	go for broke
break a promise	break wind	if it ain't broke,
break a spell	break stride	why fix it
break a story	breaking point	like a broken
break and enter	broke the mold when	record
break bread with	they made	lucky break
break curfew	broken dreams	mold-breaking
break a sweat	broken record	take a break
break into a sweat		

I have chosen certain words like *break* and *run* for the examples in this chapter to show the range of possibilities under the topic of English vocabulary, but I could have chosen hundreds, possibly thousands, of other high frequency words to make these same points. Allow me to share one more example with the word *chip* before encouraging you to do your own explorations.

The same frequency dictionary (Davies and Gardner, 2010) contains the following entry for the noun lemma CHIP (p. 129):

2218 chip *n* <u>adj</u> blue, single, hot, baked, integrated, sweet, fried, Japanese, crushed, crisp <u>noun</u> potato., chocolate., computer., wood., .cookie, tortilla., memory. <u>verb</u> use,
•fall, eat., serve, sell, contain, place, implant, toss, replace
15079 | 0.90 M

It is clear from studying the collocates above that several meaning senses of CHIP are prevalent in contemporary American English:

1 The various food-related meanings of chip (*hot, baked, sweet, fried, crisp, potato, chocolate, cookie, tortilla, eat, serve*, etc.).
2 The computer-related meanings of chip (*integrated, computer, memory, replace*, etc.).
3 The "piece" meaning of chip (*wood*, as in *wood chip*).
4 The "monetarily valuable" meaning of chip (*blue*, as in *blue chip stock*).

Each of these meanings of CHIP would constitute a separate lexeme of the language, and each would be deserving of a separate entry in a dictionary. A quick look-up in *WordNet* (see Table 2.6) verifies three of these senses (unbolded), plus several more that did not make the frequency dictionary (bolded):

5 a triangular wooden float (no. 2)
6 a cow or buffalo chip, meaning dung (no. 3)
7 the actual mark left in a big piece of something when a smaller piece has been chopped off (no. 5)
8 a poker chip (no. 6)
9 a certain type of shot in golf (no. 8).

Table 2.6 Noun senses of "chip"

Sense	Noun senses of "chip"
1	S: (n) bit, chip, flake, fleck, scrap (a small fragment of something broken off from the whole) "a bit of rock caught him in the eye"
2	**S: (n) chip (a triangular wooden float attached to the end of a log line)**
3	**S: (n) chip, cow chip, cow dung, buffalo chip (a piece of dried bovine dung)**
4	S: (n) chip, crisp, potato chip, Saratoga chip (a thin crisp slice of potato fried in deep fat)
5	**S: (n) check, chip (a mark left after a small piece has been chopped or broken off of something)**
6	**S: (n) chip, poker chip (a small disc-shaped counter used to represent money when gambling)**
7	S: (n) chip, microchip, micro chip, silicon chip, microprocessor chip (electronic equipment consisting of a small crystal of a silicon semiconductor fabricated to carry out a number of electronic functions in an integrated circuit)
8	**S: (n) chip, chip shot ([golf] a low running approach shot)**
9	S: (n) chip, chipping, splintering (the act of chipping something)

Source: Retrieved and reformatted from *WordNet* 3.0 online. Sense no. 9 is similar to sense no. 1.

Again, each of these additional senses of *chip* could be considered a separate lexeme, and would likely receive a separate entry in a dictionary. The idiomatic sense noted in the frequency dictionary (*blue chip*) appears as a separate compound noun in *WordNet* 3.0.

Table 2.7 Noun senses of "blue chip"

Sense	Noun senses of "blue chip"
1	S: (n) blue chip, blue-chip stock (a common stock of a nationally known company whose value and dividends are reliable; typically have high price and low yield) "blue chips are usually safe investments"
2	S: (n) blue chip (a blue poker chip with the highest value)

Source: retrieved and reformatted from *WordNet* 3.0 online.

It is interesting to note that there is at least one additional meaning of *blue chip* that has not been recorded in *WordNet* 3.0 – namely, the sports meaning of "extremely talented," which may have Sense 1 above as its basis, but has taken on additional meanings of its own: "In some instances, the process resembles the recruitment of *blue chip* athletes by American colleges" (from *Washington Post*, 2006, retrieved from the Corpus of Contemporary American English, 2010). In American sports lingo, we hear of *blue chippers*, *blue chip recruits*, and so forth, attesting once more to the fluid nature of English vocabulary and the need for teachers and researchers to consider the context-dependent meanings of English words and phrases that ELLs may need to negotiate. As with most higher frequency words, *chip* also plays a crucial part in many well-known idioms of the language, including:

a chip off the old block	cash in [someone's] chips
chip in	chip on [someone's] shoulder
let the chips fall where they may	when the chips are down

Here again, all of these multiword items could be considered to be unique lexemes, and all exist as fixed units, which cannot be fully understood by an analysis of their individual word parts – a concept which has come to be known as the idiom principle (Sinclair, 1991). In contrast to the open-choice principle, which explains those cases when the meanings of Individual words do contribute (literally) to the meanings of the larger phrases in which they appear, and the fact that novel sentences are constructed all the time in real language use. To illustrate the difference between the two, consider the following:

1a. *kick the bucket* (idiomatic verb unit, meaning "to die" – e.g. *The old man finally kicked the bucket and was buried*). We don't say "*The old man finally kicked the container and was buried.*"

1b. *kick the bucket* (literal verb phrase, meaning to strike a bucket with one's foot – e.g. *the old man finally kicked the bucket of apples*). Alternatively, the old man could have kicked the "container" of apples, the "pail" of apples, etc.

2a. *throw in the towel* (idiomatic verb unit, meaning "to quit" – e.g. *The player threw in the towel after falling behind by 30 points.* We don't say *"The player threw in the socks after falling behind by 30 points."*

2b. *throw in the towel* (literal verb phrase, meaning to physically throw a towel into a container, room, etc. – e.g. *the player threw in the towel, along with his socks and shoes.* Alternatively, the player could have thrown in the "ball," the "uniform," etc.

The fact that both versions (idiom and open-choice) can be realized in these two examples is further evidence that teachers and learners should not rely completely on computer-counted word forms.

Task 2.6

Using the Corpus of Contemporary American (COCA) web interface (Davies, 2008–) located at www.americancorpus.org, find the top ten collocates for the following lemmas (*crack, pick, force*).

1 What meanings of the words can be determined by examining the collocates?
2 What multiword items (fixed collocations) can be determined by examining the collocates? Note: you can click on the ? next to the collocate function in COCA to get information about how to use this function. See Appendix H at the back of this book for a sample of a typical collocate query in COCA.
3 Now look these same words up in *WordNet* to confirm and expand your conclusions (at: http://wordnetweb.princeton.edu/perl/webwn).

So far, we have discussed two very different kinds of collocations that exist in natural language: (1) following from the idiom principle – when two or more lexical items are combined (usually side by side) to form a new phrasal lexeme or grammatical structure (which we will refer to as fixed collocations), as is the case with most multiword items; and (2) when two or more lexical items (side by side or apart) contribute to establishing each other's meanings, and/or to establishing the more global theme(s) in a sentence, paragraph, or larger piece of discourse (which we will refer to as thematic collocations). To illustrate both types further, consider the following paragraph taken from the famous American children's novel *Little House on the Prairie*:

1   "Go to sleep, Laura," Ma said. "It's only the ice
2   cracking."
3   Next morning Pa said, "It's lucky we crossed

> 4   yesterday, Caroline. Wouldn't wonder if the ice
> 5   broke up today. We made a late crossing, and
> 6   we're lucky it didn't start breaking up while we
> 7   were out in the middle of it."
>
> (Wilder, 1971, p. 9 – line numbering added)

There are several candidates here for fixed collocations:

> *broke up* (ln. 5) – phrasal verb
> *breaking up* (ln. 6) – phrasal verb
> *go to sleep* (ln. 1) – stock phrase
> *next morning* (ln. 3) – stock phrase
> *it's lucky* (ln. 3) and *we're lucky* (ln. 6) – stock phrases or pre-
>   fabricated strings
> *out in the middle of* (ln. 7) – complex preposition

Each of these functions as a unit, serving both lexical functions (meaning-based) and grammatical functions (verb phrases, time adverbials, etc.) in the paragraph. On the other hand, the thematic collocations involve several of these fixed collocations, as well as other key words dispersed throughout the surrounding text (see Figure 2.2). Thus, the collocation of words involved in the theme or idea of "ice breaking up on some crossable body of water" gives clearer meanings to the otherwise ambiguous individual words and phrases such as *cracking* (13 potential verb senses in *WordNet*), *crossed* and *crossing* (eight potential verb senses in *WordNet*), and *broke up* and *break up* (19 potential verb senses of *break up* in *WordNet*). In other words, they become distinct lexemes by virtue of the company they keep (Firth, 1951). In turn, and perhaps simultaneously, these theme-specific lexemes allow the theme of the entire paragraph to be understood. In short, it is not a coincidence that brings these words together – makes them neighbors – but the need to express a certain idea or theme.

Figure 2.2 Thematic collocations.

The idea of an expandable text window (Sinclair, 2004b) is an appropriate metaphor to describe the amount of cotext or surrounding words needed to disambiguate the meanings of certain polysemous and homonymous words. From a corpus–linguistics perspective, Sinclair refers to a "maximal approach," or expanding the text window until ambiguity disappears. For meanings of the word *picked*, for example, this could be a two-word window [*picked teams*], a five-word window [*picked the whole thing apart*], or a much larger window [*We didn't know why he picked the way he did. It must have been his early training with the guitar*]. Notice how the specific meaning of *picked* in the final example is not known until the word *guitar* is read, and that knowing the meaning of *guitar* is absolutely crucial to getting the specific meaning of *picked*.

Of course, it is only in linguistically engineered examples such as those above that we find such small windows in isolation. Real communication is usually much more robust, both in terms of the linguistic contexts and the situational contexts of communication, especially in spoken English. It would be rare indeed, and perhaps cause to call a psychiatrist, for an individual to walk up to someone and simply say "picked the whole thing apart," without any context or reason for saying so. Likewise, the example from *Little House on the Prairie* above is part of a much larger story-line that has been building over many pages. For instance, approximately two pages earlier we read:

They could not stay long in the town, because they must cross the lake that day.

The enormous lake stretched flat and smooth and white all the way to the edge of the gray sky. Wagon tracks went away across it, so far that you could not see where they went; they ended in nothing at all.

Pa drove the wagon out onto the ice, following those wagon tracks. The horses' hoofs clop-clopped with a dull sound, the wagon wheels went crunching.

(Wilder, 1971, p. 7)

Reading this passage two pages earlier would certainly have created an even stronger context for the collocational meanings we noted in the later passage. Likewise, our own personal experiences with lakes and cracking ice would also contribute to our understanding. These two passages also help to illustrate the difference between context, cotext, and collocates, with context referring to the overall text, situational variables, and shared background knowledge that help establish a word's meaning, cotext referring to the windows of actual text immediately surrounding a specific word, and collocates referring to the actual lexical items (words or fixed phrases) that co-occur in a particular cotext. Collocates are part of cotexts, and both are part of contexts. These relationships and distinctions will become increasingly useful to keep in mind as we proceed to more practical discussions of ELL vocabulary training in future chapters.

While many word meanings are not understood without context, there are also many that are because of their specific meanings. For instance, the meanings of *photosynthesis, mitosis, carbonation, integer, hexagon,* and *income* are largely unambiguous, having only one primary sense (see *WordNet*), with or without context. Changing their neighbors (collocates) will not change their meanings. This will always be the case, unless we begin *photosynthesizing our priorities,* or experience *the carbonation of our character.* Of course, such meaning evolution is always possible in a fluid language like English, but it is unlikely with these types of words, and even more unlikely that our ELLs will need to deal with such changes in their lifetimes. We will therefore refer to these kinds of words as having context-free meanings. Such words are everywhere in school subjects and specialized fields. They are, on the one hand, teachable, because their meanings are so consistent, and, on the other hand, difficult to learn, because they often represent complex concepts or processes, which are often explained or defined using other difficult words. Consider the single *WordNet* 3.0 sense of *mitosis* for example:

cell division in which the nucleus divides into nuclei containing the same number of chromosomes

Typical of vocabulary with context-free meanings, *mitosis* is defined here using other terms with essentially context-free meanings themselves (*cell division, nucleus/nuclei, chromosomes*). The same is often true with the thematic collocates in normal (non-dictionary) usage, as exemplified in the following from COCA 2010 (thematic collocates with context-free meanings are bolded):

The **kinetochore** is a **multiprotein chromatin complex** at which the forces of *mitosis* work to congress, and later to separate, **chromosomes** into **daughter cells.**

These **antibodies** have been localized to **kinetochores** during *mitosis,* but also reveal "**prekinetochores**" present during interphase.

The number of conceptually difficult words in such contexts also helps to explain why it is so difficult to learn the meanings of new words by using the contexts found in informational texts (Anderson, 1996; Coté, *et al.,* 1998), and why learning to read narrative fiction (stories), containing very few such words, is not sufficient preparation for reading informational materials, including most textbooks (Gardner, 2004, 2008). Additionally, conceptually difficult words like these will require a different teaching approach than words like *break* and *run* with their multiple, but generally more learner-friendly, meanings (cf. Nation, 2008; Stahl, 2005).

Concordancing

Modern corpus linguistics has been instrumental not only in helping us identify lexical phenomena such as fixed collocations and thematic collocations, but also in providing electronic tools for the on-screen study of language. The most influential of these tools is concordancing, which essentially produces multiple examples of a key word in context (KWIC), within certain predetermined amounts of cotext, often self-selected by the users of the concordancing program. For instance, the following sample concordance lines of *break* from a 1.5 million word *Children's Corpus* (Gardner, 2004) was generated by a freeware package called *AntConc* (Anthony, 2011), downloadable at www. antlab.sci.waseda.ac.jp/software.html:

1   the island in a terrible flood? Would the weapons **break** in my hands at the moment when my life was in dan

2   rning that' because I was a woman, the bow would **break**. The sun was far in the west, but luckily my s

3   g that a bow in the hands of a woman would always **break** in a time of danger, the animal began to move tow

4   he changed direction and, though the bow did not **break**, the arrow passed harmlessly to one side. I ha

5   h. It began to stretch, and fearing that it might **break**, I walked forward, yet I made him pull me every s

6   . I could hear it stretch and I was sure it would **break**. I did not feel it cutting into my hands, though

7   ng the swish of dry needles beneath their feet to **break** the spell. Far away from their former world came

8   OK, now. 'If you say you do not love me, it will **break** my heart. So please don't. If you love me as much

9   he prescribed entrance. He couldn't let the puppy **break** the rules. It might mean bad luck for both of the

10 brother with pure delight. "A smile that could **break** your heart," Sydelle Pulaski, the tenant in 3c, a

Here, the concordancer window was set for 50 characters to the left (including spaces) and 50 characters to the right of the key word *break* (also known as the **node word**).

Task 2.7

Before continuing on, test your knowledge by carefully studying the word *break* in the ten different concordance lines above. What are the meaningful collocates of *break* in each line? Are there similar and different meanings of *break*? Do the collocates and general cotexts help you understand the meaning(s) of *break*, or are they not useful? Are there any fixed collocations containing *break* in these lines?

It is clear from the sample concordance lines above that several similar and different meanings of *break* are represented, and in several of these instances *break* is also found in fixed collocations: *break the spell* (7), *break my/your heart* (8 and 10), *break the rules* (9). As a tool, then, concordancing allows a key word to be experienced or examined in multiple contexts (cotexts, more specifically – right?), one after the other, thus eliminating the normal space and time delays between word encounters that normally occur in actual written or spoken language. However, it is not always the case that contexts aid us in deciding what a key word means. Some contexts are helpful, some give vague or little information, and some can actually steer us in the wrong direction (Beck, *et al.*, 1983) – a topic we will pursue later on.

More advanced concordancers, like those often associated with structured mega-corpora (COCA, British National Corpus (BNC), etc.), can also add useful situational information such as the dates of the concordance lines, as well as the general registers (spoken, fiction, magazine, newspaper, academic, etc.) and actual sources (*Forbes Magazine, Chicago Tribune, MSNBC*, etc.) that the concordance lines were taken from.

1 **1994 MAG Forbes**   densities double every 18 months. The new law is that the costs of a **chip** factory double with each generation of microprocessor. Moore speculated that these capital burdens might

2 **2007 NEWS Chicago**   a drab team that couldn't hit the side of a silo with a cow **chip** and thank their almighty Chief Illiniwek in the sky – bless him – that the

3 **2004 SPOK MSNBC_Matt**   well as reporter, David Zucchino of " The L.A. Times, " and NBCs **Chip** Reid. Let me ask you about – I talked to a fellow who fought in

4 **1991 SPOK ABC_SatNews**   put their own survival at risk; they're using the coup as a bargaining **chip**. KRZYSZTOF SKUBISZEWSKI: There is a definite Western interest in reinforcing democracy, free

5 **2001 FIC BkSF:OtherOnes**   No, thank you, " Althea said. Mitzie held a chocolate **chip** cookie out to her. " Try this. Mom makes the best. "

6 **1996 NEWS WashingtonPost**   In the rec room, pretending not to notice my eating every last stale potato **chip** left over from a cocktail party. In her second-floor bedroom, letting me try

7 **1997 ACAD IBMR&D**   within a PU will check-stop this PU and propagate the check-stop state to the clock **chip** and the correspondent L2. The defective PU is fenced " on the fly,

8 **2002 ACAD ForeignAffairs**   some policymakers worry that a plant producing fissile material might be used as a bargaining **chip** with foreign countries, a blackmail tactic North Korea has used in the past.

9 **2004 FIC Analog**   control and watched the magnified display as he guided the probe needle up to the **chip's** casing. A push of the button atop the stick, and the probe

10 **2002 MAG PopMech**   ) IC-enhanced cassettes, the tape itself keeps a record of time codes. The IC memory **chip** doesn't affect how the picture is recorded and won't provide a better picture

Retrieved from COCA 2010 and reformatted
for display purposes

(TC)

Task 2.8

Take the time to study the key word (*chip*) in these real-world contexts above, while answering the following questions:

1 What are the meaningful collocates of *chip*, if any, in the different concordance lines?
2 Are their similar and different meanings of *chip*?
3 Do the collocates and general cotexts help you understand the meaning(s) of **chip**, or are they not useful?
4 Are there any fixed collocations containing *chip* in these lines?
5 Does the situational information such as register and actual source help to accurately predict what the meaning(s) of *chip* will be in the concordancing lines, or are you sometimes surprised to find a certain meaning in a particular register or source?

While concordancing has well-deserved support in the study of language by language experts (Hunston, 2002; Sinclair, 1991), it has received mixed reviews as a tool to aid teachers and learners in language education (Boulton, 2009; Flowerdew, 2009). The problems with teachers seem to deal more with training, awareness, and technology savvy (cf. McCarthy, 2008), whereas with ELLs, the problems move beyond these concerns to also include language proficiency. In other words, what English skills must ELLs already possess before they can use information provided in concordancing lines to gain new vocabulary knowledge? (Gardner, 2007a). Later we will explore ways in which concordancing can be managed more productively as a vocabulary teaching and learning tool in English language education.

Summary

In this chapter, we have discussed many of the important terms used to describe vocabulary from an applied-linguistics perspective, with special attention to issues of vocabulary form, meaning, and relationships. While not exhaustive by any means, this basic vocabulary of vocabulary will give us a foundation upon which we can build our future discussions regarding the actual vocabulary needs of our ELLs (what they need to know), the vocabulary they already know, and the classroom practices that we can employ to help them bridge this gap. We will continue to add to this vocabulary of vocabulary as we proceed through the remainder of this book, and I strongly encourage you to come back to this chapter to refresh your understanding of these important concepts.

Vocabulary Project (text scanning)

You should have identified by now an instructional setting for your vocabulary project. You should also have selected a text or texts that ELLs will need to read in that setting. Your task now is to scan the text(s) into electronic format, using any reliable scanner and optical character recognition (OCR) text-scanning software available to you. Most universities have text-scanning resources, and many also have trained assistants who can help you. You might also try libraries, public schools, and private individuals. Alternatively, you could directly ask the publisher of a particular text for an electronic version for academic purposes. Some publishers are willing to provide these and others are not. Your request would certainly need an explanation of your academic purposes. If scanning is your option, you should follow "fair use" guidelines, which generally allow some degree of electronic repurposing for teaching and research purposes.

3 Core vocabulary

Problem

Since the early 1900s, many linguists have been interested in determining the "core" words of the English language. The primary motivations for pursuing the core have been to facilitate language learning (e.g. Ogden, 1934; West, 1953) and literacy development (e.g. Dolch, 1948; Fry, 1996). In short, if a handful of words can be shown to do the majority of the work, then it makes sense to teach and learn those words first. Knowing what is core is also essential in identifying what is not core. In other words, the vocabulary items that exist in a text after the core is accounted for are generally the specialized words dealing with the theme(s) of that text – a topic we will revisit in detail in Chapter 4.

The purpose of this chapter is to discuss the concepts behind a core vocabulary, and to provide some rationale for dealing with the higher frequency words of English that impact so much of what we hear, speak, read, and write in this language. We will consider such questions as:

- Is there a core vocabulary that all learners should know?
- What are some of the challenges in determining a core vocabulary?
- Are there different levels of core vocabulary?
- What is the relationship between core vocabulary lists and the corpora from which they are derived?
- What are some of the challenges in trying to teach a core vocabulary?
- What are some of the resources available for teaching core vocabulary?

Intervention and theory

Challenges in determining a core vocabulary of English

To date, the idea of a core vocabulary of English has been addressed in two major ways:

1 subjective judgments of issues such as prototypicality (words with the most core meaning in a set of related words), collocability

(words that are neighbors to many other words), substitutability (words that are not easily substituted for by other words), and so forth; and

2 usage-based determinations of relative frequency in large corpora (words with high frequency are more core) and range (words with wider distribution across different registers are more core).

Point (2) is what I am concerned with in this book, primarily because I am interested in helping you identify the actual words that our ELLs must understand and produce in their various language experiences. For those interested in detailed discussions of the first emphasis of "core," I highly recommend applicable sections in books by Carter (1998) and Hatch and Brown (1995).

By analyzing the difficulties involved in determining what belongs in the core, we learn a great deal about the nature of high frequency words, the challenges ELLs face in trying to learn and negotiate those words, and the challenges we face as teachers in trying to assist them. I like to think of this as raising our own vocabulary awareness.

Challenge 1 (multiple word meanings)

Frequency of word forms is a primary determination of whether words make a core list of general English vocabulary, yet many high frequency word forms have multiple meanings, a characteristic that increases their teaching and learning burden. We have discussed words like this in previous chapters (*break, run, chip*, etc.), and there are also many others – possibly thousands – among the highest frequency words of English (*make, back, part*, etc.). This form-meaning challenge is particularly apparent when core lists do not address issues of semantic (meaning) frequency, or do not include definitions of the meanings that should be emphasized in language training.

It is ironic that experts may have actually done a better job of addressing this issue over 50 years ago than we do today, even with all of our modern technologies. For instance, words on the famous 1953 *General Service List* (GSL) were accompanied by percentage counts of the multiple meanings of those words (West, 1953). Figure 3.1 shows the entry for the noun SENSE, a high frequency word (entry 948) with its own multiple senses.

```
SENSE             948e
sense, n.   A.   (1)    (power of receiving sensation)
                            The sense of touch, hearing, sight    13%
                 (2)    (the same, but in a wider use)
                            Sense of time, direction
                            Moral sense
                            Sense of honour, of humour             16%
                 (3)    (a general feeling of)
                            Sense of security, danger              12%
                            [ = sensation, Sense of acute pain,     7%]
            B.   (1)    (practical wisdom)
                        Good sense
                        Common sense                               13%
                        [Bring him to his senses, Frighten him
                            out of his senses,                     1.5%]
                 (2)    (of intelligibility)
                        Doesn't make sense; can't make
                        (any) sense of it
                        Talk sense (see NONSENSE)
                        ?[ = meaning, Use the word in that
                        sense]                                     38%
```

Figure 3.1 "Sense" in the *General Service List* with percentages of different meanings found in a five million word corpus (source: West, 1953, p. 440).

1 Percentages in this and other entries rarely add up to 100% because of minor meanings not included in the list.

Task 3.1

Review the entry above from the GSL and answer the questions that follow:

1 What can we learn from this entry about the nature of words on most high frequency lists in terms of (a) their multiple meanings? (b) their relative frequency because of these multiple meanings? and (c) their occurrence in multiword expressions that often have their own dictionary entries? (Look up *sense of humor, common sense*, etc. in *WordNet*.)
2 How does all of this knowledge temper the way we think about core lists based on frequency counts, and about the concept of a general core vocabulary for teaching and learning purposes?
3 What does all of this say about the linguistic reality of high frequency word lists?

Semantic counts for the word SENSE and other high frequency words of the GSL were done manually, occurrence by occurrence, in a five million word corpus. Irving Lorge, one of the principle researchers involved in the semantic count, indicates why this was necessary:

The selection of words for the teaching of English to foreigners, to a large degree, has been based on the frequency of the occurrence of words in printed English. Such facts about word frequency have been useful in the choice of basic vocabularies of specified sizes. The teaching of these words, however, left much to the judgment of the teacher, for he had to choose which meaning or meanings of these words to impart. In general, the more frequent the occurrence of a word, the greater is the variety of meanings in which it is used.

(Lorge in West, 1953, p. xi)

The point here, and one that continues today, is that a core vocabulary based on frequency counts of word forms will always underestimate the number of true words (lexemes) to be taught and learned (Gardner, 2007a). This problem is compounded by the fact that a particular meaning of a multi-meaning word form may be common in one register of the language (e.g. science) and not in another (e.g. history), thus bringing into question the idea of "coreness" altogether.

Hyland and Tse (2007) point this out in their study that questions the notion of a core academic vocabulary across major college disciplines (biology, physics, computer science, mechanical and electrical engineering, sociology, business studies, applied linguistics). While the 570 word families of Coxhead's Academic Word List (AWL – see Chapter 2) accounted for 10.6 percent of the words in their academic corpus, they found that "different disciplines showed clear preferences for particular meanings and collocations" of those words (p. 244). As a result, these researchers emphasize the identification and teaching of field-specific or subject-specific vocabulary, rather than general, multidisciplinary lists. The concern that every subject area may have its own core vocabulary has been expressed by many other experts as well (e.g. Carter, 1998; Swales, 1990).

However, this does not mean that lists of frequent words forms like the GSL or AWL should not be used at all; what it does mean is that we must interpret the findings in the context of the specific needs of our learners, so that they spend time learning content-specific words and their content-specific meanings, rather than words and meanings they are less likely to encounter or need.

Interestingly, a partial solution to the challenge of core lists containing words with multiple meanings may be found in specialized word lists that have been used to construct lexically-simplified texts for lower-proficiency English users. One such approach is *Voice of America* (VOA), which "broadcasts approximately 1,500 hours of news, information, educational, and cultural programming every week to an estimated worldwide audience of 123 million people" (from www.voanews.com/english/about-us). The linguistic appeal of these programs, and their associated written transcripts, is that the writers work within a lexicon of roughly 1,500 words, with each word clearly specified in terms of meaning (definition) and part of speech. Figure 3.2 has an example page from the actual *Word Book* used to construct the messages.

In short, this is a list of defined lexemes used to construct messages about real-world topics in areas such as world news, education, science, economics, American history, and life in the United States (www.voanews.com/learningenglish/home). The messages are broadcast over radio and satellite television (using simple sentences and slower speech), and are accessible, without cost, in both written and audio formats to anyone in the world with internet access, making them very attractive for English language education. Additionally, my own analysis shows that all but 217 of the 1,537 VOA words are found either on the high frequency *General Service List* (GSL) or the high frequency *Academic Word List* (AWL). These figures indicate that the VOA list consists primarily of high frequency words of English, but with the following added advantages over many core lists that simply provide frequent word forms:

a (an) – *ad. one; any; each*

able – *v. having the power to do something*

about – *adj. almost ("about half"); of or having a relation to ("We talk about the weather.")*

above – *ad. at a higher place*

abuse – *n. bad treatment causing harm or injury*

accept – *v. to agree to receive*

accident – *n. something that happens by chance or mistake; an unplanned event*

accuse – *v. to say a person is responsible for an act or crime; to make a statement against someone*

across – *ad. from side to side; to the other side*

act – *v. to do something*

activist – *n. one who seeks change through action*

actor – *n. someone acting in a play or show*

add – *v. to put (something) with another to make it larger; to say more*

administration – *n. the executive part of a government, usually headed by a president or prime minister*

admit – *v. to accept ("admitted to the United Nations"); to express one's guilt or responsibility ("He admitted that what he did was wrong.")*

adult – *n. a grown person*

advertise – *v. to show or present the qualities of a product to increase sales*

advise – *v. to help with information, knowledge or ideas in making a decision*

Figure 3.2 Sample from *Voice of America* (VOA) *Word Book* (source: downloaded March 1, 2011 from www.unsv.com/voanews/specialenglish/about/wordbook/VOA-Special-English-WordBook.pdf).

Advantage 1:   the meanings of the words used by authors to construct the VOA messages are clearly defined in the VOA *Word Book*, and the parts of speech of the words are also clearly indicated.

Advantage 2:   the meanings of the words (with their established definitions) and the words used in the VOA written and spoken materials are largely the same. Thus, word forms are closely correlated with word meanings, a condition which lends itself well to vocabulary learning. For example, learning the VOA words should have a direct effect on reading and listening to the VOA materials, and, conversely, when reading or listening to VOA materials, learners can access the VOA *Word Book* to find out the specific meanings of words they are not familiar with.

Advantage 3:   the words reflect current and interesting topics, and are changed from time to time so that they stay current. Regarding this last point, I have reproduced in Table 3.1 the 217 more specialized words of the current VOA *Word Book*. These are words that do not occur in the GSL (2,000) or AWL (570) high frequency lists that accompany the *Range* program used in the analysis.

Nan and Mingfang (2009) of the South China University of Technology offer a nice discussion of how to incorporate VOA materials into an English-as-a-foreign-language setting, in order to foster ELLs' productive use of high frequency English words. I encourage you to read this article for more details.

Task 3.2

1 Review the words in the table opposite, and then answer the following questions:

   a What current topics are reflected in these words?
   b Should such words be part of a core vocabulary? Why or why not? Under what conditions?
   c What are the language-learning advantages and disadvantages of using materials like VOA that are constructed from a specialized list of words with specific definitions?
   d How does this differ from using more natural materials (not controlled for vocabulary)?

2 Take the time to explore the VOA website (www.voanews.com/learningenglish/home), considering how this free resource might be used in the language classroom to help ELLs learn and practice English vocabulary. Also consider the rich English learning resources found on the *BBC World Service* site (www.bbc.co.uk/worldserviceradio) and how these resources might be used in tandem with the VOA materials.

Table 3.1 Specialized words in *VOA Word Book*

ABUSE	BUDGET	DEFICIT	FOG	LIGHTNING	PROFESSOR	SURRENDER
ACTIVIST	BULLET	DELEGATE	FUEL	MAGAZINE	PROPAGANDA	SWEAR IN
AGGRESSION	CABINET	DEMOCRACY	GENOCIDE	MATE	PROTEST	TANK
AIR FORCE	CAMPAIGN	DENOUNCE	GOODS	MATHEMATICS	RADAR	TELESCOPE
AIRPORT	CANCEL	DEPLORE	GRAY	MAYOR	RADIATION	TELEVISION
ALBUM	CANCER	DEPLOY	GUERRILLA	MICROSCOPE	RAID	TERRITORY
ALCOHOL	CANDIDATE	DETAIN	HALT	MILITANT	RAPE	TERROR
ALLY	CAPTURE	DICTATOR	HEADQUARTERS	MILITIA	REBEL	TERRORIST
AMBASSADOR	CAREER	DIET	HELICOPTER	MISSILE	RECESSION	THEATER
AMMUNITION	CEASEFIRE	DIPLOMAT	HERO	MOB	REFORM	TORTURE
ANARCHY	CELEBRATE	DISARM	HIJACK	MOURN	REFUGEE	TRAFFIC
ANCESTOR	CHAMPION	DISASTER	HORRIBLE	MOVIE	REPRESS	TRAGIC
ANNIVERSARY	CHASE	DISPUTE	HOSTAGE	NAVY	REVOLT	TREASON
ANNOUNCE	CHEMISTRY	DISSIDENT	HOSTILE	NEGOTIATE	RIOT	TREATY
APPEAL	CIVIL RIGHTS	DONATE	HUGE	NOMINATE	ROCKET	TROOPS
ARCHEOLOGY	CIVILIAN	DRUG	HUMOR	OPPRESS	RURAL	TRUCE
ARTILLERY	CLASH	ECOLOGY	IMPORT	ORBIT	SATELLITE	TRUCK
ASTRONAUT	CLERGY	EMBASSY	INCITE	OUST	SENATE	URGENT
ASTRONOMY	CLIMATE	EMBRYO	INFECT	OVERTHROW	SHRINK	VACATION
ASYLUM	COALITION	EMERGENCY	INFLATION	PARACHUTE	SKELETON	VACCINE
ATMOSPHERE	COMPROMISE	EMOTION	INJECT	PARADE	SMASH	VEGETABLE
AUTOMOBILE	CONDEMN	EVAPORATE	INNOCENT	PARLIAMENT	SPY	VETO
AWARD	CONGRESS	EXECUTE	INSANE	PASSPORT	STAB	VICTIM
BALLOON	CONSERVATIVE	EXILE	INTERNET	PHYSICS	STARVE	VIDEO
BALLOT	CONTINENT	EXPEL	INVADE	PILOT	STATUE	VISA
BAN	CORRUPTION	EXTREMIST	JAIL	PLANET	SUBMARINE	VOLCANO
BARRIER	CREW	FEED	JURY	PLASTIC	SUBVERSION	WEB SITE
BETRAY	CRISIS	FERTILE	KIDNAP	PLOT	SUICIDE	WITHDRAW
BIOLOGY	CRITICIZE	FIREWORKS	LABORATORY	POLLUTE	SUPERVISE	WRECKAGE
BOMB	CURFEW	FLEE	LAUNCH	PORT	SUPPRESS	ZOO
BOYCOTT	DAM	FLUID	LEAK	PREGNANT	SURPLUS	

Challenge 2 (multiword issues)

Core lists rarely account for multiword issues. The fact of the matter is that much about a word is lost when we allow a machine to isolate it from its various contexts for counting purposes. Not only do we risk counting completely different lexemes as if they are the same word (e.g. *chip* in *potato chip*, *computer chip*, and *rock chip*), but we also risk not including on our lists some of the more frequent multiword items (e.g. phrasal verb lemmas like GO on, CARRY out, SET up, and PICK up).

Additionally, while fewer multiword items will make a high frequency list than individual types, their impact as certain classes may be just as important (all phrasal verbs, all lexical bundles, all idioms, etc.). For instance, Mark Davies and I found that 1 in 20 lexical verbs in the British National Corpus (BNC) function in phrasal verb structures, and that the combined frequency of phrasal verb tokens in the BNC exceeds the individual frequencies of "the verb *are*, the determiners *this* or *his*, the negative *not*, the conjunction *but*, or the pronoun *they*" (Gardner and Davies, 2007, p. 347). We go on to say that, on average, a learner will encounter one phrasal verb in every 192 words of written text, or roughly two per page. Interestingly, the combinations of 20 lexical verbs and 16 particles (320 phrasal verb lemmas) constitute 53.7 percent of the 12,408 different phrasal verb lemmas we identified in the BNC (see Appendix B).

Of particular importance to our discussion is the fact that, for traditional core-list purposes, the two parts of phrasal verbs (the verb and the particle) are normally machine counted as individual words, with their frequencies added to other occurrences of the same word forms. Thus, any semantic singularity or lexeme status associated with the phrasal verb reality of the two words is essentially *wiped out*. This is also true for idioms, stock phrases, lexical bundles, compound nouns, and other multiword units.

Task 3.3

The table in Appendix B contains the list of the 20 most productive lexical verbs that form phrasal verb units in the BNC, the particles they combine with, and the frequencies of the various combinations. Carefully study the table and answer the following questions:

1 What do we learn from the table about the problem of only counting individual words forms to determine core vocabulary?
2 What do we learn about the true frequency of many individual words of English that appear on core lists?
3 What do we learn about many multiword items of English that generally do not appear on core lists?
4 What does this all say about teaching, learning, and research that rely on core vocabulary lists?

Challenge 3 (spoken vs. written)

Core vocabulary lists have been based exclusively or primarily on written English, with spoken English being greatly under-represented (McCarthy and Carter, 2001), especially in terms of more casual forms of conversation (Adolphs and Schmitt, 2003). For instance, McCarthy and Carter (1997, pp. 23–24) provide the following comparison of the highest frequency words of a written and a spoken corpus of comparable sizes (330,000 tokens each).

	Written	Spoken
1	the	the
2	to	I
3	of	you
4	a	and
5	and	to
6	in	it
7	I	a
8	was	yeah
9	for	that
10	that	of
11	it	in
12	on	was
13	he	is
14	is	it's
15	with	know
16	you	no
17	but	oh
18	at	so
19	his	but
20	as	on
21	be	they
22	my	well
23	have	what
24	from	yes
25	had	have
26	by	we
27	me	he
28	her	do
29	they	got
30	not	that's
31	are	for
32	an	this
33	this	just
34	has	all
35	been	there
36	up	like
37	we	one
38	out	be
39	when	right
40	one	not
41	their	don't
42	she	she
43	who	think
44	if	if
45	him	with
46	we	then
47	about	at
48	will	about
49	all	are
50	would	as

Task 3.4

Take a moment to compare the highest frequency words in the written and spoken columns and answer the following:

1 What role do grammatical function words play in both lists (determiners, prepositions, pronouns, auxiliary verbs, conjunctions, etc.)?
2 What role do content (lexical) words play in both lists (nouns, verbs, adjectives, adverbs)?
3 What other characteristic differences exist between words in the two lists?
4 What does this all mean for core vocabulary lists used in English Language Education?

Challenge 4 (core size is arbitrary)

Determining the size of a core vocabulary is essentially an arbitrary decision. Historically, there has been a strong precedent set for 2,000 words in the core, based mainly on the fact that general word frequencies in larger corpora tend to fall off quite sharply at around this level. Nation (2008) states that the 2,000 word families of the GSL account for 80 percent of most texts, and over "90% of the running words" of "friendly conversation" (p. 8). Regarding spoken English, McCarthy (1999) adds "that a round-figure pedagogical target of the first 2000 words in order of frequency will safely cover the everyday core with some margin for error" (pp. 235–236). The latest edition of the *Longman Dictionary of Contemporary English* (Longman, 2009) continues to use 2,000 defining words, adding additional fuel to the 2,000-word threshold. However, we must be very clear again that 2,000 word *types* (McCarthy, 1999), 2,000 word *families* (Nation, 2001), and 2,000 *defining words* (Longman, 2009) may represent quite different word counts and instructional burdens, not to mention that multiple word meanings are a persistent problem. There is also the issue that every core list has words that are not on other lists, suggesting that 2,000 does not necessarily mean the same 2,000, and that a word list is often an artifact of the corpus from which it is derived.

Another key point for our purposes is that many "core" experts have attempted to tie together frequency and coreness with instructional possibilities, acknowledging that 2,000 words is "doable" from the perspective of direct vocabulary instruction (e.g. Nation 2001, 2008). Here again, however, I have some concerns as I consider just what we get for our extensive investment in 2,000 general high frequency words of English. Does 80–90 percent coverage have any special significance, other than being higher than say 70–80 percent coverage?

To illustrate my concern, consider this example: reading research studies have indicated that learners must know 95 percent of the words in a given text in order to comprehend the general meaning, with many studies placing the figure as high as 98 percent (49 out of every 50 words) for adequate comprehension of fictional text (Carver, 1994; Hu and Nation, 2000). In other words, if our ELLs knew the 2,000 word families described above (with all of their contextualized meanings and derivational relationships), they would still be incapable of comprehending most adult fiction without assistance. In fact, Nation (2006) suggests that they would actually need to know 8,000 to 9,000 word families to comprehend adult fiction and 6,000 to 7,000 word families to comprehend spoken English, assuming that 98 percent word knowledge does the trick. Adolphs and Schmitt (2003) suggest that 5,000 types cover approximately 96 percent of casual conversation, which may or may not be enough for adequate comprehension. From my perspective, the determination of core size should take such practical considerations into account. Jumps from 2,000 to 5,000 to 9,000 word families are very substantial and bring with them a unique set of instructional challenges. All of a sudden, we may begin to question whether it is "doable" after all from the perspective of direct vocabulary instruction.

Challenge 5 (core lists become dated)

Core lists become dated. This happens in two primary ways:

1 New words enter the language and become widely used. Appendix C contains a list of words in contemporary American English that occur at least three times as often in the years 2000–2008 as they did in the 1990s. Some of these are old words with new emphases (*affiliation, adolescent*, etc.), while others are more recent on the English scene, with several actually making the 5,000 word list in the *Frequency Dictionary* (*e-mail, terrorism, homeland, host, click, online*, etc.).
2 Some words on core lists become less important over time because the content of the corpus on which they are based becomes dated (old news, old novels, old technologies, etc.). For instance, several of the second 1,000 words of the 1953 GSL have lost their relative importance in contemporary English (*telegraph, punctual, ornament*, etc.).

Task 3.5

Thinking about the first way core lists become dated, look over the newcomer word list in Appendix C while answering the following questions:

1 How do these words "reflect changes in society itself – politically, technologically, and so on?" (Davies and Gardner, 2010, p. 150).
2 What do newcomer words say about a "core" vocabulary and how we should treat lists of high frequency words for teaching and learning purposes?

For over half a century, the 2,000 word families of the General Service List (West, 1953) have served as the core for many vocabulary applications in language education and research (Gilner, 2011). The continued influence of the list in more recent times is mainly due to the ground-breaking work of Paul Nation and his colleagues. In particular, English language studies have benefitted greatly from the *Range* program (Heatley, *et al.*, 2002) that uses the first and second 1,000 words of the GSL as two of its base lists, with the third base list consisting of the 570 word families of Coxhead's (2000) Academic Word List (AWL). Not only have these 2,570 word families given some priority to general vocabulary instruction, but their use in the *Range* program has allowed language professionals to analyze the vocabulary of written and some transcribed spoken materials (e.g. Nation, 2001; Nation and Waring, 1997), produce tests of vocabulary knowledge (e.g. Laufer and Nation, 1999), and accomplish many other useful tasks.

However, acknowledgement that the GSL may be dated started in the 1960s and 70s (e.g. Engels, 1968; Richards, 1974), and has been a growing concern ever since (Carter, 1998; Hwang and Nation, 1995), especially with regard to the second 1,000 words (Hancioğlu, *et al.*, 2008). Additionally, the fact that the AWL is largely dependent on the GSL coming first in general frequency has made us wonder for some time where AWL words would fall in general frequency lists if they were not constrained by the GSL (cf. Eldridge, 2008; Hancioğlu, *et al.*, 2008).

The problem with relying on corpus-based frequency lists is that most corpora are static or frozen in time – that is, they are not updated with new material to reflect current language trends. Because of this, static corpora like those used to produce the GSL become outdated after several years of service. Again, the second 1,000 words of the GSL have often been criticized on this basis. However, only a few open or monitor corpora exist in the world, most notably the *Corpus of*

Task 3.6

Consider now the second way core lists become dated. Using the "chart" display in the *Corpus of Historical American English* (COHA – Davies, 2010–), I generated the frequency trends for the words *telegraph* and *e-mail* seen in Figure 3.3. Study the graphs and then answer the questions that follow. You may also want to visit the COHA site yourself and explore historical frequency trends for other words (http://corpus.byu.edu/coha/).

SECTION	1810	1820	1830	1840	1850	1860	1870	1880	1890	1900	1910	1920	1930	1940	1950	1960	1970	1980	1990	2000
FREQ	0	13	27	58	98	204	492	543	548	553	446	659	524	619	259	175	154	163	109	123
PER MIL	0.00	1.88	1.96	3.61	5.95	11.96	26.51	26.73	26.60	25.03	19.65	25.69	21.30	25.42	10.55	7.30	6.47	6.44	3.90	4.16
SEE ALL YEARS AT ONCE																				

Figure 3.3a Historical frequency trends for TELEGRAPH.

SECTION	1810	1820	1830	1840	1850	1860	1870	1880	1890	1900	1910	1920	1930	1940	1950	1960	1970	1980	1990	2000
FREQ	0	0	2	1	6	0	1	6	10	6	9	13	6	6	6	5	4	1	487	1758
PER MIL	0.00	0.00	0.15	0.06	0.36	0.00	0.05	0.30	0.49	0.27	0.40	0.51	0.24	0.25	0.24	0.21	0.17	0.04	17.43	59.46
SEE ALL YEARS AT ONCE																				

Figure 3.3b Historical frequency trends for E-MAIL.

Occurrences of "e-mail" prior to the 1980s are references in documents.

1   What do the frequency trends tell us about the relative importance of these two words over time?

2   How does this information inform us about the nature of core vocabulary lists based on static or frozen corpora?

Contemporary American English (Davies, 2008–) and the *Cobuild Corpus* (1980–) or *Bank of English*, where the core could be adjusted over time as the open corpora are updated and new words are then identified as being more or less important in actual usage.

The stable and unstable cores of the English lexicon

Despite the five challenges discussed above, there remains a strong need in English language education to work from the basis of a core vocabulary (Carter, 1998; Hancioğlu, *et al.*, 2008). Perhaps the most compelling reason is that ignoring a core vocabulary altogether poses an even more difficult quandary for ELLs and their teachers – namely, where does one start to build a base of English vocabulary that can support basic communication and literacy needs, as well as support additional vocabulary learning? In short, ELLs cannot function in an English-speaking environment with an empty or severely limited English lexicon, and it takes word knowledge to learn new word knowledge. With this in mind, and acknowledging the five challenges above, I propose a new approach that considers a *stable core* and an *unstable core* of English vocabulary for prioritizing general vocabulary instruction. The goals here are:

1 to address some long-standing issues surrounding general core vocabulary and instructional word lists;
2 to provide an updated core list of high frequency English words based on two large and contemporary corpora of English (COCA and BNC);
3 to provide a well-reasoned approach for addressing this new core from an instructional perspective; and
4 to provide a solid foundation for addressing specialized vocabulary issues.

To begin, the fluid nature of English necessitates that we consider two types of core vocabulary that vary not only in their relative frequency, but also in their stability over time. I illustrate the stability-over-time issue in Figure 3.4, emphasizing upfront that the diagram represents a living and dynamic English lexicon with no fixed boundaries of absolute stability.

The stable core

The stable core contains high frequency words that tend to hang around and have an impact in the language for many decades, with some being permanent core members, including function words (*the, a, of, to*, etc.) and many common content words (*go, make, time,*

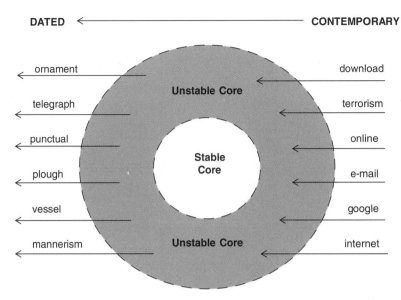

DATED ⟵————————————————————⟶ CONTEMPORARY

ornament

telegraph

punctual

plough

vessel

mannerism

Unstable Core

Stable
Core

Unstable Core

download

terrorism

online

e-mail

google

internet

Figure 3.4 English core vocabulary.

people, etc.). For example, notice in the COHA screenshot in Figure 3.5 the consistent frequency for the word *TIME* over two centuries of American English.

Some relatively stable core members may also be words like *radio, telephone,* and *television* that reflect major changes in society over long periods of time, though words in this category may eventually move out of the stable core. My *telegraph* example earlier in this chapter is an illustration of this – heavy usage in the 1870s through 1940s (roughly 70 years), and then declining quite rapidly thereafter because of a newer technology (the telephone). This is why the word *telegraph* appears in the GSL (based on texts from the early 1900s), but may not be as important in topics of current interest.

Interestingly, the COHA screenshots in Figure 3.6 show that the word *telephone* itself has been on the decline since the 1970s, but that its family member, *phone,* continues to climb the frequency charts, partially because of natural vocabulary simplification (*telephone* to *phone*), and partially because of the social impact of an even newer technology (the *cell phone*). This example shows the complexity of trying to manage a core vocabulary of English.

Additionally, there may be new words entering the stable core as they become firmly established in the language over longer periods of time. Frequency trends suggest that words like *internet, e-mail, online,* and other popular technology terms may be candidates for future stable core status.

SECTION	1810	1820	1830	1840	1850	1860	1870	1880	1890	1900	1910	1920	1930	1940	1950	1960	1970	1980	1990	2000
FREQ	1621	12107	22960	26380	28552	30825	34533	38483	38936	40730	43224	48714	47936	50490	51789	49101	46741	47250	55131	59478
PER MIL	1,372.33	1,747.75	1,666.84	1,643.78	1,733.40	1,807.40	1,860.39	1,894.22	1,890.02	1,843.19	1,904.09	1,898.90	1,948.41	2,073.69	2,109.98	2,047.82	1,962.65	1,866.41	1,973.08	2,011.61
SEE ALL YEARS AT ONCE																				

Figure 3.5 Historical frequency trends for TIME (source: COHA 2011).

SECTION	1810	1820	1830	1840	1850	1860	1870	1880	1890	1900	1910	1920	1930	1940	1950	1960	1970	1980	1990	2000
FREQ	0	0	0	0	0	4	20	170	409	1145	1585	2223	3141	3294	2743	2750	2849	2810	2234	1167
PER MIL	0.00	0.00	0.00	0.00	0.00	0.23	1.08	8.37	19.85	51.82	69.82	86.65	127.67	135.29	111.75	114.69	119.63	111.00	79.95	39.47

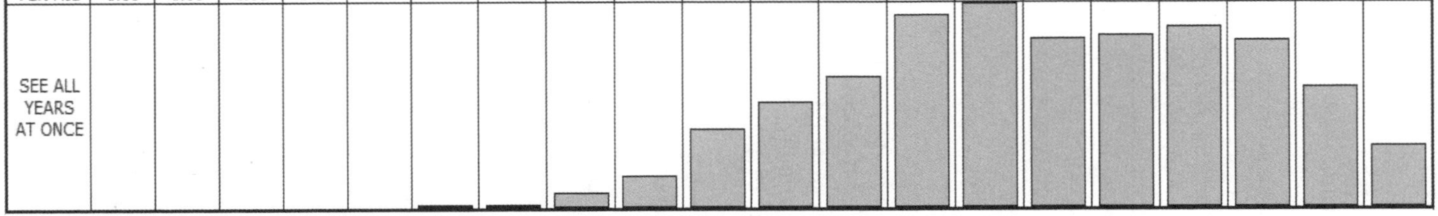

SEE ALL YEARS AT ONCE

Figure 3.6a Historical frequency trends for TELEPHONE (source: COHA 2011).

SECTION	1810	1820	1830	1840	1850	1860	1870	1880	1890	1900	1910	1920	1930	1940	1950	1960	1970	1980	1990	2000
FREQ	0	0	0	0	0	0	1	2	19	175	494	559	1424	1883	2213	3167	3579	3912	5455	7459
PER MIL	0.00	0.00	0.00	0.00	0.00	0.00	0.05	0.10	0.92	7.92	21.76	21.79	57.88	77.34	90.16	132.08	150.28	154.53	195.23	252.27

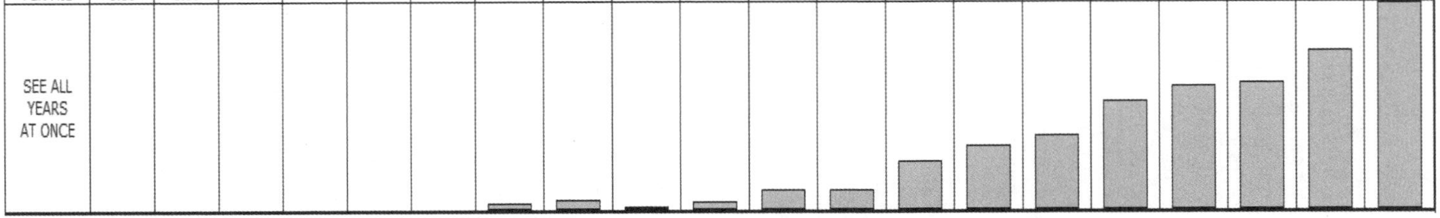

SEE ALL YEARS AT ONCE

Figure 3.6b Historical frequency trends for PHONE (source: COHA 2011).

All of these examples indicate that "stability" is a relative concept on the fringes of the stable core. I show this in the core diagram (Figure 3.4) by using a broken line around the stable core, suggesting that there may be some changes over time. Again, these will be primarily with more specific or specialized content words that hang around for a while, not with ultra-high frequency content words (*time, people, think, go, say, move*, etc.), and certainly not with the ultra-high frequency function words (*the, a, and, for, to, that, he, she*, etc.). However, to not include the more specific or specialized groups at some level of a stable core would be a mistake, because they are important words, impacting communication, literature, and so forth over relatively long periods of time, as opposed to unstable content words that may be important for a year or two, but soon fade out (*groovy, gnarly, VCR, floppy disk, zip drive*, etc.).

The unstable core

I refer to the next level of coreness as the unstable core to emphasize its variable nature. Content words (nouns, verbs, adjectives, adverbs) in the unstable core are more frequent in general than most content words of the language, but they are normally less frequent than content words in the stable core for one or more of the following reasons:

1 They are not as versatile as stable core content words in terms of their possible meanings.
2 They are not as versatile as stable core content words in terms of their impact across major English registers (e.g. American and British) and sub-registers (e.g. spoken, fiction, newspapers, magazines, academic).
3 They are not as versatile as stable core content words in terms of their collocations with other words in forming multiword items such as phrasal verbs, idioms, and other fixed phrases.
4 They are not as time-tested as stable core content words. They may be new on the English scene, or they may be on their way out in terms of their impact in English usage. Thus, they appear with less consistency in general across English samples from various time periods.

Despite these differences, they are important words in terms of a systematic approach to general vocabulary instruction, because they tend to cover a useful percentage of the language that ELLs are likely to encounter or need to use beyond the stable core.

Common Core List of English vocabulary

The call for a new core list of high frequency English words has been around for quite some time, and so have descriptions of the challenges involved in trying to produce such a list (e.g. Carter, 1998; Nation and Waring, 1997; Read, 2000). I discussed several of these challenges early in this chapter, and agree with other researchers that the task of producing a valid and reliable core list is extremely difficult. However, I am equally concerned that too much reliance has been placed on the dated GSL in vocabulary applications in language education, and that we would be better off with a new list that reflects more contemporary usage. As mentioned previously, I am also concerned that words on the popular AWL used in academic settings are assumed by many to be the next step after the GSL in terms of instructional importance, when some of the AWL words may actually supersede some GSL words in terms of their general frequency in the language.

With all of this in mind, I offer the Common Core List (CCL) of English vocabulary as a bridge from the GSL and AWL approach to a more contemporary view of English core vocabulary. The CCL is essentially a combination of the top shared words of COCA and the BNC, with words in the top 1,000 of these lists receiving higher priority than words in the next 2,000 and so forth. The basic rubric used to classify the words into sublists is displayed in Figure 3.7, with numbers representing 1,000-word tiers in the two corpora (1 = 1–1,000; 2 = 1,001–2,000; 3 = 2,001–3,000; 4 = 3,001–4,000; etc.):

SUBLIST	BNC	COCA
A	1	1
A	1	2
A	1	3
A	1	4
A	2	1
A	3	1
A	4	1
B	2	2
B	2	3
B	2	4
B	3	2
B	4	2
C	3	3
C	3	4
C	4	3
C	4	4
C	1	NONE 4
C	2	NONE 4
C	NONE 4	1
C	NONE 5	2
C	NONE 6	3

Figure 3.7 Common Core List (CCL).

The CCL headwords are reproduced in Appendix D in three Sublists (A, B, and C), based on the strength of their combined frequencies in the two corpora. I have indicated which of these words are also found in the GSL, AWL, and Dolch–Fry lists in order to determine where these older lists fit in a more contemporary core of words, and therefore how useful they continue to be for instructional purposes. Results from several pilot studies show that the CCL word families cover a greater percentage of a variety of texts than either the GSL–AWL or BNC versions of *Range*, with ongoing testing underway.

Appendix D, Sublist A (function words)

Unlike most core lists, the CCL breaks out function words from content words in the highest frequency list (A). I view this move as being crucial to our vocabulary discussion for two primary reasons:

1 The learning burdens for function words are very different than for content words, with content words requiring more attention to both meaning and form; and
2 Assessments of the vocabulary coverage of written and oral texts based on core lists can be distorted and even misleading when so much of that coverage is accounted for by the function words of the language that do not impact meaning (thus comprehension) in the same way that content words do.

I must also note that a handful of the function words on this core A list are not ultra-high frequency words (*whence, whither*, etc.), but were added to the list in order to keep all function words together for teaching and word-coverage purposes. Additionally, several of the function words in this list are actually found in the AWL (see bolded items). From my perspective, all of the function words in Sublist A should be characterized as part of a stable core.

Appendix D, Sublist A (content words)

The content words of Sublist A could also be thought of as part of a stable core because they are relatively frequent across both COCA (American English) and the BNC (British English).

> ## Task 3.7
>
> Take a moment to look over the Sublist A content words in Appendix D. Notice how this contemporary high frequency list is comprised of words from all of the older important lists (GSL 1000, GSL 2000, AWL, Dolch–Fry), as well as many newcomer words. What does this say about the nature of a "core" vocabulary over time, particularly the unstable portion of that core? What does this say about the nature of the corpora from which core-word lists are generated?

Appendix D, Sublists B and C (content words)

While no absolute distinctions can be made between stable and unstable core words, it would be fair to say that stability may be on a cline from Sublist A (most stable) to Sublist C (least stable), with Sublist B being somewhere in the middle. Of course, these lists are subject to the same changes over time that all other lists are subject to, and I would fully expect them to be adjusted in the future. I must also make it clear that my choice to work with corpora containing more contemporary English may come at a price if the needs of our ELLs are more historical in nature (reading older novels, historical documents, etc.). However, I believe the opposite situation to be even more problematic – namely, trying to meet the needs of ELLs in the contemporary world using word lists based on historical content.

> ## Task 3.8
>
> Take a few moments to look over Appendix D, Sublists B and C in order to answer the following questions:
>
> 1 Why does there appear to be far more newcomer words (not in the older lists) in Sublists B and C than in Sublist A?
> 2 Why are there only eight Dolch–Fry words in Sublist B and zero Dolch–Fry words in Sublist C, yet 262 in Sublist A? What does this say about the Dolch–Fry Lists?

Several key insights can be gained by comparing the CCL with the older core lists that have had such an impact in English Language Education, Applied Linguistics, and Second Language Acquisition:

1 Many of the *first thousand GSL word families* remain prominent in the language (appearing in Appendix D, Sublist A), while several are less prominent (appearing in Appendix D, Sublists B and C or not in the CCL at all).

	Families
Sublist A function and content	793
Sublist B content words	150
Sublist C content words	34
Not in CCL	23
TOTAL	1,000

Examples of words from the first thousand GSL that are not in the more contemporary CCL at all include *accord, castle, coin, furnish, scarce, sword, vessel,* and *virtue,* and examples that are in Sublist C (the least stable list of the CCL) include *captain, colony, empire, miner, sail, shore, wound,* and *yield.*

2 Several of the *second thousand GSL word families* are more prominent than they once were, while many do not appear to be core any longer.

	Families
Sublist A function and content	171
Sublist B content words	297
Sublist C content words	204
Not in CCL	328
TOTAL	1,000

Examples of the 328 that are not in the CCL include *arch, barber, charm, donkey, handkerchief, hurrah, saucer, spade, telegraph,* and *umbrella.*

3 Many of the *AWL word families* are among the highest frequency content and function words of the language.

	Families
Sublist A function and content	118
Sublist B content words	197
Sublist C content words	255*
Not in CCL	0*
TOTAL	570

Note
* 62 AWL word families added that were not in top 4,000 words of COCA or BNC.

Examples of the 118 AWL words in Sublist A include *area, authority, community, economy, energy, environment, goal, income, link, network, research,* and *technology.* Examples of the 197 AWL words in Sublist B include *adult, annual, channel, chapter, contrast, edit, highlight, investigate, method, overall, text,* and *virtual.* The key point here is that these academic words are in the top 1,970 words (Sublists A and B combined) of the CCL, which is derived from the modern and very large COCA and BNC corpora, thus validating our concerns that they should not be thought of as something to be learned after the GSL – a list based on much smaller and less balanced corpora from the first half of the twentieth century (cf. Hancioğlu, *et al.*, 2008).

The fact that all 570 academic word families are represented somewhere in the CCL suggests that general training with these words should be given some early priority in second-language academic settings, with those in Sublists A and B receiving higher priority than those in Sublist C. Of course, AWL words actually appearing in the texts and tasks that our particular learners will encounter should be given highest priority, with their context-specific meanings being the focus of that instruction and practice.

4 The *Dolch and Fry lists* continue to represent some of the highest frequency words of the English language.

	Types	Families
Sublist A function and content	306	262
Sublist B content words	8	8
Sublist C content words	0	0
Not in CCL	0	0
TOTAL	314	270

Based on my findings, I endorse these lists for use in second and foreign language education, not only because they pass the test of time in terms of their impact in the English core, but also because there are many resources available to learn these words, most of which come from primary literacy education.

Just how important are the 314 types of the combined Dolch and Fry lists in today's English? Adapting the *Range* program (Heatley, *et al.*, 2002), I found that the 314 Dolch–Fry types account for 58.3 percent of the nearly 1.5 million tokens of the *Children's Corpus* (Gardner, 2004). In other words, over 58 of every 100 word tokens, on average, come from this list of 314 words. Also impressive is the fact that every one of the 314 words is actually used in the corpus (not always the case with some lists), with the lowest frequency being 60 for the word *draw*, and the highest being 89,764 for the word *the*. I further determined that every word appears in both of the major narrative and expository divisions of·the *Children's Corpus*. Simply put, our ELLs need to know these words, and know them well. Interestingly, 130 of these types are grammatical function words (*the, and, to, a, of,* etc.), while the remaining 184 consist of ultra-high-frequency nouns (*ball, clothes, ear, people, woman, year,* etc.), verbs (*came, carry, eat, go, grow,* etc.), adjectives (*best, better, good, black, white, red,* etc.), adverbs (*again, also, always, early,* etc.), or crossovers that could operate under several different parts of speech (*run, saw, show, coat,* etc.). Because these words are so core and so stable over time, I strongly recommend that they be taught and practiced early in English language education. In fact, I believe they represent the best starting point for dealing with the general high frequency words of English.

5   Several *new words* appear in the CCL that are not in any of the older lists.

	Families
Sublist A function and content	64
Sublist B content words	177
Sublist C content words	395
Not in CCL	0
TOTAL	636

NEW WORDS APPEARING IN SUBLIST A (ALL 64 WORDS)

*according, **ah**, America, **aw**, awful, basis, bet, bother, brilliant, Britain, budget, campaign, candidate, career, cell, chairman, choice, Christ, client, closes, clothe, county, dad, death, decision, defence, democrat, direction, drug, Europe, evidence, executive, feed, France, Germany, guy, **ha**, hell, huge, interview, kid, knowledge, meaning, movie, museum, okay, original, ounce, pension, professor, religious, response, score, song, switch, tablespoon, teaspoon, television, traffic, trial, unit, video, x, z.*

EXAMPLES OF THE 177 NEW WORDS APPEARING IN SUBLIST B:

abuse, acid, agenda, aircraft, airport, alarm, apartment, background, battery, bike, bomb, cancer, cash, charity, chip, chocolate, conservative, crazy, crisis, diet, disaster, entitle, flight, fuel, furniture, golf, household, jacket, launch, magazine, mess, mortgage, pilot, planet, poll, pop, pregnant, sandwich, session, software, sponsor, sue, troop, urban, web, zone.

EXAMPLES OF THE 395 NEW WORDS APPEARING IN SUBLIST C:

administrator, airline, alcohol, angel, athlete, atmosphere, automobile, boyfriend, cable, campus, carbon, communist, convict, database, diagram, disc, divorce, electronic, e-mail, fibre, genetic, girlfriend, helicopter, hurricane, immigrant, internet, jeans, jet, lawsuit, medication, missile, online, pants, pill, racial, refrigerate, rocket, satellite, scandal, spokesman, suicide, terror, tragedy, workshop.

The number and characteristics of these new words emphasizes the need to use current word lists based on the most contemporary English available, and that the core of English can change over time. It is easy to see how these "up-to-date" core words could become foundationally important for ELLs attempting to negotiate current topics on the internet, in newspapers, magazines, and books, and in many other contemporary texts or tasks.

Suggestions for general core vocabulary instruction

1 Curricula for early academic English training should include regular practice with high frequency words of English, either during regular classroom instruction or as closely monitored homework assignments. Whenever possible, this practice should involve all modes of communication (listening, speaking, reading, and writing), and curricula should ensure that words are practiced in both isolation (flashcards, matching activities, etc.) and in meaningful contexts (stories, role plays, reports, etc.). The collocation possibilities with these words should also be emphasized (*jump high, down low, dark blue, good morning*, etc.).

2 In academic settings, ELLs should master the basic Dolch and Fry words, especially in early English literacy training. These words represent a substantial portion of Sublist A, and there are many resources available online for learning them (see Appendix E). The goal should be for our learners to recognize all of these words accurately and fluently, and to quickly connect forms with meanings (e.g. flashcards with English high frequency words on one side and their Spanish or other L1 equivalents on the reverse side). However, we should be careful not to introduce all meanings of a particular word in the same learning session, and to spread out the review sessions, with longer and longer time frames between sessions (Nation, 2008). Wherever possible, learners should be exposed to the native pronunciation of words at the same time they are working with the written forms of those words. Online programs like *Quizlet* (2011) are excellent resources for accomplishing this goal (see www.quizlet.com).

3 ELLs should practice with other high frequency words (including AWL words), but teachers should be selective in terms of which words to have ELLs focus on. This may require teachers to create their own flashcards or other activities using *Quizlet* or comparable programs. The primary consideration for selection should be those *high frequency words that will appear in the actual texts or tasks* that ELLs will be required to deal with (i.e. in fiction and nonfiction books, basic science projects, etc.). In early English literacy instruction, teachers may also want to consider using graded readers, which provide repetitive encounters with high frequency words in carefully designed contexts, such as simplified classics or original books written with both vocabulary presentation and interesting content in mind (e.g. *Oxford Bookworms Library*, 2011).

4 General high frequency word practice is never a waste of time because of the impact these words have in the English language, as well as the foundation they provide for basic communication and for learning additional words that become crucial to success in more specialized areas of communication (science topics, math topics, business topics, etc.). Appendix E contains many online programs (with my site ratings) for learning Dolch and Fry words, other general high frequency words, and the AWL words. Depending on your instructional situation, you should be able to find or adapt programs on the list to meet the needs of your learners. Again, these could be made part of your regular curriculum or assigned as closely monitored homework. I also wish to emphasize the power of *Quizlet* (2011, www.quizlet.com) and comparable programs to allow flexible focused practice with the words that your learners need to know.

Chapter summary

The main purpose of this chapter was to make you more aware of the difficult issues surrounding a core vocabulary of English, so that you can be better informed about what to teach in this regard, as well as how to deal with high frequency word lists that continue to be so influential in English language education. I have also introduced the *Common Core List* (CCL) as a viable new core based on two of the largest contemporary and publically available corpora in the world – COCA (American English) and the BNC (British English). However, this new core, like others before it, is not without limitations, particularly in dealing with multiword items and the multiple meanings of many high frequency word forms. These issues will require you as teachers to adapt the resources listed in Appendix E, as you implement the teaching of core words within the frameworks of your English instruction. In future chapters, we will discuss ways to create your own vocabulary tools to meet the needs of your particular learners.

While I view this chapter on core vocabulary as a necessary discussion in the area of English vocabulary, I also see it as inadequate by itself. In short, we must find ways to connect the core to the specific needs of our English language learners. In the next chapter, we will focus on this very idea, using the core to determine the more specialized words that our learners must deal with.

A new Academic Vocabulary List

At the time of publication of this book, a new *Academic Vocabulary List,* based on a corpus of over 120 million words of contemporary academic English, was under review (Gardner and Davies, under review). The list represents a core of academic English words which appear much more often in academic materials than in non-academic materials and which have excellent coverage across nine major registers of academic English: (1) education, (2) humanities, (3) history, (4) social science, (5) philosophy, religion, and psychology, (6) law and political science, (7) science and technology, (8) medicine and health, and (9) business and finance. The list is statistically-driven and is therefore not based on any preconceived assumptions about a more general list preceding it, or more technical lists following it. It contains core academic words as basic as *study, group, result,* and *change,* and as complex as *theoretical, independence, yield,* and *facilitate.* Because of the size of the corpus from which the words are drawn and the powerful statistics used to find them, these words are saturated with academic sense and represent a serious list to consider for future academic training. This core academic list is also being tied into a powerful online user interface that teachers and learners can utilize to find and study academic core vocabulary.

Vocabulary Project (downloading analysis tools)

In order to analyze the electronic texts you assembled from the assignment in Chapter 2, you will need to download and learn to use three freeware programs from the internet:

1, 2 *Range program with GSL/AWL lists* (Heatley, *et al.*, 2002) and *Range program with BNC lists* (Nation, 2004). Both are downloadable for Windows PCs at: www.victoria.ac.nz/lals/staff/paul-nation.aspx. The programs will be available on the website in downloadable ZIP files. The file comes with the actual *Range* program and several supporting resources, including "INSTRUCTIONS.doc." You should carefully read through these instruction documents to learn how to run both versions of *Range,* and then practice using *Range* with several electronic texts.

3   *kfNgram* (Fletcher, 2010). Downloadable for Windows PCs at: www.kwicfinder.com/kfNgram/kfNgramHelp.html. The *download* tab is available on the home page, as are the instruction tabs (*use, options,* etc.). After downloading the *kfNgram* program, you should completely familiarize yourself with how the program finds phrases (n-grams) in texts, and then practice using the program with several electronic texts.

4 Register-specific vocabulary

Problem

I often address groups of educators wanting to know how to meet the vocabulary needs of their English language learners. The first question I always ask is "what English do your learners need to know?" This question may seem too broad or uninteresting on the surface, but it is surprising how often it generates a discussion that leads to major reforms in the way some teachers manage the vocabulary issues in their classrooms. I have even witnessed an intensive English program completely revise their curriculum as a result of answering this simple question. On the other hand, not answering this question to begin with, especially with vocabulary issues, is like trying to drink from a fire hydrant, or like typing "anywhere" in *Google Maps* and then hoping for useful results – the task is simply too big and too complex.

The purpose of this chapter is to make a clear case for addressing the specific vocabulary needs of ELLs, whatever educational settings they may be in. I also hope to bring some sense of order and focus to English vocabulary instruction by determining "what" to teach. In turn, knowing what to teach will help us better understand "how" we might teach it. Some of the questions we will address include:

- How do registers and sub-registers affect the words my learners need to deal with?
- How do I determine the specific words my learners need to know?
- How do I determine the specific multiword items my learners need to know?

Intervention and theory

Register-specific vocabulary

Many vocabulary teaching approaches emphasize direct core vocabulary training early on, and then shift the focus to vocabulary-strategy instruction (using dictionaries, guessing meanings from context, looking at word parts, etc.), with the idea that the sheer number of non-core words cannot be dealt with in any systematic manner, and must therefore be dealt with by individual learners through natural language exposure. As evidence, these approaches tend to emphasize the size of the learning task (how many words there are in the English language, how many words typical native speakers know, how many words a learner can normally acquire in a year, how many words can be taught directly, etc.). These are typical characteristics of the view I have alluded to in this book as English for general purposes (i.e. general core, general strategies, general goals). Teaching and learning materials generated from this view tend to have a holistic feel to them, such as vocabulary examples and practice activities dealing with many different topics, needs of learners described in broad terms (listening, speaking, reading, and writing), general vocabulary assessments, and so forth. I have parted from this common approach because I believe that most ELLs have specific needs, and that they do not have unlimited time or resources to meet those needs. In turn, those needs almost invariably correspond to specific texts and tasks containing specific words with topic-focused meanings (cf. Hyland and Tse, 2007; Swales, 1990). Focusing on English for specific purposes gives us a great chance for identifying and teaching specialized words that our learners really need, together with the specific strategies that would be most beneficial for learning those words. I also believe that such an approach is more motivational for ELLs and their teachers.

Understanding and managing core vocabulary becomes very important in the context of English for specific purposes. Consider, for instance, that a useful general core list is based on a large, broad, and balanced corpus (registers equally represented), which poses two serious quandaries: (1) many words and phrases that would be high frequency in a specific register will be ignored on the core list, either because they lack sufficient range over many registers, or because they lack sufficient frequency in the overall scheme of things; and (2) many words that make the list because of general frequency and range will be of little service to the focused learner, because the non-specificity of such words (frequent forms representing many different meanings across different registers) often gets them on the list in the first place. In turn, this means that learners using such general lists to learn vocabulary may spend valuable time and energy learning some words that do not directly intersect with their specific needs or interests at the current moment.

Another concern with over-emphasizing general core English vocabulary is that most of the words of real importance to comprehension are often not high frequency words with common meanings, but specialized words in specific registers (*emancipation, proclamation, confederacy, asteroid, amoeba*, etc.), or high frequency words with specialized meanings in specific registers (*mean* = average;

mouse = handheld computer-control device) (cf. Nation, 2008). Unlike general core words such as ultra-high frequency function and content words, register-specific words tend to carry the bulk of the important meaning (Carter, 1998), and are therefore essential for achieving adequate comprehension. A simple example will serve to illustrate this point. As mentioned in Chapter 3, reading research indicates that approximately 95–98 percent of the words in a given text must be known by the reader in order to achieve adequate comprehension. With this in mind, study the message in Figure 4.1 with four different percentages of known words (non-blanks), and then attempt to answer the test question at the end.

1

When we are _____ _____, we _____ that your _____ of the _____ _____ _____ _____ _____ will be _____ _____, _____with _____ to the _____ _____ between _____ _____ and _____ _____.

44% Word Knowledge

2

When we are _____ today, we ____ that your ____ of the _____ facing _____language _____ will be _____ forever, _____ with _____ to the _____ _____ between reading _____ and vocabulary _____.

63% Word Knowledge

3

When we are finished today, we hope that your view of the _____ facing English language learners will be changed forever, _____ with _____ to the _____ relationship between reading abilities and vocabulary knowledge.

88% Word Knowledge

4

When we are finished today, we hope that your view of the challenges facing English language learners will be changed forever, especially with regard to the _____ relationship between reading abilities and vocabulary knowledge.

97% Word Knowledge

TEST QUESTION: What kind of relationship exists between vocabulary knowledge and reading abilities?

Figure 4.1 Word knowledge at lower percentages.

In this example, the register is *Applied Linguistics*, or, more specifically, *Second Language Reading*. Those not familiar with this specific field of study will likely struggle to guess the correct unknown word to pass the test question (see *reciprocal* in Figure 4.2), despite the fact that they may know the rest of the words in the surrounding cotext.

> **5**
>
> When we are finished today, we
> hope that your view of the challenges
> facing English language learners will
> be changed forever, especially with
> regard to the **reciprocal** relationship
> between reading abilities and
> vocabulary knowledge.
> **100% Word Knowledge**

Figure 4.2 Word knowledge, 100 percent.

Words like *reciprocal* carry a great deal of the meaning in certain contexts, and if we or our ELLs do not know them, or have ways of learning them, it is clear what the consequences will be in terms of comprehension. It is also true in this example that knowing only *reciprocal*, without the words surrounding it, would be of no real value when it comes to comprehension of the sentence.

Consider one more example from a competency test given to all high-school students in one U.S. state. Those who passed the test received a high-school competency designation on their official transcript. Figure 4.3 is an adapted excerpt from one of the reading passages that students (including ELLs) were expected to comprehend (through multiple-choice questions), with bolding indicating those words *not found* in the GSL or AWL high frequency lists:

STORAGE AND DISPOSAL STATEMENT

STORAGE: Store in an area inaccessible to children and away from heat or open flame.

DISPOSAL: This container may be **recycled** in the few but growing number of communities where **aerosol** can **recycling** is available. Before offering for **recycling**, empty the can by using the product according to the label. (DO NOT **PUNCTURE!**) If **recycling** is not available, do not **reuse** empty container. Wrap the container and discard in the **trash**.

PRECAUTIONARY STATEMENTS: **HAZARDS** TO HUMANS AND DOMESTIC ANIMALS CAUTION: Harmful if **absorbed** through the skin. Keep out of the reach of children. Avoid contact with skin, eyes, and clothing. Do not remain in enclosed areas after use. **Ventilate** enclosed areas before returning. Avoid **contamination** of food. Remove plants, pets, and birds before using. Cover and turn off fish **aquariums**. Wash hands thoroughly with soap and water after handling.

STATEMENT OF PRACTICAL TREATMENT: If on skin, remove with soap and water. If **irritation** persists, seek medical attention.

ENVIRONMENTAL **HAZARDS**: Do not apply directly to water. This **pesticide** is toxic to fish.

Figure 4.3 High-school comprehension test passage (source: retrieved March 13, 2003 from *Utah State Office of Education* website and adapted).

Task 4.2

Review the passage in Figure 4.3 and answer the following:

1 What is the specific topic of the reading passage?
2 How important are the bolded words in describing the topic?
3 How important are the non-bolded words in describing the topic?
4 Do any of the non-bolded words have topic-specific meanings?
5 How would reading comprehension be affected if the bolded words were not known by ELL readers (*storage, aerosol, recycling, puncture, reuse, precautionary, hazards, absorbed, ventilate, contamination, aquariums, irritation, pesticide*)?
6 What does this example say about the relationship between specific topics, core vocabulary, and vocabulary for specific purposes?

The main point of this example is that the real-world needs of our ELLs often demand knowledge of specific vocabulary for specific purposes. It is noteworthy that many of the general and academic high frequency words are also specific to the topic of the sample passage (*disposal, container, flame, product, harmful, toxic, apply,* etc.), and that passage comprehension would not be possible without knowledge of these words.

Understanding registers

The many varieties of English (spoken, newspapers, academic, etc.) all have their specific words, as well as their specific grammatical structures, discourse structures, and so on. Applied linguists refer to these varieties as registers, with each register usually consisting of sub-registers with their own special linguistic characteristics. Figure 4.4 provides an example breakdown of major written registers of English. Keep in mind that a similar layout could be done for spoken English.

Narrative (Tells a story)	Expository (Informs, defines, explains, instructs)

Fiction (novels and short stories)
    General fiction
    Romance fiction
    Adventure fiction
    Science fiction
    Historical fiction
Biographies
Autobiographies
Personal essays
Movies
Poems
Plays
Other
	Newspaper articles
	    World news
	    Local news
	    Business and economics
	    Sports
	    Editorials
	    Home and garden
	    Obituaries
	    Other
	Magazine articles
	    World issues
	    Local issues
	    Sports issues
	    Business and economics issues
	    Other
	Manuals
	    Owner's manuals
	    Instruction manuals
	Dictionaries
	    Monolingual
	    Bilingual
	    Bilingualized
	Scripted newscasts
	Informative essays
	Academic (textbooks, articles, nonfiction tradebooks)
	    History
	        World history
	        American history
	        British history
	        Australian history
	        Other
	    Science
	        Earth science
	        Physical science
	        Life science
	    Business
	        Marketing
	        Advertising
	        Accounting
	Other

Figure 4.4 Example of written English registers.

In a sense, Figure 4.4 is a graphic depiction of the question I posed at the start of the chapter: "What English?" When we consider that within each of these registers there are characteristic vocabulary items that make the register what it is – that make it different than the other registers in some way – we also must realize the necessity of finding out what those words are in order to meet the specific needs of our ELLs. As you continue to work with the idea of register-specific vocabulary, you will undoubtedly become more linguistically aware of the relative consistency with which certain terms and expressions are used by those who communicate in a particular register.

But we must not stop here either. Each of the registers noted in Figure 4.4 could be further subdivided into even more specific sub-registers, with their own specific vocabularies. For example, life science has at least the sub-classifications shown in Figure 4.5.

Some common core of life-science words is likely to be shared between all of these sub-registers (and these will be crucial to know), but each will undoubtedly have a set of very specific terms that are unique to that particular discipline. Think about it for a minute – if the words were all the same in the sub-registers, how would we be able to distinguish between those registers, and, therefore, why would they exist in the first place? This may seem like a "no brainer," but it amazes me how often vocabulary teaching and learning is attempted with some abstract level of generality in mind, when what is really needed is knowledge of words for specific purposes. A graphic representation of register-based vocabulary may look something like the one in Figure 4.6. Keep in mind that the registers in the diagram

Agrotechnology	Cell biology	Microbiology
Bio-engineering	Cognitive neuroscience	Molecular biology
Biomedical science	Computational	Nanotechnology
Biochemistry	neuroscience	Neuroinformatics
Biocomputing	Developmental biology	Neuroscience
Biocontrol	Ecology	Oncology
Biodynamics	Environmental science	Optometry
Bioinformatics	Evolutionary biology	Personalized
Biology	Evolutionary genetics	medicine
Biomaterials	Food science	Pharmacogenomics
Biomechanics	Genetics	Pharmacology
Biomedical sciences	Genomics	Physiology
Biomolecular	Health sciences	Plant sciences
engineering	Immunogenetics	Proteomics
Biomonitoring	Immunology	Structural biology
Biophysics	Immunotherapy	Systems biology
Biopolymers	Medical devices	Tissue engineering
Biotechnology	Medical imaging	Zoology
Botany	Medicine	

Figure 4.5 Partial list of life science sub-registers (source: accessed from http://en.wikipedia.org/wiki/Life_sciences on March 17, 2011).

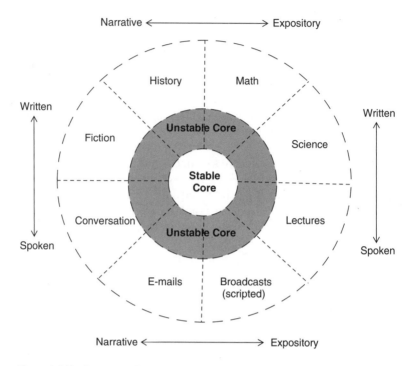

Figure 4.6 Register-specific vocabulary in the English lexicon.

are only examples, and that the actual English lexicon contains all possible registers of the language.

The sample diagram in Figure 4.6 depicts several key issues that I have determined from research:

1 Each register has its own specific vocabulary, represented by the white space in each section.
2 Each register may accept new words both from within the existing lexicon (old forms with new meanings) and from without (new words entering the language). This is represented by broken lines between sections and on the perimeter of the main lexicon circle.
3 All registers use some words from the core. Some of these words will be common to all registers (high frequency function words as *the, a, and,* etc.), while others may be high frequency forms with register-specific meanings (e.g. *mean* = average; *bug* = tiny microphone; *goal* = score in football/soccer).
4 Registers have varying degrees of similarities and differences with other registers. I indicate this by relative placement on the diagram. Registers that are next to each other tend to have vocabulary with similar characteristics (fiction and conversation, conversation and e-mails, etc.). Registers that are farther apart tend to have vocabulary

with different characteristics (e.g. fiction vs. science, conversation vs. lectures, etc.).

5 The traditional spoken–written distinction is not always a good indicator of vocabulary similarities and differences between registers. For example, conversation and fiction have many similarities, especially when a fictional text contains a lot of dialogue. Also, some written registers (e.g. e-mails) have many traditional characteristics of spoken English, while some spoken registers (e.g. scripted broadcasts) have many traditional characteristics of written English.

6 Registers tend to fall under two large macro-registers: Narrative (those with more story-like characteristics) and Expository (those that transmit facts and information) (Grabe, 2002). I indicate this by placement of the registers relative to the narrative and expository sides of the lexicon diagram (left and right respectively).

7 Some registers have more of a mixture of narrative and expository characteristics than others (cf. Biber, 1988). I indicate this by placing them closer to the middle between the narrative–expository dividing line. For example, the mathematics register is clearly expository in terms of explanations, definitions, instruction, and so on, but it also contains many story problems that have narrative characteristics, including character names, time-sequence words (*then, next*, etc.), and so on. The history register contains a lot of storytelling characteristics, but also many factual explications.

8 Any register of English can be plotted somewhere in the diagram as its own unique section of the lexicon circle.

9 Many registers can be further divided into more specific registers, or sub-registers. For example, science could be divided into earth science, life science, and physical science. Math could be divided into algebra, geometry, trigonometry, calculus, and so forth. In turn, all of these more specific registers could be divided into even more specific registers (e.g. earth science = atmosphere, biosphere, hydrosphere, etc.; calculus = differential calculus, integral calculus, etc.). Each of these sub-sub-registers will have a unique set of vocabulary items, made up of core words and subject-specific words.

Case study of register-specific vocabulary

To gain insights about vocabulary variation across registers, consider with me a case study involving books from four different reading registers in academic English: fiction, American history, mathematics, and life science. The books analyzed were written at approximately a middle-school level (11–12 year-old children). Table 4.1 provides the details of the four books:

Table 4.1 Books from four registers

Register	Book title	Author/Pub year
Fiction books	*The Westing Game*	Raskin, 1978
American history	*A History of US: Liberty for All (Book 5)*	Hakim, 1994
Mathematics	*CK-12 Middle School Math – Grade 6*	Brockett, *et al.*, 2010
Life science	*CK-12 Life Science: Honors for Middle School*	Brainard, *et al.*, 2011

To perform the case study, I used the *Range* program (Heatley, *et al.*, 2002) with my new Common Core List (CCL) as the high frequency base lists in the program. This allowed me to look at register-specific words both outside and inside the new core. I refer to those outside the core as off-list words because they do not appear in the high frequency core (see Table 4.2). Also, to emphasize the register-specific concept, I have included only those words that are in one register, but not in the other three. These are the words that would be in the respective register sections of the lexicon diagram in Figure 4.6. The frequency with which these exclusive types appear in their specific registers also indicates the impact they have in those registers.

Table 4.2 Top 75 exclusive off-list words in four different registers

Fiction	No.	Am. history	No.	Mathematics	No.	Life science	No.
WESTING	361	MISSOURI	61	DECIMAL	468	ORGANISMS	393
WEXLER	156	WAGONS	41	DECIMALS	330	JPG	365
SYDELLE	135	OREGON	38	TRIANGLE	217	WIKIMEDIA	340
THEO	133	FE	35	INTEGERS	189	BACTERIA	316
OTIS	118	JACKSON	34	DENOMINATOR	176	DNA	278
PULASKI	108	MORMONS	32	TRAVIS	146	FUNGI	188
BAUMBACH	99	KANSAS	29	RECTANGLE	145	ORGANISM	157
HEIRS	90	THOREAU	29	SUBTRACT	107	TRAITS	157
DOUG	88	OHIO	28	SUBTRACTION	106	NUTRIENTS	156
DENTON	55	WHALING	27	ZERO	100	GNU-FDL	152
THEODORAKIS	52	ELLEN	26	GRID	98	MOLECULES	137
MCSOUTHERS	51	MANJIRO	25	TANIA	97	CHROMOSOMES	131
DOORMAN	47	PIONEERS	25	CONGRUENT	95	REPRODUCTION	125
PLUM	42	VIRGINIA	24	NUMERICAL	88	MAMMALS	121
BARNEY	36	LINCOLN	23	NUMERATOR	87	REPRODUCTIVE	120
HEIR	35	ABOLITIONISTS	22	UNDERLINE	87	MEMBRANE	119
NORTHRUP	35	BOWDITCH	22	PARALLELOGRAM	84	DIGESTIVE	118
MADAME	33	SALEM	22	MEDIAN	81	PATHOGENS	114
SHIN	32	EMERSON	21	DENOMINATORS	77	DIOXIDE	113
WINDKLOPPEL	31	POLK	20	ISAAC	77	CC-BY-SA	112
INTERN	28	FORT	19	PERCENTS	76	PROTISTS	105
DRESSMAKER	24	NATHANIEL	19	MARC	75	RESPIRATORY	104
CRUTCH	23	TELEGRAPH	19	INTEGER	74	PREY	95
WINDSOR	23	JEFFERSON	18	REAL-WORLD	74	ECOSYSTEM	94
SIKES	21	MELVILLE	18	HOWSTUFFWORKS	68	IMMUNE	89

Fiction	No.	Am. history	No.	Mathematics	No.	Life science	No.
DUMB	17	OBERLIN	18	HUNDREDTHS	66	CARDIOVASCULAR	88
BABA	16	PHILADELPHIA	18	PERIMETER	65	CHROMOSOME	86
BRAID	16	PONY	18	CYLINDER	59	DARWIN	85
ALICE	15	ANDREW	17	LARRY	56	PHOTOSYNTHESIS	85
CORPSE	15	JULIA	17	POLYGON	56	LYMPH	83
ERICA	15	LOUIS	17	CIRCUMFERENCE	54	RESPIRATION	81
ROSALIE	15	TH-CENTURY	17	PARENTHESES	54	CC-BY	79
BERTHE	14	CALHOUN	16	KYLE	53	NUCLEUS	79
FIREWORKS	13	CINQUE	16	ISABELLE	51	FOSSIL	77
FLASK	13	FRONTIER	16	DILEMMA	49	ALLELE	76
RUG	13	LUCY	16	ANDERSEN	47	AMINO	74
SNOWBOUND	13	PEALE	16	SINGLE-VARIABLE	44	OFFSPRING	72
WESTINGTOWN	12	STANTON	16	GCF	43	BIOLOGY	68
GRACIE	11	ABRAHAM	15	SUBTRACTING	43	AQUATIC	67
PODIATRIST	11	MORSE	15	INVERSE	42	DOMINANT	65
CRUTCHES	10	ADAMS	14	VERTEX	41	ARCHAEA	64
LIMPED	10	DESTINY	14	QUOTIENT	40	VERTEBRATES	63
MA	10	EXPEDITION	14	HSW	39	ATP	62
RECEIPT	10	HOUSTON	14	CUBES	37	ENZYMES	62
SUSPICIOUS	10	ILLINOIS	14	DIVISOR	37	EUKARYOTIC	62
THIEF	10	OXEN	14	JONAH	37	GLUCOSE	62
WPP	10	SIERRA	14	QUADRILATERAL	37	NITROGEN	62
CHIN	9	SUTTER	14	RECTANGULAR	36	CELLULAR	61
DUMMY	9	ABOLITIONIST	13	RENAME	36	FLICKR	60
EASTMAN	9	ANTISLAVERY	13	KEVIN	35	SKELETAL	60
HALLOWEEN	9	BUREN	13	POLYGONS	35	DIABETES	59
TAPESTRY	9	ANNA	12	MATHPLAYGROUND	34	TERRESTRIAL	59
UTTERED	9	BLUBBER	12	BOX-AND-WHISKER	33	TRAIT	59
DISGUISE	8	CADY	12	PROTRACTOR	33	UTERUS	59
FLUNG	8	CATLIN	12	RECTANGLES	33	ALLELES	58
GOWN	8	CROCKETT	12	STEM-AND-LEAF	33	HOMEOSTASIS	58
HEIRESS	8	NEVADA	12	ZEROS	33	INTESTINE	58
JIMMY	8	OVERLAND	12	ALGEBRAIC	32	PHYLUM	58
LIMP	8	SECESSION	12	DIVISIBLE	32	PNG	58
MAJESTIES	8	STEAMBOAT	12	EXPONENTS	32	REPTILES	56
MUTTERED	8	WHITMAN	12	CLUBHOUSE	31	URINE	56
SQUAD	8	BUCHANAN	11	QUARTILE	31	ARTERIES	55
BROKER	7	CONCORD	11	DIVIDEND	30	ECOSYSTEMS	55
CLIPPINGS	7	CALIFORNIANS	10	PARALLELOGRAMS	30	ELECTRON	55
CLOSET	7	CLIPPER	10	LCM	29	MEIOSIS	55
DENTIST	7	COLORADO	10	CASEY	28	MOLECULE	55
FRUITED	7	NEBRASKA	10	OBTUSE	28	ALGAE	54
HIGH-SCHOOL	7	QUAKER	10	VERTICES	28	HORMONES	54
INNERSOLES	7	CLARK	9	AMUSEMENT	27	NEURONS	54
JULIAN	7	CONNECTICUT	9	QUADRILATERALS	27	KIDNEYS	52
SLUMPED	7	FUGITIVE	9	KEISHA	26	BIODIVERSITY	51
AVIATOR	6	HARDING	9	PRISMS	25	ECOLOGY	51
BLINKED	6	HARRIET	9	EXPONENT	24	VASCULAR	51
BOOKIE	6	HERMAN	9	MATH-MASTERY	24	PREDATORS	50
BRAT	6	INDIANA	9	QUOTIENTS	24	BB	49

Task 4.3

Carefully study the words in the Table 4.2, and then answer the following:

1 What are the characteristics of the words in the four different registers?
2 How can knowledge of register-specific vocabulary be useful in the ELL classroom?

The concept of register-specific vocabulary is very clear when we compare the words in these columns. Fiction is comprised of many character and place names (*Westing, Wexler, Theo, Alice, Westingtown*, etc.), along with words that describe characters (*doorman, dressmaker, dentist, heir, heiress, braid, thief*, etc.), feelings or conditions (*suspicious, dumb, muttered, snowbound, brat*, etc.), actions of people (*flung, limped, uttered, slumped*, etc.), physical items or objects (*gown, rug, tapestry, crutch*, etc.), and so forth. Many of these words can be represented by pictures and/or simple definitions or glosses (L1 equivalent words). An important distinction between these fiction words and those of the other three registers is that no clear theme (topic) emerges in the fiction words. In other words, it is hard to tell what the theme of the fiction book is by just looking at the words. This is not the case with words in the three expository (informational, nonfiction) registers that are clearly American history, mathematics, or life science respectively. This supports the suggestion that themes are a natural part of the academic content areas (Stoller and Grabe, 1997), and that theme-based words are more easily identified in expository texts than in narrative fiction (Gardner, 2008).

The American history register also contains many names of people and places, but these are very different than in fiction, because they are real people and places of historical significance (*Jackson, Thoreau, Lincoln, Jefferson, Missouri, Oregon, Virginia, Philadelphia, frontier*, etc.). Unlike most fictional names of characters that are simply an author's random choice, these historical names – with their historical significance – are likely to appear in most books on American history, and primarily for the same reasons. In other words, not knowing who Abraham Lincoln is will undoubtedly cause more comprehension issues than not knowing who Samuel Westing is. In addition to historical names, American history also contains words that describe causes, activities, philosophies, and conditions that have impacted American thought and the development of American society (*whaling, pioneers, abolitionists, antislavery, secession*, etc.). These can often represent complex concepts, not easily defined in a few words.

Interestingly, the mathematics text also contains names of people (*Travis, Tania, Isaac, Larry, clubhouse*, etc.). This is a typical characteristic of such texts when they use real-world descriptions and story problems to teach math concepts. Like fiction, these names typically have no significance beyond the particular math book itself. The most significant words of mathematics, however, are the terms used to describe math-related concepts, processes, and objects (*decimal, triangle, polygon, congruent, subtraction, circumference, divisible, exponent*, etc.). Again, understanding these words requires conceptual knowledge that goes beyond a simple definition. Many of these words contain Greek and Latin morphemes (word parts) that give some clues to word meaning (*deci = tenth*; *tri = three*; *poly = many*; *con = with*, etc.).

Finally, most of the Life Science words represent complex organisms, processes, systems, and other concepts (*bacteria, fungi, photosynthesis, respiratory, homeostasis, ecosystem, terrestrial*). Again, and perhaps even more pronounced, there is the presence of Greek and Latin morphemes (*photo = light*; *homeo = same*; *eco = environment*; *terre/terra = earth*, etc.). Additionally, it is clear in this register, more than in the others, that many of the complex terms can only be described by using other complex terms in the register, making these words the most difficult to define or describe.

If the case study were to end here, it would have served its purpose in demonstrating that specific registers have specific vocabularies with specific characteristics. However, I wish to emphasize that the effects of register impact the core as well as these off-list specialized words. Table 4.3 provides the top core words of the same four registers. Again, these are words that appear in one text and not the other three.

Task 4.4

Carefully study the words in Table 4.2 and answer the following:

1 What are the characteristics of the core words in each of the registers?
2 Is this similar to what you observed with the off-list words? Explain.
3 What does this say about the relationship between a core of general English vocabulary and vocabulary for specific purposes (registers)?

The effects of register are as clear with these higher general frequency words as they were with the off-list specialized words. In fact, most advanced native speakers of English would be able to look at the words in the columns and come up with the register they belong to

Table 4.3 Top 75 exclusive core words in four different registers

Fiction	No.	Am. history	No.	Mathematics	No.	Life science	No.
APARTMENT	56	SLAVE	99	FRACTIONS	408	COMMONS	796
TOWERS	53	SLAVERY	99	MULTIPLICATION	172	ORGANISMS	393
MURDERER	49	INDIANS	69	SIMPLIFY	135	DOMAIN	342
BOMB	25	SLAVES	55	OPERATIONS	110	ORGANS	266
STARED	25	SPANISH	32	ESTIMATION	106	OXYGEN	207
BOMBER	24	SAILORS	26	ROUNDING	92	EVOLUTION	192
ELEVATOR	21	COMPROMISE	24	SQ	71	HUMANS	167
HURRIED	13	SETTLERS	23	VIDEOS	68	FOODS	149
LEANED	13	INDEPENDENCE	23	GRAPHS	60	CYCLE	134
STUPID	12	MEXICANS	22	REWRITE	58	GENETIC	126
NODDED	12	BLACKS	21	PM	53	PROTEIN	124
STARING	11	CLAY	20	DISCOUNT	50	PROTEINS	124
WINDY	10	FOUGHT	19	ASKS	46	BONE	124
REMARKED	10	TERRITORIES	19	MULTIPLES	44	GENE	116
SHOUTING	10	DECLARATION	17	COORDINATES	42	GOV	108
VICTIM	10	ARTISTS	16	TENTHS	40	STRUCTURES	104
ATTORNEY	10	CHURCH	16	SLICES	36	ORGAN	102
DRIVEWAY	9	RAILROADS	16	THOUSANDTHS	35	SOURCES	99
PAUSED	9	MINERS	16	SUBSTITUTE	34	SELECTION	92
BET	8	CREW	15	CORRESPONDING	32	GENES	90
CORPORATION	8	TRADERS	14	SCORE	30	SUMMARY	90
CLEARED	7	TRAINS	12	WHOLES	30	PRESSURE	87
BOMBS	7	CIVIL	12	ESTIMATING	30	OBJECTIVES	85
ENGAGEMENT	7	SOUTHERNERS	12	PINTS	27	SUPPLEMENTAL	85
PARTNERS	7	CONSTITUTION	12	SIMPLIFYING	26	CHEMICALS	83
DECORATOR	7	DEMOCRACY	12	DISTRIBUTIVE	25	THEORY	82
MT	7	SAIL	12	SUPPLEMENTARY	24	INTERNAL	81
REFINE	7	SENATE	12	DEFINITELY	23	BEHAVIORS	81
TWIN	7	OWNERS	11	MILLILITERS	23	ACIDS	78
ANYHOW	6	POEM	11	PERCENTAGES	23	VIRUS	77
APPOINTMENT	6	LIBERTY	11	PLOTS	22	HYPOTHESIS	72
CHAIRMAN	6	LABOR	10	KILOMETER	21	DRUG	70
MESS	6	MARCH	10	CENTIMETER	18	POPULATIONS	69
SKIES	6	AFRICANS	10	DIMENSION	16	DISCUSSED	66
CANDLE	6	POEMS	10	FORMULAS	16	PHOTOS	62
CHEER	6	MOUNT	10	TRANSFORMATIONS	15	SUBSTANCES	60
DOORWAY	6	PASSENGERS	10	ASSOCIATIVE	14	ADAPTATIONS	59
GHOSTS	6	FREED	9	OPPOSITES	14	SEXUAL	55
MEDAL	6	HAPPINESS	9	EQUIVALENCE	14	TRANSPORT	54
PATTED	6	PRESIDENTS	9	PENNIES	14	WASTES	53
CHILDISH	5	MILLS	9	ADOPTION	13	VIRUSES	53
EXPECTING	5	MISSIONS	9	CALCULATING	13	ENVIRONMENTAL	53
GEE	5	BANKS	8	OPTIONS	13	ENVIRONMENTS	52
LAUGHING	5	DEMOCRATIC	8	THEATER	13	ATMOSPHERE	52
REMAINED	5	HEADING	8	PHRASES	13	MARINE	52
SHHH	5	LEADER	8	ABSOLUTE	12	MAINTAIN	52
TELEPHONE	5	BELONGED	8	SIDED	12	CONCENTRATION	51
APARTMENTS	5	CAMPED	8	SQUARED	12	EFFECTS	51
FRAMED	5	CIVILIZATION	8	SHADED	12	BIOLOGICAL	48
INVESTIGATOR	5	PORTRAIT	8	FRACTIONAL	11	ADAPTED	48
RESERVATIONS	5	BOATS	7	GRAPHED	11	DETECT	46
WHEELED	5	MINISTER	7	INTERVAL	11	EVOLVED	44
CONFESS	5	MINISTERS	7	EIGHTHS	10	GLOBAL	44
DISPOSABLE	5	SETTLE	7	SPENDING	10	MALES	44
PIN	5	RIDERS	7	COMPATIBLE	10	DIVERSITY	44
SQUEEZED	5	DECK	7	CLASSROOM	9	GENETICS	44
CARD	4	FLAG	7	GALLON	9	CONTROLS	44
DADDY	4	SAILING	7	REORDER	9	DISORDERS	43
RADIO	4	TRAPPERS	7	SIMPLIFIES	9	FUELS	43
SLIGHT	4	WEALTHY	7	SURVEYS	9	CONTRACT	42
UNLOCKED	4	CATCHERS	6	MULTIPLIER	9	FATS	41
YOUNGSTER	4	FAIRNESS	6	SPECIFIED	9	TUBE	41
APOLOGIZED	4	HISTORIAN	6	TILE	9	PRODUCING	41
GUILT	4	JUSTICES	6	HUNDREDTH	8	CONTACT	40
PRAY	4	NORTHWEST	6	THOUSANDTH	8	POLLUTANTS	39
QUOTATION	4	STATIONS	6	MIN	8	RELEASE	39
WAVED	4	THROW	6	PRESENTATION	8	REACTION	37
INVALID	4	TRADER	6	REWRITING	8	LUNG	36
LEAPED	4	ACADEMY	6	WALKER	8	FORMATION	36
MEDALS	4	BELLS	6	REVENUE	8	ADULTHOOD	35
GOTTA	3	EXPLORERS	6	EQUIVALENTS	8	HARMFUL	35
APPOINTMENTS	3	IRELAND	6	INTERACTIVE	8	HOST	35
EXCUSED	3	IRISH	6	SUBSTITUTING	8	INFECTIONS	35
LATEST	3	REVOLUTIONARY	6	TRANSLATIONS	8	MATURE	35
LOSER	3	MINER	6	SIXTHS	7	COMPOUNDS	35

without the column headings. Of course, word names are not a big part of the core, so very few of these appear in the lists. It is also important to emphasize here that core words are not always "easy words" from the perspective of conceptual difficulty and learnability, especially when they appear in the expository registers of the language (*independence, democracy, civilization, fraction, multiple, estimation, evolution, gene, protein, atmosphere*, etc.).

The key point I wish to emphasize in this phase of the case study is that the general core becomes much more manageable when we consider registers and English for specific purposes. If our ELLs need to read life science, then our work with them should include an emphasis on core words that could and do appear in life science, instead of core words that tend to appear in fiction, or American history, or mathematics, or any other specific register. Specific registers also tend to constrain (narrow) the meanings of high frequency word forms with multiple meanings, especially in the expository registers (Gardner, 2007a), making it easier to decide what to teach.

In the final phase of the case study, I address the multiword items that occur in the four different registers (see Table 4.4). These phrases along with their frequency counts, were obtained by using the *kfNgram* program (Fletcher, 2010), and then determining from a list which collocated words were functioning as true multiword items. The program did not allow me to determine which phrases were exclusively found in one register, but it is fairly clear from observation that the vast majority are register-specific.

Task 4.5

Carefully study the phrases in Table 4.4 and answer the following:

1 What are the characteristic differences between the phrases in the four registers?
2 How does this compare to our previous discussion about differences in off-list and core words?
3 What is gained by looking at phrases instead of individual words?
4 How does knowledge of these phrases change the way we look at some of the individual off-list and core words in the two previous tables?
5 How do phrases change the learning burden placed on ELLs?

It is clear that register-specific topics are maintained in the phrases, especially in the three expository registers, and that many of the same register characteristics apply to the phrases as they did to the off-list and core words (register-specific uses of names, descriptions of complex concepts in the expository texts, etc.). However, several new

Table 4.4 Highest frequency phrases

Fiction	No.	Am. history	No.	Mathematics	No.	Life science	No.
2-WORD PHRASES		**2-WORD PHRASES**		**2-WORD PHRASES**		**2-WORD PHRASES**	
OTIS AMBER	97	UNITED STATES	90	LOOK AT	478	SUCH AS	411
SAM WESTING	92	NEW YORK	49	FIGURE OUT	368	FOR EXAMPLE	267
FLORA BAUMBACH	72	SAN FRANCISCO	22	HOW MANY	306	PUBLIC DOMAIN	247
SYDELLE PULASKI	71	MOUNTAIN MEN	21	HOW MUCH	170	WIKI IMAGE	236
JUDGE FORD	66	THE UNION	21	THINK ABOUT	151	WIKI FILE	203
MR HOO	65	PONY EXPRESS	18	WHOLE NUMBERS	135	NERVOUS SYSTEM	154
SUNSET TOWERS	52	NEW ENGLAND	17	EQUAL TO	129	BLOOD CELLS	114
WESTING HOUSE	48	ST LOUIS	17	REAL LIFE	126	CARBON DIOXIDE	112
DENTON DEERE	45	YEARS LATER	17	MIXED NUMBERS	124	LESSON OBJECTIVES	85
GRACE WEXLER	35	SUPREME COURT	16	WHOLE NUMBER	122	LESSON SUMMARY	85
BARNEY NORTHRUP	33	ABRAHAM LINCOLN	15	MIXED NUMBER	109	REVIEW QUESTIONS	85
COFFEE SHOP	25	NEW MEXICO	15	DECIMAL POINT	104	READING SUPPLEMENTAL	83
JAKE WEXLER	25	A LOT	14	PRACTICE DIRECTIONS	95	BLOOD VESSELS	81
WESTING PAPER	25	AS WELL	14	TEACHING TIME	94	DIGESTIVE SYSTEM	69
MR MCSOUTHERS	24	ROCK ISLAND	14	ICE CREAM	91	NATURAL SELECTION	68
ALL RIGHT	23	SALT LAKE	14	TECHNOLOGY INTEGRATION	87	IMMUNE SYSTEM	67
DOUG HOO	23	MISSOURI COMPROMISE	13	MENTAL MATH	75	CARDIOVASCULAR SYSTEM	60
THANK YOU	23	ANDREW JACKSON	12	PLACE VALUE	73	LIVING THINGS	57
DELIVERY BOY	22	WAGON TRAIN	12	LESS THAN	72	AMINO ACIDS	56
GRACE WINDSOR	22	WOMEN'S RIGHTS	12	SURFACE AREA	71	RESPIRATORY SYSTEM	55
MRS WEXLER	22	NATIVE AMERICANS	11	NUMBER LINE	66	CELLULAR RESPIRATION	52
WINDSOR WEXLER	22	SANTA ANNA	11	COORDINATE GRID	65	REPRODUCTIVE SYSTEM	49
ED PLUM	20	SOUTH PASS	11	WORK ON	65	BLOOD PRESSURE	38
UNCLE SAM	17	CIVIL WAR	10	GREATER THAN	64	LIVING ORGANISMS	38
MRS WESTING	16	FREE STATES	10	LOOKING AT	59	CELL DIVISION	36
PAPER PRODUCTS	16	PACIFIC OCEAN	10	UNCLE LARRY	56	EUKARYOTIC CELLS	36
SANDY MCSOUTHERS	16	PRESIDENT POLK	10	CIRCLE GRAPH	55	LOOK AT	36
STOCK MARKET	16	SLAVE STATE	10	SIMPLEST FORM	54	THINK ABOUT	36
OF COURSE	15	MANIFEST DESTINY	9	COMMON DENOMINATOR	52	AIR POLLUTION	35
TURTLE WEXLER	15	SAM HOUSTON	9	MORE THAN	52	WATER POLLUTION	35
BERTHE ERICA	14	WHITE PEOPLE	9	WORKING ON	50	NERVE IMPULSES	31
MS PULASKI	14	DRED SCOTT	8	CUSTOMARY UNITS	49	SEEDLESS PLANTS	31
CLEANING WOMAN	13	FREE STATE	8	ACCORDING TO	48	SMALL INTESTINE	60
ERICA CROW	13	GEORGE WASHINGTON	8	SIXTH GRADE	47	BREAK DOWN	29
MR WESTING	13	NEW ORLEANS	8	MRS ANDERSEN	47	EXCRETORY SYSTEM	28
MRS BAUMBACH	13	RUN AWAY	8	REAL-WORLD PROBLEMS	44	UNITED STATES	28
TRACK MEET	12	BRIGHAM YOUNG	7	DIFFERENCE BETWEEN	40	BROKEN DOWN	27
ANGELA WEXLER	11	CAPE HORN	7	DIVIDED BY	40	LYMPHATIC SYSTEM	27
LOOK AT	11	HERMAN MELVILLE	7	FINAL ANSWER	36	ORGAN SYSTEMS	27
ORIENTAL RUG	11	IOWA CITY	7	COMMON FACTOR	36	SKELETAL SYSTEM	27
PARKING LOT	11	JAMES BUCHANAN	7	IMPROPER FRACTION	35	HEART DISEASE	26
SOUP KITCHEN	11	JEDEDIAH SMITH	7	COMMON MULTIPLE	33	SEXUAL REPRODUCTION	26
TEN THOUSAND	11	SENECA FALLS	7	AMUSEMENT PARK	31	CELL MEMBRANE	25
A FEW	10	SLAVE OWNERS	7	STEM-AND-LEAF PLOT	30	LARGE INTESTINE	25
GAME ROOM	10	SOUTH AMERICA	7	NUMERICAL EXPRESSION	27	NATURAL RESOURCES	25
VIOLET WESTING	10	UNDERGROUND RAILROAD	7	ROLLER COASTER	25	LYMPH VESSELS	24
WESTING GAME	10	CLIPPER SHIPS	6	BOX-AND-WHISKER PLOT	25	PLASMA MEMBRANE	24
FRENCH DOORS	6	KANSAS–NEBRASKA ACT	6	CIRCLE GRAPHS	25	REPRODUCTIVE ORGANS	24
LOOKING FOR	6	NATHANIEL BOWDITCH	6	DISTRIBUTIVE PROPERTY	25	ASEXUAL REPRODUCTION	23
STARING AT	6	PIKES PEAK	6	DIVIDE BY	25	BONE MARROW	23
BACK IN	5	PUBLIC SCHOOLS	6	INVERSE OPERATION	25	CARDIAC MUSCLE	23
DOWN ON	5	ROCKY MOUNTAINS	6	MULTIPLICATION PROBLEM	24	INTERNAL ORGANS	23
HAND OVER	5	SIERRA NEVADA	6	NEW YORK	24	CONNECTIVE TISSUE	22
GET AWAY	4	SPERM WHALE	6	RECTANGULAR PRISM	24	SCIENTIFIC METHOD	22
GET BACK	4	STEPHEN DOUGLAS	6	COMMON MULTIPLES	24	CIRCULATORY SYSTEM	21
HELD UP	4	WALT WHITMAN	6	PRIME FACTORIZATION	18	OXYGEN-RICH BLOOD	21

Fiction	No.	Am. history	No.	Mathematics	No.	Life science	No.
3-WORD PHRASES		**3-WORD PHRASES**		**3-WORD PHRASES**		**3-WORD PHRASES**	
SAMUEL W WESTING	26	SANTA FE TRAIL	11	CHECK YOUR WORK	172	PUBLIC DOMAIN ##	139
GRACE WINDSOR WEXLER	22	GREAT SALT LAKE	10	A FEW MINUTES	125	SHOWN IN FIGURE	124
WESTING PAPER PRODUCTS	16	ELIZABETH CADY STANTON	8	ON YOUR OWN	116	DO YOU THINK	116
BERTHE ERICA CROW	13	FUGITIVE SLAVE LAW	8	TIME TO PRACTICE	103	CHECK YOUR UNDERSTANDING	85
I DON'T KNOW	11	HENRY DAVID THOREAU	8	REAL LIFE EXAMPLE	99	AS WELL AS	54
TEN THOUSAND DOLLARS	11	AS MUCH AS	7	SUMS AND DIFFERENCES	41	WHITE BLOOD CELLS	48
		AS SOON AS	7	DOUBLE BAR GRAPH	35	RED BLOOD CELL	47
		BOYS AND GIRLS	7	FRONT END ESTIMATION	35	AS A RESULT	43
		RALPH WALDO EMERSON	7	GREATEST COMMON FACTOR	33	IN ORDER TO	36
		THE WHITE HOUSE	7	LEAST COMMON MULTIPLE	33	BE ABLE TO	30
		DECLARATION OF INDEPENDENCE	6	ADDITION AND SUBTRACTION	30	THEORY OF EVOLUTION	20
		JAMES K. POLK	6	LOWEST COMMON DENOMINATOR	27	FEMALE REPRODUCTIVE SYSTEM	12
		LEWIS AND CLARK	6	MULTIPLICATION AND DIVISION	22	MALE REPRODUCTIVE SYSTEM	12
		JOHN JAMES AUDUBON	5	READ AND UNDERSTAND	22	COMPARE AND CONTRAST	11
		JOHN QUINCY ADAMS	5	ICE CREAM STAND	21	IN RESPONSE TO	11
		MARTIN VAN BUREN	5	SOLVE THE PROBLEM	21	HUMAN GENOME PROJECT	10
		A WHOLE LOT	4	ICE CREAM CONES	18	AUTONOMIC NERVOUS SYSTEM	9
				LOSSES AND GAINS	18		
4-WORD PHRASES		**4-WORD PHRASES**		**4-WORD PHRASES**		**4-WORD PHRASES**	
TWO HUNDRED MILLION DOLLARS	7	ALL OVER THE WORLD	7	TAKE A FEW MINUTES	124	SHOWN IN FIGURE ##.##	63
WESTING PAPER PRODUCTS CORPORATION	7	SAMUEL F B MORSE	4	TAKE A MINUTE TO	56	WHAT DO YOU THINK	32
CHAIRMAN OF THE BOARD	5			YOU CAN SEE THAT	55	HOW DO YOU THINK	29
IN THE MIDDLE OF	5			THE END OF THE	44	ONE OF THE MOST	19
SECRETARY TO THE PRESIDENT	4			PART OF A WHOLE	41	AS A RESULT OF	10

issues also become highlighted when we compare phrases. For example, several of the texts contain phrasal verbs: fiction (*look at, looking for, hand over, get away, get back, held up,* etc.); mathematics (*look at, figure out, think about, work on,* etc.); and life science (*look at, think about, break down,* etc.). In the case of mathematics and life science, these phrasal verbs are primarily for giving instructions to the reader, and are register-specific and quite restrictive from that perspective. Fiction, on the other hand, tends to use phrasal verbs for general expressive and descriptive purposes.

Other common phrases found in giving instructions to readers are in mathematics (*practice directions, check your work, on your own, time to practice, read and understand, solve the problem, take a few minutes, take a minute to,* etc.) and life science (*lesson objectives, lesson summary, review questions, shown in figure, do you think, check your understanding, compare and contrast, shown in figure #, what do you think, how do you think,* etc.). Such language reminds us that many textbooks, unlike fiction, are designed primarily for instructional purposes (to teach something directly), and that instructional language is a type of language, and may actually be a register of its own. Even more importantly, we must recognize that our ELLs need to understand the language of instruction itself to successfully comprehend the language and aims of many textbooks, as well as to perform successfully in classroom assignments, tasks, and tests. Such language will almost always be expressed through a set of fixed phrases like those listed above.

Another major register difference revealed by the case-study phrases is in the area of discourse markers (logical connectors), or how authors link various pieces of information together in logical ways. The life science register is full of these markers (*such as, for example, as a result, in order to, in response to, as a result of*, etc.). Such language would almost sound stilted in the case of fiction, where the range of logical connections between ideas is much narrower – primarily temporal and causal (cf. Coté, *et al.*, 1998) – and often expressed with simple single words (*then, next, because*, etc.). The wider and more complex range of logical relationships found in life science and similar registers places one more comprehension burden on ELLs.

Finally, and more importantly, phrases in the case study point out the potential costs of looking at individual words only. For example, what important meaning is lost when *Manifest Destiny* and *Missouri Compromise* become simply *manifest, destiny, Missouri,* and *compromise* on a list of single words, or when *organ system, nervous system, circulatory system, immune system, reproductive system, excretory system, lymphatic system, skeletal system,* and *respiratory system* become simply *system* with a high frequency count on a list of core individual words? In terms of register distinctions, is there a difference in loss of meaning if we break apart *Sam Westing* (typical fiction), *George Washington* (typical history), *common factor* (typical mathematics), and *amino acid* (typical science) for word counting purposes? Hopefully, the value of considering multiword items is clear enough.

This concludes the register case study. You can apply the same analysis principles to any register of English that your particular students are trying to learn. This discussion is also intended to serve as a foundational tenet for the remainder of this book, where we will consider the vocabulary issues involved with English for specific purposes, as we attempt to link the three realities of vocabulary described in Chapter 1: the linguistic reality (the specific vocabulary our learners need to know), the psychological reality (the vocabulary our learners already know), and the pedagogical reality (the most effective vocabulary teaching methods that will help our learners move from what they know to what they need to know).

Why do I care so much about register? Why should you care?

This may seem like an unusual subheading, but with the background established so far, it is a good time for an editorial summary about why register is the focus of this particular chapter and a major focus of the book as a whole. Plain and simple, here it is:

1　When you change the register, you change the vocabulary – not in terms of the grammatical words that glue everything together (the, that, to, for, etc.), but in terms of the specialized content words that help to make a register a register in the first place (sarcophagus, mummy; red blood cells, carbon dioxide; super nova, astrophysicist; volcano, igneous rocks; Declaration of Independence, antislavery; place an order, close a deal; transmission, steering wheel, etc.).

2　When you change the vocabulary, you change the set of strategies needed to learn that vocabulary. For instance, phrasal verbs are notoriously problematic for ELLs because they consist of two words (often with multiple meanings) that may or may not be together in a sentence. They are found everywhere in fiction and conversation, but are not so frequent in scientific writing. In contrast, scientific writing is full of words with Greek- and Latin-based morphemes, but conversation and fiction have relatively few such words. These scientific words are not easily learned through contextual exposure because they themselves are often the primary problem with reading comprehension (Coté, et al., 1998), but raising learners' morphological awareness of Greek and Latin roots and affixes will certainly help in this regard.

3　Extensive practice with vocabulary in one register may not be adequate preparation for dealing with the vocabulary of another. An excellent example of this is the often-discussed "fourth-grade slump" that occurs in academic reading (Chall, 1983). Children, accustomed to reading the words and grammar of narrative fiction (stories), often find it difficult to read textbooks and other expository materials that begin to enter the classroom around the fourth grade (nine- to ten-year-old children) (Sanacore and Palumbo, 2009). Part of this slump is certainly associated with the documented vocabulary differences between the two macro-registers of narrative and expository reading materials (Gardner, 2004; Grabe, 2002).

4　ELLs need to comprehend and use the language of certain registers in order to meet their personal needs and goals (having casual conversations, learning academic subject matter, communicating well in the business world, functioning in a vocational field, etc.). We serve them well when we address the specific vocabulary that matches those needs, and when we teach them the strategies they will need to be successful in learning that particular vocabulary. Surely this is the answer to the question I posed at the start of the chapter – what English do we teach? – as well as its direct corollary – what vocabulary do we teach? I also feel it is time for all teachers of ELLs to become vocabulary teachers in their individual stewardships (science teachers, math teachers, vocational education teachers, ELL specialists, ELL paraprofessionals, reading specialists, etc.).

Vocabulary Project (creating a vocabulary inventory)

I assume at this point that you have had enough time to download and practice using the *Range* programs (GSL/AWL and BNC versions) and the *kfNgram* program as described at the end of Chapter 3. If you have not thoroughly acquainted yourself with these programs, you should do so now before continuing with this section.

The next step in the Vocabulary Project is for you to run the electronic texts you have chosen through the two *Range* programs (GSL/AWL and BNC) and the *kfNgram* program, using the output to create a vocabulary inventory to be used for curricular decision making, and direct vocabulary instruction (see Chapter 6). I highly recommend copying *Range* outputs to spreadsheets in order to sort the data more easily. You will also need to carefully select the most transparent phrases from the lists produced by the *kfNgram*. I recommend looking at the two-word, three-word, and four-word phrases (ordered by frequency). Some longer phrases may exist, but they will be rare and are not likely to have important frequencies.

There are several options that could be combined to make a robust inventory from the output of these programs:

1 *Frequency data* for types, families, and phrases. These could be similar to the case study I produced in this chapter. The information would allow you to determine priorities for vocabulary testing and training. Keep in mind that the first base lists in the two *Range* programs contain general high frequency words (including function words), so they may not be as insightful (from a content perspective) as the words on remaining lists or the specialized words that do not appear on any of the lists.
2 *Alphabetical listings* for types and families. These can be used to determine the degree of morphological relationships between the words, and they will provide useful examples for morphological-awareness training (see Chapter 6).
3 *Range data* (or coverage data) for types and families. Two types of range data would be very useful: (a) specialized (content) words that appear across different texts. Such words are prime candidates for instruction because the learners will see them in different texts; and (b) specialized (content) words that appear across different

chapters (or sections) of a single text. Again, these are important words to consider for instruction because the learners will see them multiple times and in different parts of a book or other text.

You may also elect to use the *Range* program with the new Common Core List (CCL). This version can be downloaded at www.routledge. com/cw/rial.

5 The tasks of vocabulary learning

Problem

In Chapters 3 and 4, we discussed issues involving the actual vocabulary our learners must know in order to meet their English language needs – in other words, the target. Now we must shift our attention to the learners themselves – to understanding the actual tasks they face in trying to learn that target vocabulary. If you have learned a second or foreign language yourselves, you may have naturally experienced much of what we will discuss in this chapter, but you are less likely to have understood why. As teachers or prospective teachers, the "why" becomes very important, especially if you want to become the facilitator your learners will need in order to reach their target-language vocabulary goals. Specifically, this chapter will address:

- the relationships between known and unknown vocabulary;
- the relationships between spoken and written vocabulary knowledge;
- the relationship between reading skills and vocabulary knowledge
- the various ways in which learners can come to understand new word meanings;
- the degrees of vocabulary knowledge necessary to achieve successful learning outcomes.

In all of this, the aim is to better prepare you to take your ELLs from "what they know to where they need to go."

Intervention and theory

Relationships between known and unknown vocabulary

While visiting the British Museum in London, I noticed an usually large number of people surrounding one particular display case. Inside the case was one of the greatest linguistic discoveries in history – the *Rosetta Stone*. This stone contains a single message (a decree) in three different languages – two known at the time of its discovery (Demotic and Ancient Greek) and one unknown (Egyptian hieroglyphs) – and was the key not only to unlocking the meaning of the Egyptian

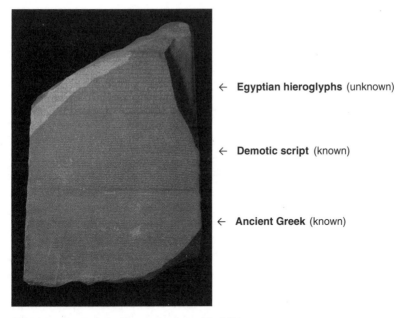

← **Egyptian hieroglyphs** (unknown)

← **Demotic script** (known)

← **Ancient Greek** (known)

Figure 5.1 The Rosetta Stone, discovered in 1799.
© The trustees of the British Museum. All rights reserved.

hieroglyphs, but also to our deeper understanding of the great civilizations that used them in their writing system.

For our purposes, the story of the Rosetta Stone and the eventual deciphering of ancient Egyptian writing is essentially a story of using known language to understand unknown language. Of course, other language systems besides vocabulary were involved in the deciphering process (grammar, discourse, etc.), but I am confident in saying that vocabulary was the key player. It is also important to note that the language experts of the time understood the message on the Rosetta Stone before making the meaning connections with the written hieroglyphs. In other words, they needed to understand new labels (Egyptian hieroglyphs) for old concepts (the contents of the same decree in the two known languages – Demotic and Ancient Greek). Had the contents (concepts) been different in the three languages, the stone would have essentially been useless as a language key.

A discussion of labels and concepts is fundamental if we are to understand the vocabulary learning tasks facing our ELLs. While I could simply refer to labels as "words," I prefer to avoid the obvious ambiguity this would create between word forms and word meanings. The term *label* also reminds us that word forms are essentially arbitrary symbols that have been agreed upon by users of a particular language (*cat* in English; *gato* in Spanish; 猫 in Chinese, 𓄿𓃭𓆑𓃠 in Egyptian hieroglyphics, etc.). The term *concept* broadly encompasses referents

(*Winston Churchill, Stonehenge, Great Barrier Reef*, etc.), classifications (*birds, doctors, cars*, etc.), processes (*mitosis, photosynthesis, decomposition*, etc.), ideologies (*communism, socialism, capitalism*, etc.), philosophies (*idealism, pragmatism, existentialism*, etc.), and so forth.

With these definitions in mind, we will consider five major relationships that exist between labels and concepts in language learners' developing L2 lexicons:

Known Labels and Known Concepts: these are known L2 words (already acquired) that can be actively used by learners to reason with and communicate with in the L2. They are also available to assist learners in gaining knowledge of new L2 words.

New Labels and Known Concepts: these are words for which learners already have a conceptual understanding (from their L1 or other language experiences), but have not learned the appropriate labels in the L2 (similar to the Rosetta Stone story), or they are new L2 synonyms for words already acquired by the learner. In this category, ELLs may sometimes have a word-learning advantage over some English L1 speakers if the ELLs already know the concepts behind the new words they encounter because of experiences with those concepts in their native languages (Grabe, 2009). In other words, they only need new labels in English for known concepts in their native languages.

Similar Labels and Known Concepts: These are also referred to as cognates, or word forms in an L2 with similar (sometimes identical) forms in learners' existing L1 lexicons (e.g. English = *angel*, German = *Engel*; English = *ball*, German = *Ball*; English = *family*, Spanish = *familia*; English = *actor*, Spanish = *actor*). Of course, cognates are much more likely to occur when two languages are similar (German and English, Spanish and English, etc.) and less likely to occur when they are different (Chinese and English, Korean and English, etc.). There are also false cognates, or words in two languages that look similar on the surface, but have different underlying meanings. For example, the German word *Art* means *manner, kind,* or *type* (not *portraits, drawings,* etc.), the German word *bald* means *soon* (not *hairless*), and the Spanish word *embarazada* means *pregnant* (not *embarrassed*). False cognates are often referred to as false friends because they give the appearance of being helpful, but are actually misleading.

Known Labels and New Concepts: These are words with known forms, but with new (unknown) meanings (e.g. homonyms and polysemes). The many meanings of the simple word forms *break, run,* and *chip* discussed earlier are examples of this relationship.

They can also be words that sound familiar, but their meanings are not yet clear to us.

New Labels and New Concepts: These are words for which learners have little or no knowledge of either their form or their meaning(s) in any language. They are often found in specialized language domains or registers, and are particularly common in the content areas of education. In fact, learning such words and the concepts behind them is one of the primary reasons for going to school in the first place (*amoeba, plankton, exponents, denominator, parliament, House of Lords, cavaliers,* etc.).

The key here is that the difficulty of learning new words will vary depending on what learners already know (or don't know) about those words in terms of both the concepts behind the words and the labels used to identify them. Accordingly, teachers must adjust the degree of attention paid to such words, making well-reasoned assumptions about which words learners will find easier or more difficult to understand and eventually acquire. Understandably, the instructional goal would be to elevate our learners' knowledge of important words to the first category (Known Labels and Known Concepts) with our biggest challenge coming from words in the last category (New Labels and New Concepts). This is especially true when the new concepts behind the new labels represent complex systems, processes, or ideas such as with the labels *biosphere, mummification,* and *Magna Carta.* The need for direct or supplementary instructional intervention increases dramatically for such words.

(TC)

Task 5.1

1 Using the relationships described above, consider the words listed below and decide for each word where you personally stand in terms of the label (known or unknown) and the concept (known or unknown).

2 For those that you feel you might know, try to determine the depth of your knowledge. Would I understand the word in a conversation or while reading? Could I produce the word when speaking or writing?

epistemological	marginalization
reciprocity	latency
concomitant	dyad
typology	iterative
schema	exogenous
hegemonic	discontinuous
canonical	contestation

The relationship between spoken and written vocabulary knowledge

Known versus unknown vocabulary must also be considered on the spoken-versus-written dimension. A personal example may serve to illustrate this point. While playing a timed word-guessing game with a group of people, I was making great progress getting my team to guess the words on a list – until I encountered the word *hors d'oeuvres*. Under time pressure, not being a reader of French, and having encountered this word very infrequently in English texts, I mentally processed it as something like *horse devors*, which made absolutely no sense to me under the constraints of playing the game. Of course, I skipped the word, my turn ended, and I endured the laughter of the group as I expressed frustration about this strange word on my list – *horse devors*. I was reminded of a valuable component of vocabulary knowledge when I finally realized that it was actually *ordurves* – a word I had heard many times and for which I had a good understanding of its meaning (*appetizer*). In short, I owned the spoken label and the concept (meaning) behind it, but not the written label – at least not well enough to recognize it when the sand in the little hour-glass timer was running out. Had I put on my limited French-word pronunciation hat, I might have come closer to the correct pronunciation and thus recognized the word.

Connecting written word forms with spoken vocabulary knowledge is a key component of the cognitive skill of reading, especially in the early developmental stages (cf. Biemiller, 2003). First language learners of English have a much easier time learning to read words they already own in their oral vocabularies, and the benefits of using letter–sound correspondences to recognize words and improve reading comprehension can only be realized with words that are already known through oral experiences (National Reading Panel, 2000). This paints a somewhat bleak picture for many young ELLs learning to read in English, because they generally have fewer English words in their oral vocabularies to make connections with. Proponents of bilingual education often point this out when they recommend teaching ELLs to read in their native languages before trying to read in English.

The crucial relationship between spoken and written vocabulary also suggests that second-language vocabulary teaching is best accomplished with an integrated-skills approach (listening, speaking, reading, and writing all emphasized together), rather than the isolated-skills approaches we find in many English-language programs (separate reading class, separate writing class, etc.). Combining an integrated-skills approach with theme-based and task-based content that meets the immediate needs of ELLs holds the greatest promise that important vocabulary will be recycled in related materials and tasks and through different modes of learning (speaking, listening, reading, and writing). The chances of a "horse-devors" experience are much less likely under such instructional conditions.

Academic reading and vocabulary knowledge

The Rosetta Stone is also a story of the roots of literacy – namely, that written symbols invented by humans (linguistic artifacts) can be used to represent and convey meaningful language, as long as everyone involved knows what those symbols stand for. I have consciously chosen to give literacy development some of my prime attention in this book on vocabulary because I view the relationship between vocabulary knowledge and academic literacy skills as being both the greatest challenge for ELLs, and the greatest area for potential language growth. Having said this, however, I would also suggest that far too little has been done to discuss the role of orally-based language in preparing ELLs to read academic materials, including the vocabulary in those materials (Biemiller, 1999) – a point we will return to in Chapter 6.

The BICS and CALP distinction

Cummins' (1979) famous distinction between BICS (Basic Interpersonal Communicative Skills) and CALP (Cognitive Academic Language Proficiency) supports the idea that major differences exist between conversational English and academic literacy, by suggesting that surface-level conversational listening and speaking skills (BICS) generally take from six months to two years for ELLs to acquire, whereas the skills necessary to acquire academic language (CALP), tied heavily to academic literacy skills, normally require five to seven years before ELLs approach grade-level proficiency. One of the primary constraints in CALP development is that ELLs are typically trying to learn both new concepts and new labels on a regular basis in "context-reduced" (context-poor situations commonly associated with written materials), such as while reading textbooks, listening to classroom lectures, writing essays, taking normed tests, and so forth (Cummins, 1981). This is in stark contrast to the "context-embedded" (context-rich) situations in which BICS is acquired, where ELLs benefit from various social interactions requiring everyday language that is not cognitively challenging, and where learners benefit from oral language features "such as intonation, body language, and shared physical surroundings" (Beck, *et al.*, 2002, p. 3). Seen another way,

> Academic language, therefore, is a tool that promotes a kind of thinking different from that employed in social settings. Learning academic language is not learning new words to do the same thing that one could have done with other words; it is learning to do new things with language and acquiring new tools for these new purposes
>
> (Nagy and Townsend, 2012, p. 93)

Proponents of bilingual education often cite the BICS–CALP distinction as a primary reason for initially teaching academic content in learners' native languages (e.g. Spanish, Hmong, Russian) before asking them to negotiate that content in a second or foreign language (e.g. English). Regardless of the educational position we might take on this issue, it is clear that CALP, based heavily on academic literacy skills, poses a serious challenge for ELLs and their teachers, especially when we consider the potential life consequences of having poor academic language skills. In fact, there is ample evidence to support the following relationships:

Academic vocabulary knowledge

Academic reading abilities

Academic success

Economic opportunity

Societal well-being

Figure 5.2 Relationships with academic language ability.

While I certainly do not wish to reduce academic reading abilities to vocabulary knowledge only, I do view it as the key player (cf. Biemiller, 2005; Chall, *et al.*, 1990; Corson, 1997; Snow and Kim, 2007). The same key-player status is true of the relationship between academic reading abilities (key) and academic success, between academic success (key) and economic opportunity, and between economic opportunity (key) and societal well-being. (cf. Chall, 2000; Goldenberg, 2008). As we continue, it is important to keep the true ends in mind (academic success, economic opportunity, and societal well-being) while we discuss more specifically the means (gaining academic vocabulary knowledge and becoming a skilled academic reader).

Task 5.2

1 What are some of the important gate-keeping tests of academic success (e.g. ACT, UKCAT, GAMSAT)?
2 What do I mean when I say that these gate-keeping tests are primarily tests of academic literacy, and, by extension, academic vocabulary?

The double arrow in Figure 5.2 suggests a reciprocal relationship between academic vocabulary knowledge and academic reading abilities – more specifically, that vocabulary knowledge is essential for reading comprehension and that reading itself can lead to vocabulary exposure and acquisition. On these two points, there is little disagreement among reading and vocabulary experts. However, just how these two factors actually coalesce to produce long-term improvements in academic vocabulary knowledge and academic reading comprehension is not so clearly understood or agreed upon. A brief review of this debate is essential, because the very reason for writing this book hangs in the balance, as it would for any book suggesting that formal vocabulary instruction (strategy training, awareness raising, etc.) and direct attention to unknown words play vital roles in advanced vocabulary acquisition.

On one side of the issue, Krashen (2010) and others continue to maintain that all that is needed is the input offered ELLs by light self-selected reading materials, without any vocabulary skill-building required. This *reading hypothesis* emphasizes that the reading of "massive amounts" of high-interest "comprehensible" books will produce the vocabulary knowledge necessary for ELLs to transition to more complex academic reading. Furthermore, the new vocabulary is assumed to be acquired "subconsciously" (Krashen, 1989) while readers are attending to basic comprehension of "authentic materials" that have not been "specially prepared" for school (Krashen, 1985, p. 93).

However, Coady (1993) points out the *beginner's paradox* that exists for ELLs attempting to use incidental word learning through contextual input as the primary means of their vocabulary growth:

> One side of the paradox is that less frequent vocabulary is almost exclusively encountered during reading. Consequently English as a second language (ESL) students have to read in order to learn the less frequent words. But the other side of the paradox is that all too often they don't know enough words to read well. How can these students learn enough to learn?
>
> (Coady, 1993, p. 7)

Adding to this paradox is the fact that students who are lacking in vocabulary to begin with "are less able to derive meaningful information from the context" of reading materials (Beck, *et al.*, 2002, p. 4). By extension, this vocabulary–reading paradox suggests that even the *unassisted* reading of books and magazines (Krashen, 2010) may cause problems for many developing ELL readers. For instance, the "adult second-language students" in the Cho and Krashen (1994) study found that the *Sweet Valley High* novels – "written at the sixth-grade level" (for 12-year-olds) – were too difficult for "free pleasure reading," causing the researchers to resort to the *Sweet Valley Kids* series – "written at the second-grade level" (for eight-year-olds) (p. 664). This picture becomes even more troubling when one considers that three of the adult subjects had studied English for six years (one actually taught English in Korea), and the fourth subject (age 21) attended ESL classes in secondary schools after arriving in the U.S. at age 13, and was mainstreamed in the tenth grade (14–15 years old). Additionally, all of the adult students appear to have had extensive literacy training and experience in their first language.

I have also argued that, for many ELLs, "the reading of more cognitively challenging academic texts (expositions), without assistance or strategies, may actually represent an oxymoron – that is, reading, in terms of comprehension, may not take place at all, or with limited usefulness" (Gardner, 1999, pp. 60–61). In turn, the subconscious learning of conceptually-challenging academic words through contextual input alone is equally problematic, as evidenced by the following conclusion by Anderson, based on the now famous study of incidental vocabulary acquisition (Nagy, *et al.*, 1987), in which he participated:

> We found small but highly reliable increments in word knowledge attributable to reading at all grades and ability levels. The overall likelihood ranged from better than 1 in 10 when children were reading *easy narratives* to *near zero* when they were reading *difficult expositions.*
>
> (Anderson, 1996, p. 61, emphases added)

Anderson highlights this experimental evidence to justify the use of "playful, stimulating experiences with good books" (p. 74) as the recommended source for sustained vocabulary development. However, the hard linguistic evidence (actual words in actual reading materials) suggests that many specialized words needed for academic development are not found in so-called easy narrative reading materials to the extent that is needed for successful academic reading (Gardner, 2004, 2008). How will these crucial academic words eventually be learned if they appear almost exclusively in lexically-dense, context-reduced materials (informational texts) that are not friendly to incidental vocabulary acquisition, especially if that acquisition is supposed to happen subconsciously, and especially if learners do not have years to wait on the "iffy" chance that they will encounter (and learn) those words through reading self-selected materials? Because some of us have pointed out this linguistic puzzle, we have been labeled as being "against reading" (Krashen, 2010, p. 36), when, in fact, we are all for reading as the major source for vocabulary *input* in academic and other advanced language contexts (cf. Beck, *et al.*, 2002). What we are against is the misleading view that ELLs do not need to pay conscious attention to many important academic words they do not already know, especially when those words are embedded in lexically-complex contexts they do not already comprehend. This is simply a logical fallacy.

Based on hard linguistic evidence, we are also against the notion that eventual access to such academic words is best promoted by a reading-only curriculum that is based on *self-selected* reading materials, consisting almost exclusively of *narrative fiction* – the notion that ELLs will have learned "all the vocabulary and syntax they required in due course from repeated interactions with good stories" without "regular analytic study and practice with the language" (Elley, 1991, pp. 378, 379), or, as Krashen himself puts it:

> The results of incidental studies suggest that *comprehensible input alone* can do the *entire job for vocabulary* and nearly the entire job for spelling... This is, I think, good news for readers. Many people, I am sure, would not read at all if they were compelled to *work on their spelling and vocabulary* while trying to *enjoy a good book*.
>
> (Krashen, 1989, p. 448, emphases added)

These and similar philosophies have had a noticeable impact in how reading and vocabulary development have been dealt with in many ELL settings worldwide, and have led to some very popular instructional practices such as *free reading, wide reading, book floods,* and *sustained silent reading,* all of which might be subsumed under the more universal term of *extensive reading* (see Day and Bamford, 1998, for overview). To be absolutely clear, there is everything right about such practices for the purposes they serve. Extensive narrative reading, for instance, is absolutely essential in all phases of reading development (narratives address engaging topics, contain and recycle many important words, foster reading fluency, etc.), but the point is that it is simply not sufficient by itself for learning many important words, nor is it sufficient preparation by itself for dealing with the vocabulary and cognitive demands of academic reading, which is rarely at a comprehension level $(i+1)$ conducive to *subconscious* incidental vocabulary acquisition – if indeed such an untestable phenomenon actually exists. As Hulstijn (2001, p. 274) points out, "simply encouraging learners to spend much time on reading and listening, although leading to some incidental vocabulary learning, will not be enough in itself," and successful vocabulary acquisition "will almost always require attention *and* awareness."

Task 5.3

1 Analyze the two contexts below from the BNC and group them according to the register you believe they come from: narrative (fiction), or expository (informational).
2 What vocabulary characteristics of the contexts led you to your conclusions?
3 Are there any noticeable differences between the two contexts in terms of their ability to convey the meaning of the highlighted word *query*?

> A This in turn can lead us to query the legitimacy of judicial review, since it appears to be an ad hoc affair.
> B "There was no room for doubt in your words, Wilson, nothing left to query?"' Oh no, ma'am, I could not have been plainer.
>
> Retrieved and repurposed from
> http://corpus.byu.edu/bnc.

The fourth-grade slump and its correlates

An over-emphasis on narrative reading in academic settings is thought to be one of the major causes of the well-documented *fourth-grade slump* in United States education (Chall, *et al.*, 1990; Chall and Jacobs, 2003; Sanacore and Palumbo, 2009), where many children, who appear to have developed basic reading skills, struggle to negotiate the more complex vocabularies and structures of informational materials such as textbooks that are introduced into the school curricula at about the fourth grade (nine- to ten-year-old children). Those particularly affected by the slump are students from the lower socio-economic classes, many of whom are ELLs, because their life experiences have not exposed them to the vocabulary and related concepts contained in the informational materials they are assigned to read (Corson, 1997; Goldenberg, 2008). Interestingly, these deficits appear to be well-entrenched before most of these at-risk children even start formal schooling (Hart and Risley,

1995, 2003). If not attended to early, they can persist through elementary school (Biemiller, 2010; Chall, 1996), middle school, (Townsend and Collins, 2009; Townsend, *et al.*, 2012), and, most likely, throughout a student's entire educational experience (Corson, 1997).

A word on self-selected reading materials

Regarding the self-selection component of a narrative-based reading curriculum, Carver expresses the following concern, which his research findings with L1 children confirm:

> When students are allowed to choose their own library books, often called free reading, it seems reasonable to assume that they will choose books at their independent reading level; that is, they will select relatively easy books... Under these conditions, it seems likely that students will encounter very few, if any, unknown words that they might learn with repeated exposures.
>
> (Carver, 1994, p. 434)

This sentiment is echoed by Beck, *et al.* (2002, p. 4) by stating that "many students in need of vocabulary development do not engage in wide reading, especially of the kinds of books that contain unfamiliar vocabulary."

In another study, Carver and Leibert add the following about vocabulary growth through self-selected narrative reading materials:

> How can students read material that is mostly, or entirely, fiction that involves words and ideas that are not challenging, and still grow in their ability to accurately comprehend material at a higher level of difficulty? How can children learn new words when they read material that rarely, if ever, involves new words?
>
> (Carver and Leibert, 1995, p. 45)

Additionally, the situation for ELLs and struggling L1 readers is even more problematic, because they are likely to have difficulties even reading the good stories for pleasure, including the vocabulary of such stories.

> Struggling readers do not read well enough to make wide reading an option. To acquire word knowledge from reading requires adequate decoding skills, the ability to recognize that a word is unknown, and the competency of being able to extract meaningful information about the word from the context. Readers cannot be engaging with the latter two if they are struggling with decoding.
>
> (Beck, *et al.*, 2002, p. 6)

Biemiller (2009) adds that even if useful decoding skills are mastered (through phonics instruction, etc.), many "less-advantaged and second-language children" will still struggle with reading comprehension because they don't already own enough vocabulary – "the words they need to know in order to understand what they're reading" (p. 29).

In short, what many experts from various fields are telling us is that reading is indeed the major source of long-term vocabulary input, but that incidental word learning cannot be relied on as the sole means for learning many new words if:

1 the words to be learned are cognitively challenging and appear exclusively, or almost exclusively, in lexically-dense reading materials such as those found in most academic settings,
2 no direct attention or assistance is given to learning such words,
3 the time frame for learning the new words is critically short (as it is in most academic settings), and
4 learners are not already skilled readers, capable of using contexts effectively when such contexts do provide helpful word-learning information – a condition that does not appear to be the norm for many naturally-occurring reading contexts (Beck, *et al.*,1983).

Regarding this last point, a more detailed discussion is warranted.

Types of contexts for potential word learning

Beck, *et al.* (2002) describe five types of contexts that an unknown word may appear in:

1 *Misdirective Contexts* – or contexts that would actually lead readers to a false or wrong conclusion about an unknown word, such as with *grudgingly* in the following context:

> Sandra had won the dance contest, and the audience's cheers brought her to the stage for an encore. "Every step she takes is so perfect and graceful," Ginny said *grudgingly* as she watched Sandra dance.
>
> (p. 4)

2 *Nondirective Contexts* – or contexts that give readers virtually no assistance in learning the meaning of an unknown word, such as with *lumbering* in the following context:

> Dan heard the door open and wondered who had arrived. He couldn't make out the voices. Then he recognized the *lumbering* footsteps on the stairs and knew it was Aunt Grace.
>
> (p. 5)

3 *General Contexts* – or contexts that give readers enough information about an unknown word to allow them to form only general notions (positive, negative, etc.) about the meaning of that word, such as with *gregarious* in the following context:

> Joe and Stan arrived at the party at 7 o'clock. By 9:30, the evening seemed to drag for Stan. But Joe really seemed to be having a good time at the party. "I wish I could be as *gregarious* as he is, thought Stan.
>
> (p. 5)

4 *Directive Contexts* – or contexts that would appear to lead readers to a clear and specific meaning of an unknown word, such as with *commotion* in the following context:

> When the cat pounced on the dog, he leapt up, yelping, and knocked down a shelf of books. The animals ran past Wendy, tripping her. She cried out and fell to the floor. As the noise and confusion mounted, Mother hollered upstairs, "What's all that *commotion?*"
>
> (p. 5)

5 *Instructional Contexts* – or contexts that have been *linguistically designed* to deliberately point readers to the clear and specific meaning of an unknown word, such as with *improvise* in the following context:

> Anna was making some chocolate chip cookies. She was almost done with the dough when she noticed that her little brother had eaten all of the chocolate chips. She decided to *improvise* by using raisins instead of chocolate chips. Anna's mother was very happy with her decision. The cookies were delicious.
>
> (Gardner, 2007b, p. 368)

As Beck and her colleagues point out, the difference between directive contexts (4) and instructional contexts (5) is that the authors of the former are simply telling a story or conveying an idea, with no intention of teaching particular words. This is the case with most, if not all, "authentic" narrative writing like that used in the examples above. In fact, I would add that authors of most "authentic" narrative contexts (1–4 above) naturally assume that their words are already known by those who will read them. This is not always the case with expository (informational) text in many academic subjects such as science, mathematics, and history, where often the very purpose of a particular text is to draw readers' direct attention to important new vocabulary items and the concepts they represent. A simple example of the characteristic differences between narrative and expository contexts will illustrate this point. Figure 5.3 provides comparisons of what an ELL reader might encounter when trying to learn the word *mummy* using typical narrative and expository contexts written for children approximately 11 years old. Several crucial points emerge from this comparison:

1 The word *mummy* in the six expository passages (7–12) is either directly defined, or the facts about how mummies are created, preserved, and studied are explicitly explained. In the six narrative passages, the word *mummy* is simply used descriptively in the storytelling, and even takes on a clearly fictional meaning in Context 3 – a Hollywood-like description of a mummy that has come back to life and wants to harm or scare people. If you ever see such a mummy yourselves – BEWARE!

2 The fact that the expository contexts point more clearly and directly to the meaning of *mummy* might suggest that they are the best contexts for word learning, except for three crucial issues: (a) many of the words used in defining *mummy* are conceptually difficult themselves (*decay, soft tissues, fossil, bacteria, fungi, bitumen, built-in atomic clock, atoms, radioactive, carbon-14*, etc.); (b) the authors actually use elaborations to define some of these words for the reader (see *soft tissues* in 7, *bitumen* in 9, and *carbon-14* in 11); and (c) the mummy-related processes that many of these words help to describe are complex (mummification, decay, carbon-dating, etc.) and would definitely require readers to come to the learning table with some key knowledge and skills already in place (elaborate content knowledge, more advanced reading skills, etc.).

3 From the perspective of incidental vocabulary acquisition, learners would simply have to know many more difficult words in the authentic expository contexts than in the authentic narrative contexts to achieve basic comprehension.

Thus, the idea of using naturally-occurring academic context as the primary mechanism for learning new academic words is a risky proposition that will undoubtedly require ELLs to: (a) use conscious word-guessing strategies while actually reading (analyze the cotexts, look at parts of words, consider known collocates, etc.); (b) use supplementary aids such as dictionaries, glosses, diagrams, photos, tables, charts, and internet resources; or (c) ask a teacher, parent, classmate, friend, etc. In short, the assumption that subconscious acquisition of words encountered in context will do the entire job for vocabulary learning is an oversimplification of a much more complex issue, especially in academic settings. The research-backed reality is much closer to the following:

Narrative Contexts	Expository Contexts
The Mummy, the Will, and the Crypt (Bellairs, 1983)	*Mummies and Their Mysteries* (Wilcox, 1993)
1. "The young man paused and grinned unpleasantly. 'Do you know what a **mummy** looks like after it's been unwrapped? Just a dried brown husk that used to be a human being, with holes for eyes?'"	7. "A **mummy** is the body of a human or animal in which some of the soft tissues (skin, muscles, or organs) did not decay after death. This makes a **mummy** different from a skeleton or a fossil."
2. "The other was stretched out, and his hand was layed flat on the floor. It was brown and withered, like the hand of a **mummy**."	8. "Drying isn't the only way to turn a body into a **mummy**. Taking away all air from around the body will stop decay, since bacteria and fungi need air as well as water to live."
3. "A figure with hollow **mummy** eyes and a withered **mummy** face and clawlike **mummy** hands. Moving with an awful, tottering, unsteady gait, it came toward him."	9. "When the word **mummy** was first used in the English language in the early 1400s, it did not mean a body as it does now. Instead, it was the name of a medicine. **Mummy** comes from mumiyah, an Arabic word for bitumen, a sticky oil now used to make roads."
The Vandemark Mummy (Voight, 1991)	*Tales Mummies Tell* (Lauber, 1985)
4. "Phineas looked across the table, across the **mummy's** face, to his father. Mr. Hall stared down at the wrapped figure, and at the portrait face that was held in place by wrappings, and then back down the length of the **mummy** to its feet, where Althea stood staring."	10. "The ground froze and stayed frozen, except for the top few inches, which thawed each summer. In this natural deep freeze, the body of the baby mammoth was preserved for thousands of years. It became a **mummy**, which is the term now used for any well-preserved body, whether animal or human."
5. "He wasn't sure he exactly understood that now, but he felt as if this ancient **mummy** stood for something truer than…all the money he could imagine winning in the lottery, truer than Donald Trump, truer even than the threat of nuclear war and nuclear accidents, AIDS, or the waste crisis."	11. "To find the age of the **mummy**, scientists made use of a built-in atomic clock. This is how the clock works: Certain kinds of atoms are radioactive they keep breaking down by giving off tiny parts of themselves. Among these atoms are those of carbon 14, which is a radioactive variety of carbon."
6. "'The Collection, as you will find, is a hodgepodge. There will be some pleasant surprises for you, or so I like to think. The **mummy**, which is its centerpiece, has a certain wistful appeal, being from the Roman era.'"	12. "Copper Man is a South American **mummy** that formed naturally with the help of dry air and salts. This **mummy** was once a copper miner who lived and worked around AD 800 in the Atacama Desert of northern Chile."

Figure 5.3 Narrative versus expository context (source: adapted from Gardner, 2004, p. 23, emphases all added).

> vocabulary acquisition will benefit from reading only when readers consciously engage in inferring the meaning of unfamiliar words, and when the text does contain cues allowing the meaning of unfamiliar words to be inferred
>
> (Hulstijn, 2001, p. 272)

It is also true that many unfamiliar academic words may be learned through classroom discussions and other means before or after they are encountered in academic texts. In such cases, the unfamiliar words are processed by learners both "elaborately and repeatedly" (Hulstijn, 2001, p. 272).

Vocabulary knowledge in "learning to read" and "reading to learn"

This is an optimal point to discuss the tasks of vocabulary learning in terms of two popular orientations to reading: *learning to read* and *reading to learn*. These two concepts have been viewed as being end points on a reading-skills continuum (Anderson, 2008), with *learning to read* involving foundational skills (print represents spoken language, words have phonetic parts, words have meaning-based parts, words combine to make sentences, etc.), and *reading to learn* involving the mature reading skills used in gaining new knowledge from printed materials (intensive reading skills, strategy usage, skimming, scanning, etc.).

What is crucial for us to understand as ELL teachers is that vocabulary knowledge is essential at every point on this reading-skills continuum. In fact, it is so important that it simply cannot be left to chance or incidental possibilities only, and it often deserves our direct attention and intervention (Beck, *et al.*, 2002). For example, in the beginning stages of reading, we know that our ELLs will need focused practice with the foundational or "core" vocabulary of English, both out of context (memorizing sight words, working with rhyming words, etc.) and in context (reading simple books mostly comprised of these core words). Most of us have no trouble with the concept that this "critical mass" of recognizable vocabulary is necessary to read even basic materials, and to develop the skill of reading in the first place. It should not be difficult, therefore, to believe that a critical mass of vocabulary knowledge is necessary to read more advanced materials? Simply put, if our ELLs do not know enough words to comprehend what they are reading, at whatever level of difficulty a text may be, they will either need to learn more applicable words, choose a new book to read, or stop reading altogether. Where book choice is not available (often the case in academic settings where a curriculum is already set), then the only options are to learn more applicable words,

Task 5.4

1 If you do not know the meaning of *anachronism*, try to utilize the ten contexts below to learn its meaning. If you already know the word, move to Step 2.
2 For each context, decide which of the Beck, *et al.* (2002) types best describes that context in terms of helping you understand *anachronism* (*misdirective, nondirective, general, directive*).

1	use only on the road. The Sport Utility Vehicle is a porcine, menacing **anachronism** in the 21st century. Diminution in their number on public thoroughfares correspondingly would improve
2	More and more, the whole forage fish reduction industry is looking like an **anachronism**. A report released in March by the Lenfest Ocean Program, financed through the
3	many of us the ease of buying digital music has rendered file sharing a quaint **anachronism**, a past transgression stored away next to memories of that drug-fueled summer following sophomore
4	has changed surprisingly little since its Depression-era build-out. Consequently, it's an industrial **anachronism**, a failure-prone, dumb, and output-only power net- work that should be more
5	up a lot more these days. Home canning and preserving – practically a culinary **anachronism** in this fast food nation – is on the rise. As more Americans embrace
6	, fat, soft-terrain-flotation tires. (Clearly, conventional reference in this context purest **anachronism**: Nose-wheel-based tricycle gear, as seen on jetliners, military aircraft, etc. including
7	way if you prefer it." "No. I won't be an **anachronism** in the world. I'm okay with genetic engineering now." He smiled
8	Chesapeake Bay. # There are bridges to the south and north, but this **anachronism** can save motorists about 15 minutes' driving time. # Most of the time
9	for movie stars on Hollywood Boulevard. The Oracle had been their star, an **anachronism** from another era of policing, from long before the Rodney King riots and Rampart
10	perhaps bad for America, but it was good for Billy. Although a self-declared **anachronism**, lacking the appurtenances of what might be called a regular job, Billy acted

Source: retrieved and repurposed from http://corpus.byu.edu/coca.

or stop reading. In turn, if our ELLs do not own enough vocabulary to achieve basic reading comprehension of a given text, they cannot use reading as a means of gaining new knowledge, including the vocabulary used to label that new knowledge.

Additionally, learning to read in our first language does not mean we can automatically read in another language. As the formula below depicts, the *Threshold Hypothesis* (Alderson, 1984; Clarke, 1979; Cummins, 1979) suggests that adequate knowledge of a second language is necessary before first language reading skills can transfer to second-language reading.

$$\text{L2 Reading Abilities} = \text{L1 Reading Abilities} + \text{L2 Knowledge}$$

Furthermore, research in this area points to second-language vocabulary as the most important component of that requisite L2 knowledge (Bossers, 1992; Nassaji, 2003; Schoonen, *et al.*, 1998; Verhoeven, 2000). In short, lack of second-language vocabulary knowledge (along with insufficient grammar knowledge, discourse knowledge, etc.) can "short circuit" (Clarke, 1980) the transfer of good first language reading skills to second-language reading. To illustrate this point, we need not go further than the example I opened the chapter with. For centuries, linguistic scholars – arguably some of the most literate individuals on the planet – could not read the Egyptian hieroglyphs, until the Rosetta Stone gave them the clues they needed to understand enough of the unknown language to figure out the rest, using their expert skills. No amount of immersion in or exposure to the ancient print could have changed this situation. Again, the key point for us is that a critical mass of vocabulary knowledge – for any given text, in any given language, and with any given skills base – is necessary before readers can adequately comprehend what they are reading. Of course, more is required than sufficient vocabulary knowledge, but without it, there is certainly little hope for success.

To conclude this particular section, I have chosen to give you a first-hand experience with short circuits and thresholds. If you are already a reader of Chinese, you will not be able to participate like other readers, but I am sure you can apply this discussion to other languages that are not familiar to you. During this exercise, it is crucial for you to think about the teaching implications of what you are experiencing, and what this means in terms of the vocabulary support your ELLs will need. To begin with, take a minute to look at Figure 5.4 – a text in simplified Chinese (Mandarin). If you are not a reader of Chinese, this text will likely have no meaning for you. If you had 100 pages of this kind of text to study, would you ever be able to read Chinese without assistance? How about 1,000 pages? A million pages? If this script were all around you every day, would you be able to read

温度告诉我们有些

东西的热或冷。 在

夏天，空气的温度常常

是热的，但是在冬天，

空气的温度常 常是冷的。

Figure 5.4 Simplified Chinese characters (source: from Gardner and Nance, 2001).

Chinese without support? This was the similar task facing the great linguists studying the Egyptian hieroglyphics before the Rosetta Stone was unearthed, and this is also the similar task facing many beginning readers of English if they do not receive support. So, which of your great literacy skills are you able to utilize at this point? Perhaps you are able to surmise that the printed characters must have some meaning, even though you have no idea what that meaning is. You might even see global sentence structuring, indicated by commas, periods, etc. If you look carefully, you might also see that some of the characters repeat themselves, but beyond this you are likely mystified by this script. Your great literacy skills are short-circuited by a lack of Chinese vocabulary knowledge, or, in other words, you have not met the threshold (critical mass) of Chinese vocabulary knowledge necessary to comprehend this text. The bottom line here is that vocabulary is more than symbols or text on a written page, although such items are essential for written word recognition to take place. This also serves as a reminder that vocabulary is truly an artifact of a particular culture that we may or may not participate in.

Now study Figure 5.5, containing the same Chinese text. What has changed? You now see a familiar-looking script (the Romanized pronunciation guides for the characters), and you might even try your hand at pronouncing these more familiar forms, although a native Chinese speaker may not understand what you are saying, unless you have been trained to pronounce the Romanized forms correctly. Even if you *were* able to pronounce the Romanized forms correctly, would you be able to comprehend Chinese text if you had 100 pages like this to study? How about 1,000 pages? A million? The bottom line here is that vocabulary is also much more than the sounds of words, although

温度告诉我们有些
wēn dù gào sù   wǒ mén yǒu xiē

东西的热或冷.   在
dōng xi de rè huò lěng   zài

夏天,   空气的温度常常
xià tiān   kōng qì de wēn dù cháng cháng

是热的,   但是在冬天,
shì rè de   dàn shì zài dōng tiān

空气的温度常 常是冷的.
kōng qì de wēn dù cháng cháng shì lěng de

Figure 5.5 Simplified Chinese characters with Romanizations (source: from Gardner and Nance, 2001).

such sounds are essential for spoken word recognition. While symbols and sounds (the forms of words) are fundamental components of vocabulary, they are quite arbitrary and useless if we cannot attach meanings to them. Conversely, we may know meanings or concepts (in our native language), but have insufficient knowledge of the forms (the symbols and the sounds) representing those meanings and concepts in another language, and we therefore struggle to make the necessary form-meaning connections.

Now study Figure 5.6, which contains the same information as Figure 5.5, plus some rough English translations (glosses) of the Chinese characters. What has changed? Suddenly, the arbitrary characters and pronunciation aids (Romanizations) have meaning attached to them. Do you think you could learn to read some Chinese with 100 pages of such material? How about 1,000 pages? A million? If I asked you to tell me the Chinese word for *temperature*, could you do it? Could you write the Chinese characters for the word *air*? In one sense, you have experienced your own simplified version of the Rosetta Stone, and hopefully you have come to a better understanding of thresholds and short circuits as they relate to second and foreign language vocabulary. Before leaving this example, however, it is crucial to point out that your existing literacy skills in English eventually allowed you to find some success in reading Chinese. Keep in mind that beginning ELLs who do not have literacy skills in their native language will face a much harder task than you did, because they lack two parts of the equation – L2 knowledge (vocabulary, etc.) and L1 literacy itself.

Figure 5.6 Simplified Chinese characters with Romanizations and English glosses (source: adapted from Gardner and Nance, 2001).

Breadth and depth of vocabulary knowledge

The relationship between *breadth* of vocabulary knowledge (numbers of words known at a basic level) and *depth* of vocabulary knowledge (quality of word knowledge) has been an important discussion in English language education since the early 1900s (Read, 2004), but was given a particular boost in recent decades in articles by Anderson and Freebody (1981) and Wesche and Paribakht (1996). While a full discussion of this topic is beyond the scope of this book, suffice it to say that our ELLs must not only learn a large number of words to be successful in English language education and many occupational settings (breadth of vocabulary knowledge), but they must also learn important dimensions of those words (depth of vocabulary knowledge) in order to function at high levels of proficiency and to compete with native English-speaking peers. These depth dimensions include (a) knowledge of a word's phonological and orthographic representations, (b) knowledge of the various ways that a word is used in syntax (parts of speech, collocations, etc.), (c) knowledge of a word's morphological characteristics and possibilities, (d) knowledge of a word's semantic representations, including its core meanings, connotations, and alternative meanings (polysemy), and (e) knowledge of a word's pragmatic functions, including its relative formality, its context-based appropriateness, and its register-related tendencies (Ordóñez, *et al.*, 2002; cf. Nation, 2001).

Not surprisingly, some researchers point to frequency of input (sheer exposure) as the solution to both sides of the breadth–depth equation (e.g. Vermeer, 2001), and extensive reading, in its various forms, as the best way to achieve both breadth and depth of new word knowledge (e.g. Krashen, 2010; Elley, 1991; Day and Bamford, 1998; Nagy and Herman, 1987). Unfortunately, the value of reading input as a means of gaining new word knowledge is often pitted against direct vocabulary instruction, with the primary criticisms being that direct instruction is too slow to account for the vocabulary growth noted in first language children (Nagy and Herman, 1987), or that direct instruction somehow leads to inferior vocabulary learning instead of true acquisition (Krashen, 2010). Again, if these claims are taken at face value, then the role of the teacher would be reduced to providing ELLs with a vast amount of reading materials at various difficulty levels and simply inviting them to read – an approach that we have already discussed as being problematic with many ELLs and struggling first language readers, especially in academic settings, and certainly if time is of the essence.

However, some advocates of the *reading hypothesis* also see the value of awareness and direct instruction for many vocabulary purposes (e.g. Nagy, 2007; Stahl and Nagy, 2006). Still other experts take an even stronger position on the side of direct instruction, viewing it as essentially mandatory, especially in the case of ELLs and struggling first language readers (e.g. Biemiller, 2009; Beck *et al.*, 2002; Chall, *et al.*, 1990; Zimmerman, 1997). While not discounting the value of reading as a means of gaining word knowledge, they emphasize that direct instruction can greatly facilitate vocabulary learning, especially if such instruction contains large doses of vocabulary-strategy training that learners can eventually use on their own when they encounter new words (morphological analysis, dictionary look-up, cognate recognition, contextual guessing strategies, etc.). Too often, direct instruction is simply viewed as learning lists of decontextualized words – a view that certainly does not do justice to the range of possibilities with direct instruction.

So what is a teacher to do? "To teach, or not to teach: that is the question"

As discussed earlier, many advocates of the *reading hypothesis* claim that the "sheer volume" of encounters with unknown words through reading input produces the necessary conditions for both breadth and depth of vocabulary acquisition. From an academic perspective, the real problem with this position is that "authentic" reading materials do a poor job of recycling words once we get past the 3,000 to 5,000 highest frequency words of the language. In the absence of an elaborate systematic approach to language-content presentation in textbooks and other materials (Decoo, 2011), or the restructuring of existing content through technological interventions such as concordancing programs that unnaturally drive together contexts containing unknown words (Cobb, 1999), there is simply no guarantee that important academic words will be recycled in transparent reading contexts within a reasonable time frame for acquisition and retention. This is a linguistic reality. It is therefore crucial that ELLs have strategies for dealing with unknown words beyond the learning possibilities that come from natural exposure in context.

We have also discussed together, with examples, how differences even exist between the high frequency content words of reading materials from different registers (e.g. fiction vs. history vs. mathematics vs. science textbooks), and, as a result, that reading in one register may not be adequate preparation for reading in another register. This is a linguistic reality. The bottom line is that direct vocabulary instruction (the teaching of words themselves and the teaching of strategies for independent word learning) is not only justified, but may very well be essential for our ELLs in academic and occupational settings. A combination of direct vocabulary instruction coupled with actual opportunities for our learners to read and interact extensively in the language offers our best hope for success. The next chapter is devoted to a discussion of how we might accomplish such a task, as we take our learners from "what they know to where they need to go" in terms of their vocabulary knowledge.

Vocabulary Project (learning about vocabulary tools)

At the end of Chapter 4, you were encouraged to produce a vocabulary inventory for the texts used in the specific instructional setting you chose for your vocabulary project. You should now familiarize yourself with online resources that can be used by you and your learners to teach and learn the key words you discovered through the inventory process. I encourage you to take some time now to search the internet widely for online tools that can assist in these efforts. Keep in mind that you specifically want tools that allow you to enter your own vocabulary lists and texts, rather than those that have predetermined content. My personal favorites are listed below, but they are by no means all that is available.

1 Quizlet – available at www.quizlet.com.
2 Word and Phrase – available at http://corpus.byu.edu/coca.
3 Compleat Lexical Tutor – available at www.lextutor.ca.
4 AntLab Tools – available at www.antlab.sci.waseda.ac.jp/software. html

6 Building vocabulary knowledge

Problem

My philosophy of ELL education in general has always been that teachers must first have a basic understanding themselves of the linguistic and psychological challenges involved in learning English, so that they are capable of assessing which instructional approaches will work or not work for their particular learners. While it is tempting to reach immediately for the many language activity books on the market – with their predetermined content and lesson plans for the classroom – we may find that what is proposed in such materials does not match either the global or specific goals of our particular learners, the skill levels of our particular learners, or the backgrounds they bring with them to our classrooms. Much better, from my perspective, is a knowledgeable teacher who can take any group of ELLs and address their vocabulary and other language needs directly and flexibly. With the basic background established in the previous chapters, I believe you are ready to discuss how we can take our learners from "what they know to where they need to go" in terms of English vocabulary knowledge.

The following questions will serve as our guide:

1 What is a useful overall approach for addressing the vocabulary needs of my particular learners?
2 How do I deal with the immediate vocabulary needs of my learners?
3 How do I prepare my students to be independent word learners and to negotiate unknown vocabulary they will encounter outside of my instructional influence?
4 What specific vocabulary strategies are essential for my learners to know?

Intervention and theory

The "big picture" with vocabulary teaching

It should be clear by now that vocabulary knowledge is crucial at every stage of English language education. There is simply no way that ELLs can function effectively without a critical mass of vocabulary knowledge for specific English purposes. Efficient and effective teaching of English vocabulary must be considered from the viewpoint of actual learner needs, as well as the associated vocabulary demands that will be placed on learners as they attempt to meet those needs. I like to ask the following questions every time I make curricular decisions involving vocabulary:

1 What English do my particular ELLs need in the short run and in the long run?
2 What are the texts and/or tasks associated with meeting those needs?
3 What is the actual vocabulary in those texts and tasks?
4 How much of that actual vocabulary do my learners already know?
5 What vocabulary will my learners still need to learn in order to successfully negotiate the texts and tasks that will fulfill their English language needs?
6 How can I best help my learners gain this new knowledge?

On the surface, these questions may seem very simplistic, but the answers involve some of the most careful analysis and planning that a teacher can ever perform. Hopefully, the preceding chapters have helped to clarify some of the complexities associated with answering these questions. These basic questions also direct us away from the common perspective of vocabulary for general purposes toward the more practical perspective of vocabulary for specific purposes – to actual needs, to actual texts and tasks, and to actual words. They also inspire needed flexibility in instructional approaches and designs to vocabulary training.

In Chapter 3 we discussed the need for our ELLs to have a foundational (core) vocabulary consisting of high frequency function and content words, which enables them to get around in the language, and upon which they can build more vocabulary knowledge. At the end of Chapter 3, I also provided some suggestions and links to tools for helping our learners with the core. I recommend that you review these as you consider the particular needs of your learners, and in designing an appropriate curriculum for them. The remainder of this chapter will focus on words beyond the core – the large number of content words in texts and tasks that are likely to cause the most comprehension and production challenges for our ELLs, particularly in academic and other specialized settings.

Designing a vocabulary-centered curriculum

To begin this section on curriculum decisions relating to vocabulary, I wish to echo the following from Biemiller (2009, p. 32): "I strongly recommend a more teacher-directed and curriculum-directed approach to fostering vocabulary and language growth. If education is going to have a serious "compensatory" function, we must do more to promote vocabulary."

Biemiller is specifically talking here about the early grades of primary education, but I see no reason why this same sentiment should not apply to every level of education. In fact, there are many logical reasons why we should organize classroom instruction from the beginning with vocabulary in mind. For one, it plays such a critical role in the oral discourse of the classroom (oral instructions, explanations, lectures, discussions, group and pair work, etc.), as well as the written discourse (written instructions, homework assignments, content readings, writing tasks, etc.). Additionally, we have discussed previously how vocabulary learning is intricately related to the aims of education in the first place, especially in academic settings where the learning of key content terms and their associated concepts becomes the very focus of our attention (*mitosis, longitude, denominator, eclipse, democracy, igneous, economy*, etc.).

The following are instructional decisions that can give us some measure of control over the vocabulary in our classrooms, and improve our ELLs' chances of being successful with that vocabulary.

Identifying important vocabulary

Deciding what words to focus on with our particular learners is perhaps the most important decision we have to make. The Vocabulary Project option of this book was designed to develop skills in this regard. I cannot emphasize enough the importance of having target-language materials in electronic format if possible. So much can be done with modern technology to take the guesswork out of the vocabulary selection process, but we must first have at least the target written materials in electronic format. The excellent programs discussed in the Vocabulary Project sections of this book (*Range, kfNgram*, etc.) allow us to create a vocabulary inventory, specific to the needs of a particular learner group. If you have not already done so, I would encourage you to review those programs now by reading through the Vocabulary Project instructions at the end of each chapter. In addition to the programs mentioned in the Vocabulary Project, there are several other useful online resources for *quickly* identifying important vocabulary. One of my favorites is the *KeyWords Extractor*, part of the *Compleat Lexical Tutor* suite (Cobb, 2012). This program allows the user to paste in up to 50,000 words of text (a good-sized novel or informational text), and then it determines the words that appear statistically more often in that text than in a large general corpus of English. This all happens within a few seconds. Figure 6.1 contains examples of the output from this program, using three different texts.

To Space and Back (Ride and Okie, 1986)	The Secrets of Vesuvius (Bisel, 1990)	Whales: Great Creatures of the World (Dow, 1990)
astronaut weight airlock shuttle sally suction airplane sunrise treadmill orbit rendezvous trash tether satellite carton cargo robot hatch cabin gravity helmet pouch float launch runway sunset toothpaste peanut flight earth space razor locker telescope pants urine deck crew harness planet capture rocket dispense atmosphere Dale drift mask norm tray spoon	pumice tunic balustrade magma whimper cupid millstone artifact weight glint volcano mosaic shrill awning avalanche skeleton erupt tremor trowel lavish stench mistress blindfold excavate debris slave wail skull vineyard mound alcove tavern ancient surge pelvis cavity anthropology bronze suffocate topple statue eggshell leash huddle scorch banquet archaeology murmur fragile shriek	blubber whale blowhole bowhead crustacean scrimshaw weight minke harpoon dorsal fluke flipper porpoise whalebone barnacle Eskimo cask mammary temperate genus flense kayak ovulate subarctic pygmy sperm Basque louse squid courtship dolphin arctic Antarctica lunge decompose snout swarm vertebra stranded underwater slug calf mammal harem ovary slit intestine suckle hemisphere groove

Figure 6.1 Sample outputs from the *Compleat Lexical Tutor* program.
Note
1 Only top 50 words listed.

The program clearly does an excellent job of identifying key terms in each of the books. In an instant, we know a great deal about the important vocabulary in these books, and we can begin to think more clearly about what our learners need to know in order to read the respective books and participate in discussions about the content of those books. We also have a good idea what to pay attention to in our attempts to provide some direct vocabulary instruction – a topic we will take up shortly.

Theme-based instruction

By choosing to organize around themes, we are giving our curriculum a mathematically-higher probability of recycling specialized content words, thus making it easier for us to isolate important vocabulary for direct instruction, improving our ability to predict which words our learners will encounter next, and analyzing which words they will likely have the most trouble with. However, not all themes are created equal and it is therefore imperative to choose them wisely (Gardner, 2004, 2008). For instance, in my own extensive research with themed book collections in primary education, I discovered that the relative "tightness" of the theme made a tremendous difference in specialized vocabulary sharing and recycling in expository (informational) book collections, as shown in Table 6.1.

Table 6.1 Rank of vocabulary recycling in expository theme-based book collections

Theme	Thematic tightness	Authorship	Average rank[1]
Mummy	Tight	Uniauthor	1.3
Mummy	Tight	Multiauthor	1.7
Westward movement	Semi-tight	Multiauthor	4.5
Westward movement	Semi-tight	Uniauthor	6.3
Mystery	Loose	Multiauthor	7.0
Mystery	Loose	Uniauthor	10.7
Control	Control	Multiauthor	14.0

Source: adapted from Gardner (2008).

Note

1 Average rank was based on three critical vocabulary recycling measures.

My *Mummy* book collections (tight theme) were much better at sharing and recycling specialized mummy words like *mummy, sarcophagus, pyramid, pharaoh*, and *tomb* than my *Mystery* collections (loose theme), which shared and recycled mystery words like *bones, evidence, creature, horror*, and *evil* at lower frequency levels. Both of these theme-based collections were better than my expository *Control* collection (no thematic relationships between books), which shared and recycled unrelated words, and at even lower frequency levels (*areas, apart, Atlantic, education, gradually*, etc.). The semi-tight *Westward movement* collections were ranked between *Mummy* and *Mystery*, sharing and recycling words like *trail, cattle, fort, territory*, and *California*.

However, as seen in Table 6.2, this same tightness-of-theme finding did not hold true for my theme-based narrative collections, consisting of fictional children's books. In fact, one of my fictional *Mummy* collections ranked last in terms of specialized vocabulary recycling among theme-based narrative collections. On the other hand, the key variable for recycling specialized words in fiction was authorship, or number of authors (uniauthor vs. multiauthor). Collections of fiction containing books written by one author (e.g. a series) shared and recycled specialized vocabulary better than collections consisting of books written by several authors. The same was not true with the informational (expository) collections, as can be seen in Table 6.1. It is also important to note that the shared specialized fiction words were characteristically different than those in the expository collections. Rather than theme-specific words like *mummy, sarcophagus, pyramid, pharaoh*, and *tomb*, the shared fiction words were primarily "characters (*Laura, Pa, Ma, Rosie, Kayo, Anthony, Eells, Almonzo*, etc.), places (*prairie, creek, museum, porch*, etc.), simple action verbs (*nodded, grabbed, yelled, grinned, peered*, etc.) or expressions (*okay, yeah*, etc.)" (Gardner, 2004, p. 22).

Table 6.2 Rank of vocabulary recycling in narrative theme-based book collections (fiction)

Theme	Thematic tightness	Authorship	Average rank[1]
Westward movement	Semi-Tight	Uniauthor	3.3
Mystery	Loose	Uniauthor	5.2
Mummy	Tight	Uniauthor	6.8
Westward movement	Semi-Tight	Multiauthor	8.8
Control	Control	Multiauthor	10.8
Mystery	Loose	Multiauthor	11.8
Mummy	Tight	Multiauthor	12.7

Source: adapted from Gardner (2008).

Note
1 Average rank was based on three critical recycling measures.

Several important points for designing vocabulary-focused curricula in academic settings accrue from these findings:

1 Theme-based instructional units improve overall vocabulary recycling, and the tighter the theme, the better the recycling. *Mummy* (tight) would be better than *Mystery* (loose). The *Gold Rush* (tight) would be better than *Westward Movement* (semi-tight), which, in turn, would be better than *American History* (loose). *Bees* (tight) would be better than *Insects* (loose). However, all of these (even loose themes) would be better than no themes at all (e.g. unrelated books and topics). For vocabulary recycling purposes, it is also advantageous to have a curriculum consisting of several tight themes that are related to each other, creating a condition where common threads of vocabulary weave throughout the various thematic units (Stoller and Grabe, 1997). For instance, a loose science theme such as *plants* could be broken down into several tighter themes like *plant anatomy*, *plant growth*, *plant classifications*, *poisonous plants*, etc. Each of these tighter sub-themes will have unique vocabulary that could be recycled through several different readings, discussions, etc. but they will also have a great deal of shared vocabulary that will reduce the overall cognitive load placed on the learners and provide much needed practice with newly-learned terms.

2 Given the marked vocabulary differences between expository (informational) and narrative (fictional) reading materials, it is crucial to focus curricular attention on the vocabulary of informational texts, using theme-related fiction to supplement and enrich. Focusing heavily on fictional reading will not be adequate preparation for the vocabulary demands of informational texts or informational vocabulary in general, although reading fiction for pleasure should also be encouraged on its own merits (building fluency with high frequency words, increasing and enriching

vocabulary knowledge relating to social and personal experiences). In this regard, and adapting Cummin's terminology (see Chapter 5), I refer to fiction as the "BICS of literacy," providing ELLs with a rich source of non-academic word-learning possibilities.

3 The content areas of education are naturally theme-based (Stoller and Grabe, 1997), and these themes and their sub-themes are often reflected in educational core requirements, as seen in examples like those in Figure 6.2 taken from the California grade eight (adolescents) science content standards.

- In this example, thematic words like *galaxy, clusters, solar system, planets, planetary satellites, comets,* and *asteroids* are identifiable and therefore candidates for direct vocabulary instruction and explicit learning. The front-loading of such vocabulary will certainly allow ELLs to be more successful reading texts, performing tasks, and participating in discussions associated with this theme of *Earth in the Solar System.*
- Themes are also fairly easy to define in business English (*the sales pitch, the job interview, marketing plans, hiring and firing,* etc.) and vocational English (*mechanics, plumbing, building construction, job safety,* etc.). Even life-skills English lends itself well to theme-based units (*the grocery store, asking for directions, dealing with landlords,* etc.). Additionally, research suggests that learning vocabulary in these thematic units is more effective than learning vocabulary in semantic sets like color words (*red, yellow, green, blue,* etc.), emotion words (*happy, sad, ecstatic, depressed,* etc.), shape words (*round, square, triangle, rectangle,* etc.), and so forth (see Folse, 2004, for review).

Earth in the Solar System (Earth Sciences)

4. The structure and composition of the universe can be learned from studying stars and galaxies and their evolution. As a basis for understanding this concept:

   a. Students know galaxies are clusters of billions of stars and may have different shapes.

   b. Students know that the Sun is one of many stars in the Milky Way galaxy and that stars may differ in size, temperature, and color.

   c. Students know how to use astronomical units and light years as measures of distances between the Sun, stars, and Earth.

   d. Students know that stars are the source of light for all bright objects in outer space and that the Moon and planets shine by reflected sunlight, not by their own light.

   e. Students know the appearance, general composition, relative position and size, and motion of objects in the solar system, including planets, planetary satellites, comets, and asteroids.

Figure 6.2 Sample of science content standards (source: retrieved August 20, 2012 from www.cde.ca.gov/be/st/ss).

Integrated skills

Another critical curricular decision for vocabulary recycling is to integrate language skills (listening, speaking, reading, and writing) in the classroom, rather than having isolated modules or separate classes for these skills. The key here is that our ELLs will benefit greatly from hearing, speaking, reading, and writing the same vocabulary dealing with the same themes or topics. If integration is not possible because of institutional mandates at your particular school – a common situation in many intensive English programs and private language schools – then the next best choice would be to have similar themes in the various skills classes. For example, use *Mummy* topics in the separate listening, speaking, reading, and writing, classrooms. This will reduce the cognitive vocabulary load that is naturally placed on our ELLs by having different topics in all their classes.

Another problem in many primary and secondary educational contexts is that ELLs are often pulled out of the mainstream classroom to receive remedial help in a skill such as reading, but the content of the remedial reading class is not the same as the content of the classroom from which they were pulled out. A classic example is taking struggling science and math readers out of their classrooms, helping them to read *Harry Potter* or some other fictional text, and then sending them back into the science or math classroom to falter again.

The best scenario is to organize around important content themes, and then focus all oral and written tasks around those themes. For instance, watch a documentary about mummies, have a follow-up discussions about mummies, read a short book or article about mummies, and assign a writing task (research paper, reaction paper, synthesis paper, etc.) about mummies.

Three important benefits accrue from such a curriculum:

1 The cognitive vocabulary load is greatly reduced because a smaller set of specialized words is recycled throughout the curriculum. Remember, when we change the topic, we change the vocabulary.
2 A smaller set of specialized vocabulary can be focused on through direct instruction and focused practice. Some ELLs will need to learn a great deal of content vocabulary before they will be able to successfully participate in a particular educational discussion or task. This pre-learning or *front-loading* of vocabulary is not optional for their success in the classroom, nor can we afford to take the chance that they will gain enough words by reading self-selected books at their current skill level or through unfocused private vocabulary study.

3 The combination of themes and integrated skills, with its ability to recycle important vocabulary, can be a powerful enhancement to Nation's (2008) four strands of successful ELL vocabulary instruction, which I strongly endorse:
   - *Meaning-focused input* (learning new words and enriching knowledge of known words through listening and reading).
   - *Meaning-focused output* (enriching and establishing vocabulary knowledge through speaking and writing).
   - *Language-focused learning* (deliberately learning new words and studying more about known words).
   - *Fluency development* (extensive practice with known vocabulary to become proficient in all language skills).

When these four strands are coupled with the natural vocabulary recycling afforded by theme-based content and integrated skills, we have our greatest chances for successful vocabulary learning and teaching.

Leveled reading materials

Part of the challenge involved in designing vocabulary-centered curricula is that all learners are not at the same skill level in the same classroom. A text or task that could be dealt with successfully by some ELLs may be beyond the current capacity of others. In this regard, I believe we can benefit greatly from a special adaptation of the groundbreaking work by Fountas and Pinnell (2006), in which they provide a rationale for assessing the relative difficulty levels of books, in order to match texts with learners at their current skill levels. Not surprisingly, many of the text characteristics analyzed in the leveling scheme have direct or indirect ties to vocabulary. The special adaptation I propose is to establish collections of leveled books for a certain theme (e.g. all books are about "plants" but they are at different levels of difficulty). This allows us to better meet the skill-level vocabulary-reading needs of our learners, without distracting us from our content-knowledge classroom objectives. In other words, we can all be on the same page (learning about plants), while improving the chances that more students will have a successful learning experience, especially when we ask them to read about plants. In turn, any direct vocabulary instruction (front-loading) we provide about plants will be relevant for the entire class.

The following is a summary of the ten major factors to consider when leveling books (determining their relative difficulty), as forwarded by Fountas and Pinnell (2006, pp. 51–52). I have attempted to synthesize and summarize some of their key descriptors. For the complete leveling system (with examples), I encourage you to consult their actual book. As you review this list, carefully consider the many possible roles of vocabulary (explicit and implied) in determining text difficulty.

1 *Genre and forms*: type of fiction or nonfiction; each genre has unique characteristics.
2 *Text structure*: text organization (narrative, categorical, topical, description; also underlying structures such as chronological sequence, compare/contrast, cause/effect, problem/solution that can individually and collectively increase text difficulty (the presence and combinations of these increase text difficulty). Structures are often realized through vocabulary items (*first, second, while, yet; because, since, thus: conclude, the evidence is, furthermore*),
3 *Content*: the subject matter/concepts that learners need to understand; the relationship between the content of the text and the background knowledge of the readers (the less they match, the more difficult the text will be).
4 *Themes and ideas*: the big ideas being communicated; main themes and their sub-themes.
5 *Language and literary features*: written versus spoken language considerations; fiction versus factual versus hybrid texts (texts that combine several different features).
6 *Sentence complexity*: the degree of simple sentences versus complex sentences.
7 *Vocabulary*: the degree to which the words of the text are already understood by the readers; the relative complexity of word meanings; the degree of content and technical words; the extent of words associated with written versus oral language.
8 *Words*: the number and difficulty of words that readers must recognize and decode: the degree of high frequency words (texts containing more high frequency words assumed to be easier reading).
9 *Illustrations*: the placement and relationship to text; the degree to which readers must integrate illustrations with the text (photos, graphs, etc.).
10 *Book and print features*: the physical characteristics of the text (size, length, punctuation, print size, print style, spacing, format, indexes, glossaries, etc.).

Section conclusion

The primary purpose for designing a vocabulary-centered curriculum is to make explicit and manageable the vocabulary demands that will be placed on our learners, thus empowering us as teachers to directly address those demands. In my experience, the sheer numbers and possible combinations of English vocabulary items render more general vocabulary approaches ineffective and inefficient, often leading to frustrated learners and teachers. Following the suggestions given in this past section can bring some control over classroom vocabulary demands, and will enable us to better isolate important vocabulary for direct teaching and learning.

Direct vocabulary instruction

An exhaustive discussion of effective techniques and approaches for explicit vocabulary teaching and learning is worthy of an entire book on its own. In recent years, several excellent books with just such a focus have come onto the scene. I highly recommend those in Table 6.3 for a more in-depth study of actual classroom applications.

In the remaining sections, I draw from many of the best practices in the books listed in Table 6.3, along with my own experience and research, to highlight six key areas of direct vocabulary instruction (DVI):

1 conceptualization;
2 form and meaning practice;
3 context-based word-learning strategies;
4 dictionary definition training;
5 morphological awareness raising; and
6 collocation training.

Before beginning, however, it is crucial to understand that I view DVI as an essential but insufficient approach to building vocabulary knowledge. The value of extensive reading for vocabulary growth, as well as other experiences with rich, contextualized language – *meaning-focused input, meaning-focused output, and fluency development*

Table 6.3 Recommended books on vocabulary teaching

Title	Author/s	Publication year	Publisher
Word Knowledge	Cheryl Boyd Zimmerman	2009	Oxford
Teaching Vocabulary: Strategies and Techniques	I. S. Paul Nation	2008	Heinle Cengage Learning
The Vocabulary Book: Learning and Instruction	Michael Graves	2006	International Reading Association
Vocabulary (2nd edition)	John Morgan and Mario Rinvolucri	2004	Oxford

(Nation, 2008) – must be emphasized at all levels of English language education and made an integral part of a vocabulary-centered curriculum. However, the crucial educational and personal resources of time, money, and energy also call for a more concerted and guided effort if our ELLs are to meet their immediate high-stakes vocabulary needs, especially in academic and occupational settings. This is where DVI is essential.

> most L2 learners have to learn large numbers of words beyond the core vocabulary, words to which they are not frequently exposed during normal reading or listening activities. For the retention of these words it is necessary that learners are made aware of the nature and extent of their formidable word learning task and are taught effective strategies for coding and memorizing new words.
>
> (Hulstijn, 2001, p. 276)

> Every piece of research comparing deliberate learning with incidental learning has shown that deliberate word learning easily beats incidental vocabulary learning in terms of time taken to learn and the amount learned. The deliberate learning studies also show that such learning lasts for a very long time.
>
> (Nation, 2008, p. 104)

It is important to note that DVI comes in essentially three major forms:

1 teachers directly teaching important vocabulary to their learners (on the whiteboard, through explanation, discussion, lecture, demonstration, etc.);
2 teachers directing learners to materials and learning tools that allow them to learn vocabulary on their own (flashcards, online resources, etc.). Some of these resources already exist, while others are created by teachers to meet specific needs; and
3 teachers teaching learners strategies they can use for independent word learning outside of the classroom (using contextual clues, looking up words in various types of dictionaries, maintaining a personal vocabulary log, etc.).

All three forms of DVI are crucial and serve unique purposes in the overall education of ELLs. When all three are working together, they create a powerful foundation for extensive vocabulary training. The first form is teacher intensive and should be reserved for only the most important words that ELLs need to know right now to function well in their particular situations. The second and third forms initially require teachers' time and energy, but they eventually lead to autonomous word learning – the ultimate goal of any serious vocabulary training.

As we proceed, you should carefully consider where the key areas of DVI we discuss fall in terms of these three major forms. Also, it is crucial to understand that everything we ask our learners to do themselves should be modeled by us and revisited many times during the course of our instruction.

Conceptualization

Perhaps the most important element of effective DVI is to ensure that ELLs are actually conceptualizing the words they are trying to learn. The concepts behind some English words can be made clear by simply using an L1 gloss, but this assumes that the learners know the concept already in their L1. If they do not, then the task becomes more difficult and involved, and we must determine the best way to teach the word (through discussion in English, through discussion in the learner's L1, through pictures, through definitions, etc.). The concepts behind some words can also be made clear by using pictures or series of pictures (photos, drawings, movie clips, etc.). Keep in mind, however, that there is a difference between using pictures to remind learners of concepts they already know, and using pictures to teach new concepts. The former requires the learner to simply associate a new label (English word) with a known concept (depicted in the picture). The latter requires the learner to learn a new concept by studying the picture, and then associating that new concept with a new label (English word).

Revisiting our discussion in Chapter 5, we will remember that word learning is always dependent on what an individual learner knows or does not know about labels and concepts:

1 *Known labels and known concepts* (words only need to be practiced for fluency).
2 *New labels and known concepts* (only new forms need to be learned).
3 *Similar labels and known concepts* (cognates – only new similar forms need to be learned).
4 *Known labels and new concepts* (new meanings for old forms must be learned).
5 *New labels and new concepts* (both new forms and their associated meanings must be learned).

Once we have determined that a word is worth direct instructional time and energy, we must determine which of the five conditions above exists and organize our DVI approach accordingly. Conceptualization should guide all DVI decisions; otherwise, we may design instruction that is inefficient or ineffective.

Form and meaning practice

As we have discussed several times in this book, there is an interdependent relationship between the forms of words (written or oral) and the meanings of those words. For ELLs to be successful vocabulary learners, they will need a great deal of practice in rapidly recognizing word forms and automatically connecting forms with their meanings. Several activities and approaches lend themselves well to making these connections.

FLASHCARDS

This activity has been a staple in vocabulary learning since the first half of the nineteenth century. More recently, however, the power and versatility of flashcards has been greatly enhanced through technology. Online flashcard programs such as the freely accessible *Quizlet* (www.Quizlet.com) allow easy creation of card sets, the importing of photos, pronunciation of written words, multiple language possibilities, instant gaming for repetitive practice, and instant testing of vocabulary knowledge. Additionally, such technologies (and their mobile applications) often have shared word learning capabilities through Facebook, blogs, and other resources, and most allow cards to be printed for manual use and maximum portability. I have several suggestions for flashcard content that leads to successful learning outcomes:

1 The content of the cards should match the current skill level of the learner to make meaning available through different avenues, and to allow deeper processing of meanings to take place. Table 6.4 contains some card set possibilities, and we should keep in mind that combinations of these different versions are possible, and that the different card sets work better for some words than others.
2 When choosing L1 glosses (sets 1 and 2 in Table 6.4), careful consideration should be given to the meaning of the target word that needs to be learned, as some words have several meanings. This will be less of an issue in English for specific purposes than in English for general purposes. Also, we must always remember that the assumption behind an L1 gloss is that the learner knows the meaning of the L1 gloss and can read (recognize) the L1 gloss in print. Otherwise, it is of no value in learning the target word. This is a particularly sticky problem with the many content terms in education that often have context-free meanings. For instance, the words *carbonation, photosynthesis* and *mitosis* have German glosses of *Karbonatisierung, Fotosynthese*, and *Mitose* respectively.

If the concepts behind the words are not known in either language, the L1 glosses (German) will be of little value in learning the target English words, even if they are cognates like these in the example. In such cases, the definition card sets (4, 5, 6, and 7) would be a better option for learning new words, and possibly the picture card set (3). However, once the concepts are mastered, card sets 1 and 2 could be used for fluency practice.

3 Some programs like *Quizlet* also have sound capabilities, which should be taken full advantage of. ELLs will benefit greatly from clicking on words and definitions and hearing them pronounced. The *Quizlet* "Speller" function actually speaks a word and asks the user to write it. Experiencing the target words in multiple modalities like this produces deeper levels of processing and improves the chances that learners will properly encode the sound of new written words and make other useful connections between the written and oral forms of words in the target language.

Table 6.4 Some flashcard possibilities

Set	Front of Card	Back of Card	Purpose
1	Target word	L1 gloss	Matching word forms with their meanings (receptive target word knowledge)
2	L1 gloss	Target word	Matching word meanings with their forms (productive target word knowledge)
3	Picture(s)[1]	Target word	Matching word meanings with their forms (productive target word knowledge)
4	L1 definition	Target word	Matching word meanings with their forms (productive target word knowledge)
5	Target word	L1 definition (simplified)	Matching word forms with their meanings (receptive target word knowledge)
6	L1 definition (simplified)	Target word	Matching word meanings with their forms (productive target word knowledge)
7	Target word	L2 definition (simplified)	Matching word forms with their meanings (receptive target word knowledge)

Note
1 Only possible with picturable words/concepts (*nebula, aqueduct, mitosis, fission,* etc.)

Task 6.1

1 Set up and account on *Quizlet* (www.quizlet.com)
2 Study the features of *Quizlet* at http://quizlet.com/features
3 Create at least one set of flashcards.

Concordancing Programs

If used wisely, concordancing can also be an effective tool to teach form and meaning relationships. In this case, a target word can be displayed in several actual contexts, one after the other, as demonstrated in Table 6.5 for the word *segue*.

The concordance lines overcome the target-word spacing problems that occur in natural reading conditions, and provide a situation where focused attention can be given to both the form and contextualized meaning of a specific word. Large searchable corpora like COCA usually contain many examples of actual target word usage. However, this approach is not as direct as the flashcard activities noted above because learners must understand the meaning of words like *segue* from the contexts, some of which provide clearer clues than others. Putting on our vocabulary teaching hats, we will also realize that, without assistance, our ELLs would already need to (1) be at a high-level of English reading proficiency to take advantage of these natural

Table 6.5 Example of concordancing for "segue"

1	" as its two most enduringly popular tunes. That ninth-inning success provided a confidence boosting **segue** into a solo career that got off to a triumphant start with 1970's three-LP
2	offered by FreshPasta.com. CHEESE-A cheese or two after the main course makes a lovely **segue** to dessert. Jarlsberg is a buttery cheese imported from Norway that's now widely
3	cancerous tumors. Both approaches offer benefits, and Weil's eclecticism enables him to **segue** between Oriental and Occidental techniques in ways that unidimensional healers of either stripe can not
4	I have presented this influential argument of Christian history as a prologue to the following **segue** inserted to remind readers about the most boring of all topics for essayists, as
5	, and with scientific endeavors. # As to whether this Space Service should someday **segue** into Star Trek's Star Fleet... who knows? For the moment, let
6	He explained that changing her act would burnish her image and prepare her for a **segue** into the movies. Cher was excited about Geffen's plans. To celebrate her
7	wonk. He could charm his way through an audience large or small, then **segue** effortlessly to the intricacies of education reform and national health insurance. " Now is
8	long regarded yogurt as an anti-anxiety food, making this dessert a wonderful way to **segue** from a stressful day to sweet dreams. ½ cup cake flour 2 tablespoons sugar
9	why I always propose it in a blunt, undisguised way, abjuring wit or **segue** or preparation or coloratura in the pronunciation of the contractual possibility. I want to
10	. But soon after strapping on climbing skins and avalanche beacons, we find the **segue** through the sagebrush more satisfying than the skiing. Ahead of us is Basin Peak

Source: retrieved and modified from COCA (http://corpus.byu.edu/coca).

contexts, (2) have skills in learning word meanings from context, including dealing with different meanings of the same word form, and (3) be computer literate in order to access the concordance lines in the first place. If our learners meet these conditions, they should be encouraged to use concordancing programs to assist them in learning unknown words. If they are less skilled, several adaptations could be made to take advantage of concordancing:

1 Teachers could perform the searches themselves and only provide their learners with contexts that are beneficial to learning a particular target word. Some editing may also need to be performed.
2 Teachers could scan or obtain electronic versions of the materials that their students will be reading, and use programs like AntConc (Anthony, 2011) to create their own concordancing lines. This has many advantages because the teachers and learners will be working with contexts that are directly applicable to the needs in the classroom. This also fits nicely into the call by McCarthy (2008) for more classroom-based corpora created by teachers themselves.
3 Teachers could utilize concordancing lines as the source for teaching word learning skills such as guessing word meanings from context, examining collocations of target words, studying typical gram- matical functions of target words, etc.

Context-based word-learning strategies

Using context as a means of gaining temporary understanding of an unfamiliar word (guessing) to aid in reading comprehension is fairly well accepted among vocabulary experts, whereas using context to actually learn and remember words is not (e.g. Folse, 2004; Zimmerman, 2009). As we saw in Chapter 5, many contexts are not helpful in learning the meanings of new words, and some can even be misleading (Beck, *et al.*, 2002). However, the fact that some contexts are useful suggests that learners should be equipped with strategies to utilize them as an additional aid in learning vocabulary. It is important to distinguish here between the context strategies I am proposing for DVI and the incidental acquisition of vocabulary that naturally occurs when learners encounter unknown words in many different contexts during extensive reading (e.g. Krashen, 1989, 1993). The difference is that in DVI we want ELLs to *consciously* and *explicitly* focus on using contexts based on the concern that time is of the essence for vocabulary learning, especially in high-stakes situations like school and the workplace. In other words, ELLs do not have the luxury of time to hope that they will eventually gain the necessary vocabulary to deal with their immediate language needs. It is also important to remember from Chapters 3 and 4 that learning words from context is only possible if ELLs are capable readers already, and that unknown words are contained in texts that are appropriately matched with learners' current skill levels – that is, ELLs need to know a minimum of 95 percent of the words in a given context to have any hope of using that context to learn the words they do not know (Laufer, 1997; Liu and Nation, 1985; Nation, 1993). While explicit instruction in using contexts clues has received mixed reviews in the research literature, the most recent consensus appears to be that gains can be made if instruction is "well-planned, powerful, and relatively lengthy" (Graves, 2006, p. 27).

With these ideas in mind, I believe the following six basic strategies for context-based word learning can be very beneficial for our ELLs. These strategies are not intended to be a panacea, but they represent a basic starting point to help learners pay more consistent attention to words they encounter in context, and to help them better understand what to do when context is helpful or not helpful. I present the strategies as questions that ELLs should learn to ask themselves when they encounter an unfamiliar word in context:

1 **Is this word important for me to know?** The answer to this question should be determined quickly and usually depends on the importance of the unknown word in achieving adequate comprehension, but it can also involve other determinations such as the number of previous encounters with the word (e.g. it keeps showing up), the amount of time the learner has available to learn the word, or even the personal desire the learner has to own the word and be able to use it in the future. If the answer to the question is "no," then the appropriate strategy would be to move on, possibly recording the word and the page it was found on for future reference. If the answer is "yes," then the rest of the strategies could apply.

2 **What was my first impression of what this word means? (First Guess).** With this question, I have purposely avoided the typical approach to context-guessing strategies which is to encourage the learner to use the sentence-level and paragraph-level clues to learn the meaning of an unknown word. Why should we ask them to do something they have already done naturally – namely, to try to understand the meaning of an unknown word in the context they have been reading? It is very rare for any of us to encounter an unfamiliar word during reading and not notice it. It is also very rare for us to not have an initial impression of what that word might mean. What are the sources of this initial impression? The most obvious answers include the *context* in which the word is embedded,

followed closely by aspects of the word itself (what it sounds like, what it looks like, etc.). You might ask then why Question 2 is necessary at all. The answer is that, by asking the question, learners must pay additional attention to the new word and its meaning. It is in this reprocessing that growth in word knowledge is likely to occur.

3 **What is my second impression of what this word means? (Second Guess).** This question should inspire learners to re-read the context in which the word is embedded, taking advantage of any and all meaning clues, whether they are sentence level or paragraph level. This requires attention and deep processing. Learners should mentally note whether and why their answers to Questions 2 and 3 are similar or different.

4 **Do I know any word parts that can help me guess the meaning? (Third Guess).** This word-level strategy could also be the first line of attack. Many words, especially in academic settings, have meaningful roots or affixes, but they are often found in densely-packed contexts that offer little help in learning their meanings. If learners recognize familiar morphemes in these words, they could use this information to form a hypothesis about the word's meaning and then test it against the context. Because of its importance, a more detailed discussion of raising morphological awareness will come later in the chapter.

5 **How confident am I that I know what this word means?** We must keep in mind that the end result of any of these strategies is still a "guess," which may be accurate, partially accurate, or even an error. It is also possible that no clues exist in either the context or the word itself. ELLs should be taught to accept this quickly and move on. The key, however, is that some words can and will be learned this way, and at a much more rapid rate because they were consciously attended to.

6 **Should I confirm my guess?** It is also important to teach our ELLs to confirm their guesses if they determine that the words are important enough to warrant their extra time and effort. In the absence of a teacher, parent, or associate who might quickly be asked for confirmation, our ELLs should be taught to consult an appropriate dictionary. In my own research I have found that single contextual exposures to a unknown word can sometimes lead to immediate gains in word knowledge if the contexts are directive (i.e. give clear meaning clues), but simple definitions have a significantly greater impact than contexts on immediate understanding of unfamiliar words (Gardner, 2007b).

Task 6.2

1 Using the context below, follow the six steps described above to determine the meaning of *anathema*. Assume that the answer to Step 1 is "yes." If you already know the meaning of this word, try to look at it through the lens of an English language learner who does not know the meaning.

2 Actually look up the word *anathema* in a hard-copy or online dictionary to confirm its meaning (Step 6).

> For most biologists who've worked with island foxes, that idea is **anathema**. Fox populations on the northern islands are recovering despite their low genetic diversity.
>
> Retrieved and repurposed from
> http://corpus.byu.edu/coca/

Dictionary definition training

Most of us have looked up the meaning of words in a dictionary or encountered definitions of technical words in the prose or glossaries of subject-area textbooks. For native speakers of English with robust vocabularies already in place (e.g. adolescents and adults), most definitions provide useful information about the meaning(s) of a given word, thus providing us with a very efficient means of gaining or confirming knowledge of unfamiliar words. On the other hand, many children and ELLs often find that the definitions are as troublesome as the words they explain. The problem is that many definitions contain vocabulary that these groups have not yet mastered, and they are often written in formal styles that the groups are not yet accustomed to. For instance, consider the sets of definitions for the words *typical* and *vicarious*, below, from my study involving fifth-grade children in a public school in Arizona (Gardner, 2007b). The original definitions were taken from dictionaries actually being used in the children's classroom.

The differences in vocabulary load between the original definitions and McKeown's (1993) revised definitions are quite pronounced. Words like *combining, exhibiting, essential,* and *characteristics* in the original definition for *typical* are not basic themselves, nor is the word *undergone* in the original definition for *vicarious*. In that same definition, the phrase "as if one were taking part in" is also very formal, and reflects the style used in many dictionaries. As McKeown discovered, and I confirmed, revised and simplified definitions are much better (statistically superior) than unsimplified originals in aiding young readers with the meanings of unknown words. Using McKeown's simplification scheme, Nist and Olejnik (1995) also found this to be

---

Typical

Original Definition: Combining or exhibiting the essential characteristics of a group (Webster's New Elementary Dictionary, 1970)

Revised Definition: Describes something that is a good example of a person or thing because it shows what that person or thing is usually like. (McKeown, 1993)

Vicarious

Original Definition: Felt or undergone as if one were taking part in the experiences or feeling of another. (The American Heritage School Dictionary, 1977).

Revised Definition: Sharing the feelings of an experience by watching or reading about someone else doing it. (McKeown, 1993)

Figure 6.3 Sample definitions of "typical" and "vicarious" (source: Gardner, 2007b, p. 370).

true for adults (186 college freshmen). For our purposes, it is crucial to understand that certain characteristics make one definition more salient than another for word learning. Whether we are creating our own definitions for a specific set of vocabulary items in our curriculum, selecting definitions from an existing dictionary, or recommending a type of dictionary as a whole to our learners, we would do well to consider McKeown's four primary guidelines for effective definitions:

1　**Identify the role of the word** – "consideration of the essence of the word and its role in the language; when do speakers use *this* in particular."
2　**Characterize the word** – "for a definition to be optimally helpful for developing a representation for a word's meaning, it should pinpoint the word's meaning by explaining its characteristics or prototypical use."
3　**Make the word's meaning accessible** – "if a definition is to serve as an explanation of a word's meaning, it should be framed to make meaning accessible for a young learner. Definitions, even in student dictionaries, are often phrased in ways that seem to require learners to go through many steps of interpretation."
4　**Arrange for attention to be on the whole definition** – "To reduce the likelihood of interpretation based on a fragment, definitions should be phrased to diffuse the effect of particularly salient terms in order to direct attention to the whole definition."

(McKeown, 1993, pp. 21–22)

Definitions that have these characteristics will be the most useful for our learners, especially if they do not have advanced English skills. Modern learner dictionaries come the closest to meeting the McKeown guidelines for definitions on a larger scale. Three excellent examples are the *Longman Dictionary of Contemporary English* (2009 – portions accessible online at www.ldoceonline.com), the *Cambridge Learner's Dictionary* (2012 – portions accessible at http://dictionary.cambridge.org/dictionary/learner-english), and the *Oxford Advanced Learner's Dictionary* (2012 – portions accessible at (http://oald8.oxfordlearnersdictionaries.com/dictionary). Efforts are made in these dictionaries to use simple language, including a relatively small set of common words, in formulating their definitions. In fact, Longman only uses a lexicon of 2,000 common words to write all of their definitions. Laufer and Hadar (1997) found that such definitions were equally effective for both "preadvanced and advanced learners" (p. 195).

The following are examples for the word *vicarious* in these three learner dictionaries:

Longman Example

vi·car·i·ous [only before noun]
experienced by watching or reading about someone else doing something, rather than by doing it yourself

vicarious pleasure/satisfaction/excitement etc.

the vicarious pleasure that parents get from their children's success

Retrieved and adapted from
www.ldoceonline.com/dictionary

Cambridge Example

vicarious
/vɪˈkeəriəs/ adjective [always before noun]

Definition
› A vicarious feeling is one you get from seeing or hearing about another person's experiences:

It gives me vicarious pleasure to watch him eat.

Retrieved and adapted from
http://dictionary.cambridge.org/dictionary/learner-english

Oxford Example

vicarious ADJECTIVE
vɪˈkeəriəs vaɪˈkeriəs
[only before noun]

felt or experienced by watching or reading about somebody else doing something, rather than by doing it yourself

He got a vicarious thrill out of watching his son score the winning goal.

Retrieved and adapted from
http://oald8.oxfordlearnersdictionaries.com/dictionary

These definitions are clear and simple. There are also several other valuable tools for learners in these entries, such as information about the pronunciation of the word, the general placement of the word (e.g. *always before noun*), some common collocations (e.g. *vicarious pleasure/satisfaction/excitement*) and a simple example sentence (e.g. *It gives me vicarious pleasure to watch him eat*). Because these dictionaries are in electronic format, there is the added benefit of being able to hear the words pronounced in either British or American English. Our learners should be taught to take advantage of all of this information in learning new words and deepening their understanding of familiar words.

Task 6.3   (TC)

1 Analyze the following pairs of definitions to determine which one is an original (unsimplified) definition and which one is a simplified definition.
2 Try to describe how you made these determinations. What is it about the definitions that led you to your conclusions?
3 Which of the definitions in each pair do you personally prefer? Why?
4 Which do you think most beginning ELLs would prefer? Why?

Conspicuous
1 Attracting attention; striking the eye.
2 Describes something you notice right away because it stands out.

Devious
1 Using tricky and secretive ways to do something dishonest.
2 Done in an underhand manner; tricky; shifty.

Prudent
1 Thinking things over carefully before making decisions.
2 Having or showing good judgment; well-advised; sensible.

Repurposed from Gardner (2007b).

To this point, we have discussed monolingual dictionaries and definitions (English only). The assumption behind this type of dictionary is that learners have a large enough English vocabulary already in place to actually utilize the definitions as a source of information to learn new words. More advanced learners, like native English speakers, can often take advantage of more complex definitions, whereas learners at low and intermediate levels of proficiency are likely to deal better with the simplified definitions found in learner dictionaries. In addition to monolingual dictionaries, there are two other primary options that are particularly useful for ELLs – bilingual dictionaries and bilingualized dictionaries. The distinction between the two is that bilingual dictionaries simply contain an L1 gloss (e.g. in Spanish) of a target word (e.g. in English), whereas bilingualized dictionaries contain the L1 gloss along with an L2 definition (in English) and often an L2 example sentence containing the target word (in English).

Laufer and Hadar (1997) found that overall test scores for new word comprehension and production were higher for bilingualized dictionary entries than for either monolingual or bilingual dictionary entries. However, they qualified their findings by suggesting that learners at different skill levels used the bilingualized entries in different ways. Unskilled users likely used only the L1 gloss of the entry, not the monolingual definition. Learners with average skills used both parts, but the monolingual definition seemed to only help them with comprehension (not production) of target words. Finally, learners with good skills took advantage of all aspects of the bilingualized entries for both comprehension and production of new English words. This is valuable information as we consider how to match dictionaries and dictionary entries with our particular learners.

Morphological awareness raising

Because English has so many words related through morphology, another important key to building English vocabulary is knowledge of word parts and relationships between words. As we saw in our discussion of lemmas and word families (Chapter 2), relationships can be inflectional (e.g. the verb lemma *climb, climbs, climbing*, and *climbed*; the noun lemma *dog, dogs, dog's*, and *dogs'*, or derivational, e.g. *climb* – the verb, and *climber* – the noun; *knowledge* – the noun, *knowledgeable* – the adjective, and *unknowledgeable* – the negative adjective). Academic English in particular has a great deal of morphological complexity (Nagy and Townsend, 2012), and the acquisition of derivational suffixes generally comes quite late for school-aged learners and adult second-language learners. (See Gardner, 2007a, for review.) Corson (1997) also points out that many ELLs struggle to control the morphologically-heavy Greek- and Latin-based vocabulary of academics. It is therefore crucial that we pay specific instructional attention to raising our learners' awareness of the morphological aspects of words, in order for them to learn and recognize many more words than they normally would. As with other word-learning strategies, morphological analysis can also lead to misinformation, like *"beanstalk: beans talk; manslaughter: man's laughter; nowhere: now here; bargain: bar gain; surgeon: surge on; roughage: rough age"* (Zimmerman, 2009, p. 77). Therefore, learners should be taught to look at morphological analysis as just one more word-learning strategy that must be used flexibly and often in combination with other strategies.

Before beginning morphology training with our ELLs, we should consider two key points:

1 **The first language backgrounds of our learners.** Learners that come from first language backgrounds where grammatical changes are not signaled through morphology (e.g. Chinese, Samoan, Vietnamese) will likely have a harder time with morphological training than those that come from morphologically-rich backgrounds (Spanish, French, etc.) (Zimmerman, 2009). Learners whose first language has many cognates with English (Spanish, French, German, etc.) will likely have an easier time with instruction of morphemic roots, particularly Latin- and Greek-based roots.

2 **The current English skill levels of our learners.** Pay particular attention to whether they actually know the meanings of the words they are trying to relate through morphology (Zimmerman, 2009). If they don't know the meanings, instruction in relating words through morphology will be of minimal value.

The most useful set of guidelines and strategies I have found for teaching morphology come from Cunningham (1998). Although they are not specifically meant for ELLs, they seem equally appropriate for such learners with some slight modifications. I summarize them here:

1 **"Help students become word detectives on the lookout for the meaning, spelling, and decoding relationships shared by words."** Cunningham's emphasis on meaning, spelling, and decoding fits nicely into the view that learners need extensive practice with both the form and meaning aspects of vocabulary. She also suggests that all learners be taught to ask themselves two questions: (1) "Do I know any other words that look and sound like this word?" and (2) "Are any of these look-alike/sound-alike words related to each other?" (p. 204). The aim here is to get learners to process any knowledge they already have about possible word relations, allowing the teacher to use the learners' own word knowledge as a springboard to morphology training. This type of instruction "takes advantage of whatever words occur in the course of content-area instruction" (p. 206). For ELLs, I would add that this strategy may also require teachers to produce a few examples of words related to the target word (similar roots, similar affixes), teach the meanings of those new words, and then show the learners the morphological relationships that exist.

2 "Teach the prefixes that are most useful from a meaning standpoint."
   Here the idea is to explicitly teach some of the most common
   prefixes and their meanings by writing sets of words with shared
   prefixes on cards and then helping the students see what meaning
   changes occur with the prefixes. The following sets are given as an
   example (p. 206):

rebound	redo	record
return	replay	refuse
replace	rework	reveal

Cunningham suggests that the learners be taught that the "re" in
the different columns does different meaning work. The "re" in the
first column of words can be replaced by the word "back," and the
"re" in the second column can be replaced by "again," but the "re"
in the last column cannot be replaced by either of these words (i.e.
we do not "cord" or "fuse" or "veal" something "back" or
"again"). This is because the roots in such words are bound roots.
In this case, students can be taught that the prefix "re" helps with
spelling and pronunciation of these words, but not with the
meaning. Additional words beginning with "re" can be associated
with their appropriate columns.

   Cunningham also provides the following list of common prefixes
within her framework of meaning, spelling, and pronunciation:

Prefix	Meaning	Meaning example	Spelling-pronunciation only
re	back	replace	reward
re	again	repaint	refrigerator
un	opposite	unhappy	uncle
in (im, ir, il)	not	inactive	incident
		immature	imagine
		irregular	irritate
		illegal	illustrate
in (im)	in	inhale	instant
		import	immense
dis	opposite	disappear	distress
non	opposite	nonessential	
en (em)	in	enclose	entire
		embrace	empire
mis	bad	misbehave	miscellaneous
mis	wrong	misdeal	mistletoe
pre	before	pretest	present
inter	between	international	interesting
de	down	depress	delight
sub	under	subway	subsist
fore	front/ahead	forecast	forest
trans	across	transcontinental	translate

Prefix	Meaning	Meaning example	Spelling-pronunciation only
super	more than	superman	superintendent
semi	half	semifinal	seminar
mid	middle	midcourt	midget
over	too much	overeat	
over	over	overhead	
under	too little	underweight	
under	under	underground	
anti	against	antifreeze	antique

Repurposed from Cunningham, 1998, p. 208.

I would add to this that modern corpora can be rich sources for finding and analyzing morphological affixes (prefixes and suffixes) as well as common roots. For instance a simple wildcard search like anti* (or show me all words beginning with "anti") yields the following words (in frequency order) in the British National Corpus (only top 30 listed):

anticipated	anticipating	**antithesis**
antique	**antislavery**	**anti-government**
antibody	antigens	antipathy
anticipation	**anti-semitism**	**anti-semitic**
antibodies	**antibiotic**	anticipates
anticipate	antiquities	**antiseptic**
antiques	antics	**anti-aircraft**
antibiotics	anti	antiquarian
antigen	**anti-social**	antiquated
antiquity	antidote	**anti-fascist**

Retrieved and repurposed from http://corpus.byu.edu/bnc.

It is clear from this example that the bolded words have the true prefix "anti" (meaning *against*), and that the other words have less transparent connections to the prefix "anti." Teachers could use this information in many effective ways based on the Cunningham approach of meaning, spelling, and pronunciation, and the same types of simple queries could be done for suffixes (*tion, *sion, *ment, etc.) and roots (e.g. photo*, astro*, acro*, etc.).

3   "Teach the suffixes (and spelling changes) that are most useful." Suffixes tend to change grammatical meaning, rather than lexical meaning, or, as Cunningham suggests, they signal "a change in how and what position the word can be used in the sentence" (p. 208). She uses the example of *compose* ("what a person does"), the *composer* ("the person doing it"), and *composition* ("what a person has once he or she has composed"). Helping students see these

relationships, along with changes that might occur in root-word pronunciation when suffixes are added, are keys to effective suffix training. Cunningham also provides a list of common suffixes within her framework of meaning, spelling, and pronunciation:

Suffix	Meaning	Meaning example	Spelling-pronunciation only
s es	plural change	pencils parties	
s es ed ing en	verb endings	laughs carries painted crying forgotten	kitten
er/est	more/most	happier richest	character interest
less	without	hopeless	unless
ful	full of	joyful	
able ible	able or able to be	fashionable digestible	miserable dribble
tion sion	thing or state	reaction confusion	station passion
ly	in that manner	happily	family
er or	person or thing	inspector generator	mirror horror
ance ence ment ness y	state or act of	ignorance obedience argument laziness honesty	balance silence document witness pretty
ant ent al ive ous ic	related to	ignorant confident comical creative nervous heroic	elephant moment animal motive delicious public

Repurposed from Cunningham, 1998, p. 210

4 **"Teach a few useful root words."** Here Cunningham suggests making learners aware that simple words like *play, work, agree,* and *create* become "big words" when suffixes and prefixes are added (*plays, playful, playfulness, outplay, ballplayer,* etc.; *workable, unworkable, paperwork, workshop, outwork,* etc.; *agreeing, agreeable, agreement, disagreement, disagreeableness,* etc.; *creates, creator, creativity, creation, recreation,* etc.). This helps learners make important connections between roots, affixes (prefixes and suffixes), and word families. She emphasizes again the importance of making learners aware that the pronunciation of root words sometimes changes when suffixes are added.

To this I would add that we must help learners understand that the spelling of many roots also changes depending on the relationships between roots and affixes. For instance, the Greek root *annus* (meaning *year*) is realized in English as *annu* (*annual, annuity*), *anni* (*anniversary*), and *enn* (*perennial, millennium*). These variations are known as allomorphs, and they are extremely prevalent in the language, affecting some prefixes (e.g. *in, im, ir, il* are allomorphs meaning "not," as in *inactive, immature, irregular,* and *illegal*), some suffixes (e.g. *tion* and *sion* are allomorphs, meaning "thing or state," as in *reaction* and *confusion*), and many roots (e.g. *astro* and *aster* are allomorphs, meaning "star," as in *astronaut* and *asterisk*). However, to ask our ELLs to memorize all of the different root allomorphs would be counterproductive, because there are literally thousands. A better plan would be to teach them the skill of looking for familiar root parts by showing them some clear examples and then pointing them out during the course of our instruction.

5 **"Teach students to spell a set of big words that have high utility for meaning, spelling, and decoding."** This last suggestion by Cunningham may be the most important when it comes to raising morphological awareness. By focusing intensely on a relatively small set of words containing high-utility morphological parts, learners and their teachers will have a rich shared resource from which to build additional morphological and vocabulary knowledge. Cunningham's research of what this high-utility list might look like led to her *Nifty Thrifty Fifty*, which appear below. Essentially, these are words with high-utility parts. She found that the list and its parts could account for "more than 800 analyzable words – words whose meaning, spelling, and pronunciation could be determined by combining various parts of the *Nifty Thrifty Fifty*" (p. 216).

Cunningham points out that all 50 of these words are known by two-thirds of fourth graders (ten-year-old children). The first task with these words is to ensure that the learners can spell and pronounce them all. For ELLs, we may also need to work more with the actual meanings of these words. Once this is all in place, many options for building morphological knowledge and related vocabulary knowledge become available.

A final area of morphological awareness raising that deserves our attention as teachers is the role of compounding in English. English has literally thousands of compound words and compounding is a major source of new words entering the language (*website, internet, spreadsheet,* etc.). This is also an area that forms a nice bridge between parts of words (morphology) and multiword items – the topic of the

The Nifty Thrifty Fifty

Word	Transferable prefixes	Transferable suffixes
antifreeze	anti	
beautiful		ful (y-i)
celebrate		ate
classify		ify
communities	com	es (y-i)
composer	com	er
continuous	con	ous
conversation	con	tion
deodorize	de	ize
different		ent
discovery	dis	y
dishonest	dis	
electricity	e	ity
employee	em	ee
encouragement	en	ment
expensive	ex	ive
forecast	fore	
forgotten		en (double t)
governor		or
happiness		ness (y-i)
hopeless		less
illegal	il	
impossible	im	ible
impression	im	sion
independence	in	ence
international	inter	al
invasion	in	sion
irresponsible	ir	ible
midnight	mid	
misunderstand	mis	
musician		ian
nonliving	non	ing (drop e)
overpower	over	
performance	per	ance
prehistoric	pre	ic
prettier		er (y-i)
rearrange	re	
replacement	re	ment
richest		est
semifinal	semi	
signature		ture
submarine	sub	
supermarkets	super	s
swimming		ing (double m)
transportation	trans	tion
underweight	under	
unfinished	un	ed
unfriendly	un	ly
unpleasant	un	ant
valuable		able (drop e)

Repurposed from Cunningham, 1998, p. 215.

next section. The key here is that compound words almost always consist of two free roots that could stand on their own (*backache – back, ache; battleship – battle, ship; seashore – sea, shore; thunderstorm – thunder, storm;* etc.). As these examples point out, the parts of compound words are helpful in understanding the overall meanings of many compounds, and many of these parts are basic words of the language. This is why learning about compounding can have such a profound effect on vocabulary growth for our ELLs. Practice in separating the parts of compounds into individual words and combining words to form compounds will be very helpful. There are many websites containing lists of English compound words that could be used for lesson ideas and practice. For quick referencing, Appendix F contains an excellent list of 1,126 basic compound words from *First School Years* (2006).

Our learners should also be taught that compounds consist of closed compounds (like the examples we have seen so far), hyphenated compounds (*son-in-law, long-term, large-scale, over-the-counter, five-year-old, mass-produced,* etc.) and open compounds (*post office, school bus, real estate, half brother,* etc.), with the latter also being a classification of multiword items. They may also encounter a particular compound in various forms (e.g. *baby sitter, baby-sitter, babysitter*). Practice with all three of the compound types will open up many doors for productive vocabulary growth. Appendix G contains the top 100 hyphenated words in the BNC and COCA, and could serve as a quick reference. Practice with these higher frequency hyphenated words will also have higher utility than a more random list. As always, however, finding example compounds in the actual materials or tasks that our learners will be asked to negotiate would be the best approach.

Collocation training

Corpus linguistics has shed a great deal of light in recent years on the role of multiword items and other collocations (Sinclair 1987, 1991). Perhaps the greatest insight has been the extent of these phenomena in the English language, with some scholars suggesting that there are more multiword items in English than individual words (Erman and Warren, 2000). It is therefore crucial for our ELLs to become aware of this issue and learn appropriate strategies for dealing with collocations. As we discussed in Chapter 2, there are fixed collocations (idioms, phrasal verbs, stock phrases, prefabrications, etc.), and thematic collocations (words that often appear together, but are not actual lexical items themselves). In the remainder of this section, I group these two different types together under the term collocations for ease of discussion.

Task 6.4

1 Create two or three new words by combining a prefix, root(s), and suffix(es) from the lists given below. Also give a definition for each new word.

   Examples: *hyperchronology*: "the study of excessive time"
   pseudomortism: "the practice of faking death"
2 Share your words and definitions with someone else.
3 What does this task tell you about your own morphological awareness?

Prefixes	Meaning	Roots	Meaning	Suffixes	Meaning
hyper-	"excessive"	-saur-	"lizard"	-ism	"the practice of"
philo-	"love"	-mania-	"madness"	-phile	"one who loves"
demi-	"half"	-luna-	"moon"	-ist	"one who does"
micro-	"small"	-chron-	"time"	-ology	"study of"
pan-	"all"	-morph-	"form"	-ate	forms verbs
mega-	"large"	-phon-	"sound"	-ize	forms verbs
pseudo-	"false"	-lith-	"stone"	-tion	forms nouns
counter-	"opposite"	-terr-	"land"	-ment	forms nouns
proto-	"first"	-psyche-	"mind"	-ness	forms nouns
hypo-	"under"	-mort-	"death"	-able	forms adjectives
inter-	"between"	-urb-	"city"	-al	forms adjectives
miso-	"hate"	-logo-	"word"	-ish	forms adjectives
neo-	"new"	-paleo-	"old"	-ic	forms adjectives

The biggest challenge we face as teachers is in trying to narrow the scope of the problem, because there are simply too many collocations, and, in general, they appear relatively infrequently in the language. Teaching practices like "an idiom a day," while providing some important enrichment, are actually just another "slow boat to China" when it comes to addressing the bigger issue – although I certainly encourage any efforts (flashcards, etc.) to build ELLs' knowledge of English idioms and other collocations that bring them closer to native-like fluency. In this regard, the *BBC World Service* offers some useful vocabulary training that often involves idioms in video-based contexts (see *BBC Learning English* at www.bbc.co.uk/worldservice/learning english/language).

Interestingly, research has shown that multiword items "are not learned well through ordinary language experience" (Coady, 1997, p. 282), and that ELLs often avoid using them altogether (see Liao and Fukuya, 2004, for review). My own preference for dealing with this issue is three-fold:

1 directly teach the most prolific phrasal verbs of English;
2 use corpora as the source for finding collocations and for collocation training; and
3 signal idioms and other multiword items in reading materials.

We will consider each of these in turn, but I also recommend that you consult the books listed in Table 6.3 for other specific strategies dealing with collocations.

Of all lexical collocations, phrasal verbs are the most frequent as a whole. As discussed in Chapter 2, it is not uncommon to encounter at least one phrasal verb on every page of reading material, especially in certain registers of English. Historically, however, the problem for phrasal-verb training is that we have not been able to predict which of the thousands of phrasal verbs will show up next.

In an attempt to address this issue, Mark Davies and I performed a phrasal verb (PV) count in the British National Corpus (BNC) to determine if a smaller set of high frequency phrasal verbs could be identified for instruction (Gardner and Davies, 2007). We also wanted the list to have maximum utility with a minimum number of lexical verbs that learners could be taught to look for. We discovered that only 20 simple lexical verb lemmas (GO, COME, TAKE, GET, etc.) combine with 16 adverbial particles (*out, up, on, back*, etc.) to account for 53.7 percent of the PVs in the BNC (see Appendix B). Several examples of these combinations, which we refer to as phrasal verb lemmas, are TAKE out (includes *take out, takes out, taking out, took out, taken out*), TAKE over (includes *take over, takes over, taking over, took over, taken over*), TAKE on (includes *take on, takes on, taking on, took on, taken on*), BREAK out (includes *break out, breaks out, breaking out, broke out, broken out*) and BREAK up (includes *break up, breaks up, breaking up, broke up, broken up*). We saw this as a very low number of PV combinations (320) for such high coverage, especially when we considered that we had identified 12,508 distinct PV lemmas in the BNC. In short, 320 PV lemmas accounted for more coverage than the remaining 12,188. In a subsequent analysis, we actually determined that the same "20 lexical verb lemmas combine with only 8 of the particles (*out, up, on, back, down, in, over*, and *off*) – a total of 160 combinations

– to account for more than half (50.4 percent) of the PVs in the BNC" (p. 349). This was a shockingly low number for such high coverage.

We also found in this same study that certain word forms function more often as adverbial particles (AVPs) than as prepositions, meaning that learners could take advantage of this in terms of finding phrasal verbs. The forms *out* (97.3 percent as AVPs), *up* (87.4 percent as AVPs), *down* (79.2 percent as AVPs), *back* (77.4 percent as AVPs), and *off* (55.9 percent as AVPs) all function more as adverbial particles in phrasal verb constructions than as simple prepositions.

The point here is that we can take advantage of all of this information to provide some focused training on phrasal verbs that will give our ELLs a great jump start when it comes to collocation awareness, in general, and phrasal verb knowledge, more specifically. Learners should be taught the following:

1 The 20 lexical verb and 16 particle combinations (320) in Appendix B, with primary focus on the first eight adverbial particles (160 combinations), and noting that some verb-particle combinations are relatively infrequent (*look off, set over, break back*, etc.). This last point suggests that it may be equally as important to know when the 20 high frequency lexical verbs are not likely to be functioning in phrasal verb constructions.

2 The fact that many phrasal verbs can be separated (e.g. ***take out*** *the rubbish* vs. ***take*** *the rubbish* ***out***).

3 The fact that phrasal verbs, like many single-word verbs, often have multiple meanings, some literal and some figurative (e.g. ***break up*** *the ice* vs. ***break up*** *the relationship*). In this regard, resources like *WordNet* (http://wordnetweb.princeton.edu/perl/webwn) and learner dictionaries (see dictionary section above) could be consulted for different meanings. *WordNet* also has a setting which gives a rough idea of the relative frequencies of the various meanings.

4 The concept that the phrasal verb lemmas are actually comprised of many lemma family members (PICK up = *pick up, picks up, picking up, picked up*).

5 The concept that certain simple forms function more often in phrasal verb constructions than as prepositions (*out, up, down, back,* and *off*). For instance, if learners encounter the word *out*, there is a good chance that they are also encountering a phrasal verb either on our short list, or otherwise (e.g. *The coach* ***chewed*** *the entire team* ***out*** *for their poor play*).

The second of my three preferences for teaching collocations is the use of corpora for finding examples and for actual training. In several sections of this book, I have referred to a frequency dictionary that I co-authored with Mark Davies (Davies and Gardner 2010). This dictionary, based on 400 million words of contemporary American English, contains valuable collocation information for the top 5,000 words (lemmas) in the corpus. I should emphasize that it takes a large corpus like COCA to have enough data to find collocates and the nuances that exist with them. The following are sample entries for the noun lemma *wave* and the verb lemma *wave*:

1447 wave *n*
adj new, tidal, gravitational, huge, light, recent, current, crashing, successive, gentle *noun* shock., radio., heat., sound., .future, water, brain., crime. *verb* ride., send., hit, break, .sweep, .crash, roll, create, catch., cause 24486 | 0.95

Source: Davies and Gardner, 2010, p. 86.

2631 wave *v*
noun .hand, .arm, flag, .finger, .gun, car, crowd, .wand, air, door, banner, hair, .paper, .goodbye, camera *misc* .at, her, him, .back, .away, .off, .toward, .over, .front, stand., .through, frantically
12447 | 0.88 F

Source: Davies and Gardner, 2010, p. 151.

Examples like these, along with concordance lines containing actual examples (see below), could be used to instruct our ELLs about principles of collocation by raising their awareness of the issue, so that they can begin to think and look beyond single words to find essential meanings. Several key points for learning and instruction can be made by examining these examples:

1 Collocation is heavily tied to parts of speech (nouns, verbs, adjectives, adverbs, etc.). In our two examples, we see a completely different set of collocates for the noun *wave* than for the verb *wave*. Also, if the node word (key word) is a noun, then its primary meaning collocates will be adjectives, other nouns, and verbs. If the node word is a lexical verb, then its primary meaning collocates will be nouns and structures like adverbs, adverbial particles, prepositions, etc. which we chose to combine under the heading of miscellaneous because of space constraints in the dictionary.

2 Collocates are tied heavily to meaning. In fact, it is difficult to know the meaning of many words until we are able to look at their neighbors. Consider, for example, the differences between *catch*

some waves and *cause* *some waves*, or between *wave her off* and *wave her over*.

3 Some collocates tend to come before node words, some tend to follow node words, and some tend to show no particular preference. A dot (•) preceding a collocate in the examples indicates that the collocate follows the node word 80 percent of the time or more (e.g. *wave your hand; wave your arm; wave a gun*), whereas a dot following a collocate indicates that the collocate precedes the node word 80 percent of the time or more (e.g. *shock wave; radio wave; heat wave*). No dot simply means that the node word is likely to occur on either side of the collocate (e.g. *the crowd waved; she waved at the crowd*).

It is important to note that much of the information we provided in the actual dictionary can be obtained through simple queries in the online version of COCA (http://corpus.byu.edu/coca/), although I should also mention that some careful editing was performed for the collocates appearing in the dictionary.

The online version of COCA also allows us to see collocations in concordance lines. This can be a valuable tool for training learners about collocations, and offers a powerful word-learning tool for more advanced learners. To carry our *wave*-example one more step, I queried the collocates of *wave* (as a noun) in the online version of COCA, selected *crime* as the collocate, and chose ten examples from the concordance lines to reproduce in Table 6.6. I repeated the process for *wave* (as a verb), selecting *off* as the collocate for Table 6.7.

Task 6.5

1 Using the following entry from the frequency dictionary, determine the likely collocations between the node word *call* and its collocates (e.g. **call** for *help*; *phone* **call**; **call** the *shots*; **call** out *her name*).
2 What does this task tell you about your own knowledge of collocations?

> **121 call** *v*
> *noun* name, police, information, phone, .attention, doctor, meeting, .help, .shot, witness, telephone., .cop, critic., technique., reservation *misc* .himself, .themselves, sometimes., please., .quit, commonly., .toll-free, repeatedly, affectionately., jokingly.
> **out** .name, voice., .help, wave, .greeting, .softly, .warning, .loudly, cheerfully, announcer. **in** military, listener., caller., .investigate, .advise **up** reserve, reservist, .image, .memory, somebody
> 285031 | 0.97

Source: Davies and Gardner, 2010, p.14.

Table 6.6 COCA concordancing lines with "wave" (noun) as node word and "crime" as collocate

1	of them got ripped off during that period. " # " A major **crime wave**, " Sir Parsilal responded. " Two arrests made, with one person dying
2	2010 conviction. # The two were on the leading edge of a still growing **wave of crime** operations fleeing aggressive federal enforcement in Florida to set up health care fraud
3	, Libby Schaaf, said Dexter is not the only person unsettled by the **crime wave**. # " I am hearing an unprecedented level of frustration and fear, "
4	before following Trayvon on foot support the idea that Zimmerman's frustration with a **crime wave** in the Retreat at Twin Lakes had boiled over into vigilantism. # Zimmerman
5	has contended
	release of thousands of criminals from jails around the country have led to a **crime wave**.
6	Robberies, carjackings, and kidnappings have skyrocketed. In April gunmen abducted the
	that British police attitudes to public order are problematic. Even before August's **crime**
7	**wave**, the police lost or surrendered control in three major public-order incidents in London over
8	MORNING NEWS, calling in the National Guard to put the brakes on a **crime wave** in Chicago. Plus, the angry debate over Arizonas tough new law against undocumented
9	been forced to lay off thousands of police officers, which contributed to the **crime wave**, especially in downtrodden neighborhoods. Lucile had watched Flatbush Avenue rise and
10	fall and
	# Between around 1910 and 1950 England was in the grip of a genteel **crime wave**; a seemingly endless output of murder mysteries, generally set among the upper and
	was penalized for distracting a penalty kicker by expelling gas. In Switzerland the **crime wave** continues, with Swiss police utterly flummoxed in their effort to thwart twin brothers who

Source: retrieved and repurposed from http://corpus.byu.edu/coca.

Table 6.7 COCA concordancing lines with "wave" (verb) as node word and "off" as collocate

11	of the way in. The smell of fire smoke rushes your face and you **wave off** the haze. You stop. That's not your brother lying dead on
12	avant-garde blouses, and dresses made of digitally manipulated prints make collectors swoon. Critics **wave** it **off** as evidence of fine handicraft, and nothing more. # John Buchanan
13	she said, for misleading you. Really. " He started to **wave off** her concern- even if the Depression was officially over, he still wasn't
14	it, anyway. He puts up his hand to retract the question, to **wave off** the not quite Dutch girl, but before he can speak he's jolted
15	there, Chapman Jones was pinned between lethal peril from above and below. " **Wave** them **off**, Captain Phillips, I beg you. " Buck said, "
16	finger (with the bill wedged between them) at Stephen, who tried to **wave** her **off**. " It's either you or Anne, " Michael said.
17	and they tend to err on the side of caution. He's seen crews **wave off** a target because they feared hitting bystanders. # " There's very strong procedures
18	made ghastly noises from its throat I thought only that I had been stupid to **wave off** the money so readily, without knowing what she wanted of me. "
19	been putting in long hours to help save the company. # He prefers to **wave off** any discussion about his role as a central player in those efforts.'
20	to retrieve another. The second case is just as big. He tries to **wave off** the four old men clambering about him, their little carriages at their sides

Source: retrieved and repurposed from http://corpus.byu.edu/coca.

In the first set of ten concordance lines (Table 6.6), we find evidence of useful contexts for learning the meaning of *crime wave*. We also see an example of a change in the position of the collocate, relative to the node word (line 2 uses *wave of crime*, instead of *crime wave*). In these first ten, we also see that the predominate positioning is *crime wave* (nine out of ten of the lines, or 90 percent). The second set of ten (Table 6.7) also has several useful contexts that point to the meaning(s) of *wave off*, and we have multiple examples of the verb *wave* being separated from the particle *off* (lines, 12, 15, and 16). These are just a few examples of how we and our learners might use corpora and concordancing to improve breadth and depth of vocabulary knowledge (cf. Cobb, 1999).

The last of my three preferences for collocation training is the use of signaling, especially with idioms and phrasal verbs. Part of the problem our learners face is being able to identify the boundaries of multiword items – that is, actually realizing that they are dealing with lexical items that are composed of more than one word (what some have termed grammaticalized lexis), instead of individual words related simply by the grammar rules or word order of English (what some have termed lexicalized grammar). This is also the basis for the distinction between the idiom principle and the open-choice principle (Sinclair, 1991) that we discussed in Chapter 2. For instance, in the sentence "Bill wanted Tom to chew the fat for a while, but Tom said he didn't have time right then," many ELLs will process *chew* as a verb, *the* as a determiner, and *fat* as an object (noun). If they are unfamiliar with the idiom (*chew the fat*), they are likely to be confused, trying to understand what fat Bill wants to chew, and why Bill has a desire to chew fat with Tom in the first place. If, on the other hand, we were to underline such multiword expressions (or signal them in some other meaningful way), and inform our learners that underlining means idiomatic language, they are more likely to shift to an idiomatic processing mode and come closer to understanding the true meaning of the idiom by processing it as a unit, meaning something like "talk": "Bill wanted Tom to chew the fat for a while, but Tom said he didn't have time right then." Knowing where idioms start and end, knowing that idioms are often nonliteral, and knowing that idioms are actually lexical items that can often be replaced with single words (*talk* in the example above), allows our learners to take advantage of contexts to learn many idioms, phrasal verbs, and other multiword items.

In a study I conducted with 81 adult ELLs (Gardner, 1994), I found that pre-underlining of non-decomposable idioms (*chew the fat, kick the bucket, turn over a new leaf, beat around the bush*, etc.) had a significant effect on adult ELLs' ability to process such items correctly as multiword units and gain more understanding of their meanings in context. I also determined that the more underlining of multiword items on a given page, the more learners tended to shift to an idiomatic processing mode.

Signaling of multiword items can be a regular part of our instruction, and there are several ways this can be done. For instance, we can read ahead to find useful multiword items in the materials that we are asking our learners to read, and point them out to our learners. We can stop on certain multiword items we encounter during the course of our normal instruction, and take the time to look at them with our learners. We can take a more direct approach by using concordance lines from large corpora to isolate a particular idiom and study it with our learners. The following sample for *chew the fat* comes from the BNC:

---

1   there so just pick up the phone and hear as we sit and talk and **chew the fat** and stuff like that hello? (SP:PS3DH) Hello. (SP:PS3DB) Who's that

2   it was.' Thought it might be as good a time as any to **chew the fat**, talk over the current status of Cuckoo,' Hayman started,

3   how did you do that? How... er...'' Sure like to **chew the fat** with you, fella, but I got a busy day on.

4   . And during his flying visit to Belfast, Mr Grade took time out to **chew the fat** about the old days. He has fond memories of Irish tenor Joseph

---

Retrieved and repurposed from http://corpus.byu.edu/bnc.

Because there are so many multiword items in English that repeat so infrequently, I view the primary benefit of signaling as being one of awareness raising of multiword items, with a secondary benefit being the actual learning of specific idioms. Signaling can be done with idioms, phrasal verbs, prefabrications, compound nouns, or any other collocations.

Final thoughts

To end this chapter on building vocabulary knowledge, I wish to emphasize how important it is for teachers to determine what they need to do personally in vocabulary training and what their learners can and should do for themselves. With all of the strategies and curricular decisions discussed in the chapter, and the many that were not discussed, we must always be aware of this division of labor, taking into account the current skill levels of our ELLs, the tasks they need to accomplish, the time we and they have available, the other resources we and they have available, etc.

Finally, space does not permit a detailed discussion of motivation in vocabulary training, but it is clear that much of vocabulary learning requires hard work, especially in our ELL settings where time is often not a luxury we or our learners have. Making sure that we are properly motivated to spend essential time with vocabulary training and that our learners are taught, through our example and insights, to be motivated learners of vocabulary may ultimately make the difference between successful and unsuccessful outcomes.

Vocabulary Project (creating personalized vocabulary tools)

Now that you have an actual vocabulary inventory and have familiarized yourself with online tools for vocabulary training, it is time to actually create some learning materials that meet the immediate vocabulary needs of your targeted learners. You may, for example, want to create sets of flashcards in *Quizlet* (www.quizlet.com) based on key vocabulary in a particular text or thematic unit. The learning materials you create could be used by you or another instructor during classroom instruction, or used by learners during their independent study. The key is that you and your learners will be working with words that have a direct impact on your learners' current English needs.

7 Conclusions

As we draw our shared experience with vocabulary to a close, I wish to bring us back to where we started. Vocabulary acquisition for English language learners is a complex relationship between what the target language demands (*Linguistic Reality*), what the learners already bring to the table and are capable of negotiating in that language (*Psychological Reality*), and how we as teachers help them bridge the gap between the two (*Pedagogical Reality*) – that is, how we "take them from what they know to where they need to go." Informed teachers will carefully consider all three legs of this vocabulary stool as they design their instruction.

I have also emphasized in this book the need for teachers to meet the specific English vocabulary needs of their learners, as opposed to approaching vocabulary training from a more general perspective. Many of our learners do not have the luxury of acquiring needed English skills over long periods of time, particularly in school and the workplace. This focus on English for specific purposes requires that we are willing to participate in the art of linguistic analysis, carefully considering what vocabulary our particular learners will encounter in the texts and tasks associated with their particular English-language needs. English vocabulary instruction for specific purposes also fits naturally within the curricular framework of theme-based and integrated-skills instruction – a framework which, in my view, gives our learners the best chances for success with English vocabulary.

Finally, the major task I faced in writing this book was to decide which of all the topics on vocabulary to include. My primary consideration was to make you think deeply about the topic of English vocabulary acquisition, and to provide you with foundational knowledge that would allow you to effectively address the needs of any learners you are asked to teach, rather than to provide you with just another set of predetermined lesson plans or activities. It is my sincere hope that we have accomplished this goal together.

Task commentaries

Chapter 2

Task 2.1

The point here is that many of the highest frequency words of English do not sound the way they are spelled (*the, friend, could, know, pretty, flood,* etc.), but many actually do (*am, and, ask, man, him, no, ran, red,* etc.). Of course, our ELLs will need extensive sight practice with the opaque words (matching whole-word written forms with their correct spoken forms), but they would also benefit greatly from learning some basic phonics rules that would allow them to sound out those words that have transparent letter-sound correspondences. These skills could then be used to sound out many other transparent English words. Another key would be to teach our ELLs to be flexible with phonics tools, realizing that they may or may not work.

Task 2.2

The purpose of this task is to help you better understand the multiple-meaning potential of many high frequency words of English, and to make you more conscious of the degrees of meaning variation, with some meanings of a word being totally distinct or homonymous (e.g. *a firm handshake* vs. *a firm we work for*) and some being related or polysemous. In the latter case, these meaning relationships can be close (e.g. *a hard situation; a hard run*), more distant (***move the car; move the audience***), and everywhere in between. Part of our task as teachers is to determine how well our ELLs will be able to distinguish the various relationships between a word form and its variant meanings, and to teach them skills that will aid them in this endeavor.

Task 2.3

Answers to terminology test:

1 = E	5 = C
2 = A	6 = G
3 = F	7 = B
4 = D	

Task 2.4

Native speakers of English should be able to generate partial or complete sentences with little or no difficulty (*break out in a **sweat**, the **branch** broke off*, etc.). This tells us something about the power of collocation in our mental lexicons. This also emphasizes that fixed collocations like phrasal verbs can have strong collocations themselves. Our ELLs need to understand this principle.

Task 2.5

Shaded senses are those that I consider to be more figurative in nature. You may or may not agree.

Sense	Phrasal verb senses of "break up"
1	S: (v) disperse, dissipate, dispel, break up, scatter (to cause to separate and go in different directions) "She waved her hand and scattered the crowds"
2	S: (v) separate, part, split up, split, break, break up (discontinue an association or relation; go different ways) "The business partners broke over a tax question"; "The couple separated after 25 years of marriage"; "My friend and I split up"
3	S: (v) break up (come apart) "the group broke up"
4	S: (v) crash, break up, break apart (break violently or noisily; smash)
5	S: (v) interrupt, disrupt, break up, cut off (make a break in) "We interrupt the program for the following messages"
6	S: (v) dissolve, resolve, break up (cause to go into a solution) "The recipe says that we should dissolve a cup of sugar in two cups of water"
7	S: (v) crack up, crack, crock up, break up, collapse (suffer a nervous breakdown)
8	S: (v) disassemble, dismantle, take apart, break up, break apart (take apart into its constituent pieces)
9	S: (v) break, break up (destroy the completeness of a set of related items) "The book dealer would not break the set"
10	S: (v) sever, break up (set or keep apart) "sever a relationship"
11	S: (v) pick, break up (attack with or as if with a pickaxe of ice or rocky ground, for example) "Pick open the ice"

Sense	Phrasal verb senses of "break up"
12	S: (v) calve, break up (release ice) "The icebergs and glaciers calve"
13	S: (v) adjourn, recess, break up (close at the end of a session) "The court adjourned"
14	S: (v) dissolve, break up (bring the association of to an end or cause to break up) "The decree officially dissolved the marriage"; "the judge dissolved the tobacco company"
15	S: (v) dissolve, break up (come to an end) "Their marriage dissolved"; "The tobacco monopoly broke up"
16	S: (v) break up, fragment, fragmentize, fragmentise (break or cause to break into pieces) "The plate fragmented"
17	S: (v) break up, disperse, scatter (cause to separate) "break up kidney stones"; "disperse particles"
18	S: (v) decompose, break up, break down (separate [substances] into constituent elements or parts)
19	S: (v) break up, crack up (laugh unrestrainedly)

Source: retrieved and reformatted from *WordNet* 3.0 online.

Task 2.6

You should have found something similar to the following lists for the top ten collocates of each word. In my search, I wanted to find and count *lemmatized* collocates (all inflectionally-related forms; e.g. *voice, voices*) of the *lemmatized* words (all inflectionally-related forms; e.g. *crack, cracks, cracking, cracked*). Such queries are possible in COCA.

CRACK	PICK	FORCE
down	up	air
open	phone	task
cocaine	draft	armed
door	first-round	military
fall	overall	security
voice	bend	police
wall	pace	Iraqi
crack	tab	special
smile	winner	labor
joke	wooden	driving

With these collocate lists, you should be able to determine some of the most important meanings of *"crack"* (*crack **down** on something, crack **open** the door, crack **cocaine**,* etc.), *"pick"* (*pick **up** the pieces, pick **up** the **phone**, a first round **draft** pick,* etc.), and *"force"* (*air force, task force, driving force,* etc.).

Task 2.7

Possible meaningful collocates of *break* in each concordance line:

1 weapons
2 bow
3 bow
4 bow, arrow
5 stretch
6 stretch
7 spell
8 heart
9 rules
10 heart

Fixed collocations with *break* are the idioms *break the spell, break my/ your heart*, and *break the rules*.

Task 2.8

Possible meaningful collocates of chip in each concordance line:

1 microprocessor
2 silo, cow
3 Reid (name of person = Chip Reid)
4 bargaining
5 chocolate, cookie
6 stale, potato
7 clock
8 bargaining
9 casing
10 memory

Possible fixed collocations are *cow chip, Chip Reid, bargaining chip, chocolate chip, potato chip*, and *memory chip*. Remember, fixed collocations often take on a single, unique meaning, and may actually occur in a traditional or phrasal dictionary as a unique entry.

Chapter 3

Task 3.1

The point of this task is to raise your awareness of the fact that many high frequency words are high frequency because they have multiple meanings and are therefore found in many registers of the language. Many also function in multiword items and become part of the unique meanings of those items. The GSL was established using manual counts of words with their various meanings, but more modern frequency counts usually rely on technology to do the counting, thus essentially disintegrating any distinct or nuanced meaning differences that a particular word form might have. In short, the computers simply count forms without consideration of meanings. It is therefore crucial for teachers and learners to understand that learning the core of English is much more than learning the most frequent forms of the language.

Task 3.2

Current topics reflected in the VOA specialized words include **government and politics** (*ambassador, anarchy, boycott, cabinet, candidate, democracy*, etc.), **economics** (*deficit, inflation, goods, import, recession, surplus*), **military and national security** (*aggression, air force, ammunition, artillery, bomb, ceasefire, disarm, extremist, genocide, militant, overthrow, terrorist*, etc.), **science** (*archeology, astronaut, biology, chemistry, laboratory, physics, microscope, satellite*, etc.), **crime** (*abuse, jail, jury, kidnap, rape, stab, victim*, etc.), **health** (*cancer, diet, pregnant, suicide, vaccine*, etc.).

The question of whether such words should be part of a core vocabulary can perhaps best be answered by analyzing the topics they come from. Are the topics central to societal issues – in this case, to American issues and interests? My own view is that they are central, and therefore the key words used to convey information about those topics should also be considered core. The important point is that they are only core for now. As the concerns in society change, the topic-related words will likely change as well.

The use of materials based on controlled vocabulary (like VOA) has many advantages, especially for ELLs at low and intermediate proficiency levels. For one, such materials present a more consistent English for the learners to negotiate as they work on building fluency with the language. Controlled materials also allow teachers to better predict the vocabulary demands placed on their learners, thus encouraging more aggressive efforts to pre-teach vocabulary that the learners will likely encounter in the actual materials they will read.

Task 3.3

This task should remind us that a great deal of English is phrasal in nature, and many phrases are composed of two or more simple high frequency words. Counting individual words, without consideration of their phrasal possibilities, often does not address the linguistic reality of the language. The distortions that result from this oversight can have serious implications for teaching, learning, and researching vocabulary and its associated skill areas (reading, writing, listening, speaking). If nothing else, this task should remind us as teachers to be cautious about how we use core vocabulary lists that do not address phrasal issues, but it should also remind us of our responsibility to raise our learners' awareness of the phrasal aspects of the English lexicon.

Task 3.4

The table below shows the shared highest frequency words and the unique highest frequency words of written and spoken English based on the McCarthy and Carter (1997) study. The key for us is that while many high frequency words are the same (31 of 50), there are others that are not. Of particular interest is that spoken has several contractions in its top 50 (*don't, it's, that's*), and several informal words and expressions (*got, just, like, oh, right, so, yeah*, etc.). If such differences exist in the highest frequency words, there must certainly be many more differences beyond the top 50. For our purposes, it is crucial that we understand what often happens when high frequency core lists are determined from written materials only.

SHARED	WRITTEN ONLY	SPOKEN ONLY
a	an	do
about	been	don't
all	by	got
and	from	it's
are	had	just
as	has	know
at	her	like
be	him	no
but	his	oh
for	me	right
have	my	so
he	out	that's
i	their	then
if	up	there
in	when	think
is	who	well
it	will	what
not	would	yeah
of		yes
on		
one		
she		
that		
the		
they		
this		
to		
was		
we		
with		
you		

Task 3.5

The newcomer list reflects several themes in current American culture, such as "terrorism" (*terrorism, terrorist, homeland, Taliban, insurgent, anthrax*, etc.), "technology" (*e-mail, website, wireless, cellphone, download, reconnect, upload, broadband, dot-com*, etc.), and "health and well-being" (*yoga, vaccinate, pandemic, steroid, healthfully*, etc.).

These words and their associated themes should help us better understand the fluid nature of a core vocabulary of English, especially those words that have a high impact because of certain changes or emphases in society. This also reminds us that we need to be cautious of high frequency word lists that are based on older texts and earlier times in history.

Task 3.6

The purpose of this task is to help you see a typical cycle with many words that enter the core of English. As you can see from the graphs, *telegraph* enjoyed some prominence in English for almost a century (from roughly 1860 to 1960), but continues to decline in significance as we move into the twenty-first century. Conversely, *e-mail* started its climb in the 1980s, gained momentum in the 1990s, and made a major jump in significance in recent years. Will it continue to be important for the next 100 years like *telegraph* once was? Only time will tell.

This task should also help us understand the problems that exist when a word-frequency list is based on a corpus that is frozen and eventually becomes dated. Such a list may very well contain dated words like *telegraph* and omit important contemporary words like *e-mail*.

Task 3.7

This task should make it abundantly clear that some core vocabulary items of English are very stable over time (i.e. they appear on both older and more contemporary lists), while others are new and we do not yet know how stable they will be over time. In fact, certain words move in and out of the core as societies evolve and find new ways to express their ideas, innovations, and so forth. Therefore, creating word lists based on contemporary and truly representative corpora gets us closer to the linguistic reality of a core vocabulary.

Task 3.8

The fact that Sublists B and C contain more newcomer words than Sublist A is evidence that the former are less stable overall. We must keep in mind, however, that words on less stable lists could eventually move to more stable lists if they continue to be used in the language over long periods of time and at higher and higher frequencies.

The fact that 262 of the 270 Dolch–Fry words (97 percent) are in Sublist A, with the remaining eight in Sublist B, suggests that these are very stable core words, and that time spent teaching and learning them is still warranted.

Chapter 4

Task 4.1

The words in Box 1 are core function words. Nothing about the meaning of the message can be learned from these words alone. In Boxes 2 and 3, some content words are added, and we begin to understand more about what the message might be. Still, our comprehension is not complete. Note that Box 3 at 88 percent is still below the 95–98 percent threshold necessary for basic comprehension. With Box 4 at 97 percent, we now have a good idea of the general meaning of the message, and we might even venture a guess about what the one unknown word might be, based on our understanding of the rest of the context. As the example points out, however, not knowing the one word, *reciprocal*, may still have a direct bearing on our ability to answer the specific test question. This is a typical scenario in academic contexts, where the one unknown word often carries the bulk of the meaning. From this task, we should better understand the differences between core function words (perform primarily grammatical functions), core content words (provide essential meanings for global comprehension), and register-specific content words (provide essential meanings for specific comprehension).

Task 4.2

The purpose of this task is to raise your awareness of different kinds of vocabulary that make up any passage of English. Some are essential to the topic(s) of the passage (register or topic-specific words), some help us understand the relationships between words and ideas (core function words), and some fill in gaps and provide additional meanings (other content words).

Task 4.3

The key here is that each register has characteristic vocabulary. (See my explanations in Chapter 4 itself.) This is another example of what I mean when I say that "all vocabulary is not created equal." The register-specific words of fiction, American history, mathematics, and life science are inherently different. If we understand these differences, we stand a much better chance of designing useful vocabulary instruction to help our ELLs.

Task 4.4

The purpose of this task is to show that even the core vocabulary shows register-specific tendencies and characteristics. (See my explanations in Chapter 4 itself.) We often forget that a 2,000–3,000 word core contains many content words, some of which are quite sophisticated themselves (*chairman, corporation, constitution, democracy, fractions, distributive, environmental, genetics*, etc.). This is especially true when the core words are actually expansive word families, containing many derivational word forms. To emphasize, when we change the register, we change the vocabulary, even within the core vocabulary of English.

Task 4.5

The same register differences exist when phrases are analyzed rather than individual words. (See my explanations in Chapter 4 itself.) However, considering phrases is a sobering reminder that much is lost when the unit of analysis is individual words. In short, we lose linguistic reality when we break up fixed phrases like *stock market* (*stock, market*), *manifest destiny* (*manifest, destiny*), *common denominator* (*common, denominator*), and *red blood cells* (*red, blood, cells*). This fact has important educational consequences for using word lists comprised of individual words, for direct vocabulary instruction, for developing English reading abilities, and so forth.

Chapter 5

Task 5.1

The purpose of this task is to raise your own awareness of labels and concepts you may or may not know. You may also become more aware of your ability to look at parts of words (morphemes) to help in determining word meanings. If you are like me, some of the labels and meanings are more familiar than others. As advanced users of English, we should also be able to tell that these words are less frequent and more sophisticated than many other words we know. Keep in mind, however, that lower-proficiency ELLs will not necessarily have these same abilities. In fact, such learners will have the same label-meaning experiences with common words that we experienced with words in this task.

Task 5.2

In answering the question about gate-keeping tests of academic success, you may have come up with such acronyms as STAT, UMAT, GAT (in Australia and New Zealand), LNAT, UKCAT, GAMSAT, HAT, BMAT, ELAT (in the United Kingdom), SAT, ACT, GMAT, LSAT, GRE, MCAT (in the United States and Canada), and many more. If you think about your own experiences with these kinds of tests, you may agree with me that they are primarily tests of reading and writing abilities at their most sophisticated levels. If we consider this even more carefully, we will realize that at the heart of this literacy ability is academic vocabulary knowledge – the ability to understand key terms and their underlying concepts.

Task 5.3

Context A comes from an expository (informational) text and Context B comes from a narrative (fictional) text. Clues you might have used to make this determination include: (a) discourse markers in A such as *in turn* and *since*; (b) formality of vocabulary in A (*legitimacy, judicial review, ad hoc affair,* etc.); and (c) simple vocabulary in B (*Oh, ma'am*). Additionally, the dialogue structure in B marks it as being more narrative in nature.

Task 5.4

Deciding which type of context each example represents is a subjective matter. My own personal ratings are below. You may or may not agree with them. The point is that contexts vary in terms of their helpfulness in learning new word meanings. It is also important to consider that a word like *anachronism* is not likely to occur many times in the same text like it does in the ten concordance lines in this task. In fact, it may be quite some time between encounters. Consider what this means if our initial encounter with the word is in a non-helpful context. Then time passes, and our next encounter is also in a non-helpful context. If we are fortunate enough to encounter the word in a helpful context, will it be enough help for us to actually learn and retain the meaning of the new word, or will we need another helpful encounter that may or may not occur within a reasonable time frame. We must also consider that in this task we are paying conscious attention to word learning. What would the effect be if we simply encountered the word without trying to process its meaning more deeply?

My personal ratings of the contexts are as follows:

1 misdirective (meaning seems more like *problem* or *eyesore*)
2 nondirective
3 directive
4 general
5 directive
6 nondirective
7 general
8 misdirective (meaning seems more like *innovation* or possibly *alternative route*)
9 directive
10 misdirective (meaning seems more like *nonconformist* or *couch potato*)

Chapter 6

Task 6.1

The purpose of this task is to familiarize you with one of many online flashcard programs. I have chosen Quizlet because it is free to users, and it has many robust features for helping ELLs learn new words, including sound features, gaming, multiple language support, smart phone applications, and social media capabilities. I encourage you to search for other online vocabulary learning tools as well.

Task 6.2

The purpose of this task is to have you experience what it is like to consciously use context to learn new word meanings. The steps I outline in Chapter 6, if routinely followed, should at least help ELLs develop a higher level of awareness for how to use contexts in word learning.

For your information, there are informative word parts in *anathema* (Step 4), with *ana* meaning *against* and *thema* meaning *theme*, or possibly *idea* or *premise*. Thus *anathema* can roughly be defined by its parts as *against an idea or premise*. This seems to fit with the context.

Our confidence at this point might be fairly high as to what the word means, but we would certainly have an even clearer picture if we also consulted the following dictionary definition (Step 6):

Definition from Longman Learner Dictionary online = *something that is completely the opposite of what you believe in*
        Retrieved from www.ldoceonline.com/dictionary/anathema.

With this definition, the word parts, and the context itself, we should have a good idea of what *anathema* means.

Task 6.3

Answers to original versus simplified:

Conspicuous: 1 (original); 2 (simplified)
Devious: 1 (simplified); 2 (original)
Prudent: 1 (simplified); 2 (original)

It should be fairly clear from the examples that the simplified definitions use more basic language and contain one simple idea – characteristics that will likely be more effective for ELLs and first language learners with more limited existing vocabularies. However, the original definitions tend to have more synonyms, a characteristic that may appeal to more advanced learners with well-established English vocabularies.

Task 6.4

I have used this task in many classes, and it always proves to be both useful and entertaining. I see no reason that our ELLs could not benefit from this as well, although more advanced learners will have a definite advantage and require less support from you. The lists can certainly be expanded to include other important roots and affixes.

For fun, I offer one more word creation for your consideration:

misomaniasaurist = one who hates crazy lizards.

Task 6.5

Some of the many possible collocations include:

call the <u>police</u>	**call** to your <u>attention</u>	**call** as a <u>witness</u>
call the <u>cops</u>	**call** for a <u>reservation</u>	please **call**
call it <u>quits</u>	**call** <u>toll-free</u>	the <u>announcer</u> **called out**
a <u>listener</u> **called in**	**call up** the <u>reserves</u>	**call up** the <u>image</u>

This task should help us understand how much our own mental lexicons are influenced by collocations. We also become aware of the multiple meanings of a word when we carefully consider its frequent collocations. We should also realize that our ELLs will need a great deal of practice and interaction with the language in order to take advantage of this crucial aspect of vocabulary knowledge. Making them consciously aware of collocations (as often as we can) will surely help in this regard.

Appendices

Appendix A: Dolch (D) and Fry (F) ultra-high frequency sight words (function words are bolded)

A	D-F	COME	D-F	GREEN	D-F	MAN	F	RIDE	D-F	**TO**	D-F
ABOUT	D-F	**COULD**	D-F	GROW	D-F	**MANY**	D-F	RIGHT	D-F	TODAY	D-F
AFTER	D-F	CUT	D-F	**HAD**	D-F	**MAY**	D-F	**ROUND**	D-F	TOGETHER	D
AGAIN	D-F	DAY	F	HAND	F	**ME**	D-F	RUN	D-F	**TOO**	D-F
ALL	D-F	DEAR	F	HAPPY	F	MEN	F	SAID	D-F	TOOK	F
ALONG	F	**DID**	D-F	HARD	F	**MIGHT**	F	SAME	F	TOWN	F
ALSO	F	**DIDN'T**	F	**HAS**	D-F	MONEY	F	SAT	F	TREE	F
ALWAYS	D-F	**DO**	D-F	HAT	F	**MORE**	F	SAW	D-F	TRY	F
AM	D-F	**DOES**	D-F	**HAVE**	D-F	MORNING	F	SAY	D-F	TURN	F
AN	D-F	DOG	F	**HE**	D-F	**MOST**	F	SCHOOL	F	**TWO**	D-F
AND	D-F	**DONE**	D	HEAD	F	MOTHER	F	**SECOND**	F	**UNDER**	D-F
ANOTHER	F	**DON'T**	D-F	HEAR	F	**MUCH**	D-F	SEE	D-F	**UNTIL**	F
ANY	D-F	DOOR	F	**HELP**	D-F	**MUST**	D-F	SEEM	F	**UP**	D-F
ANYTHING	F	**DOWN**	D-F	**HER**	D-F	**MY**	D-F	SET	F	**UPON**	D-F
ARE	D-F	DRAW	D	**HERE**	D-F	**MYSELF**	D-F	SEVEN	D-F	**US**	D-F
AROUND	D-F	DRESS	F	HIGH	F	NAME	F	**SHALL**	D-F	USE	F
AS	D-F	DRINK	F	**HIM**	D-F	NEAR	F	**SHE**	D-F	VERY	F
ASK	D-F	**EACH**	F	**HIS**	D-F	NEVER	D-F	**SHOULD**	F	WALK	F
AT	D-F	EAR	F	HOLD	D-F	NEW	D-F	SHOW	D-F	**WANT**	D-F
ATE	D-F	EARLY	F	**HOME**	F	**NEXT**	F	SING	D-F	WARM	F
AWAY	D-F	EAT	F	HOPE	F	NIGHT	F	SISTER	F	**WAS**	D-F
BACK	F	**EIGHT**	D-F	HOT	D-F	**NO**	D-F	SIT	D-F	WASH	F
BALL	F	END	F	HOUSE	F	**NOT**	D-F	**SIX**	D-F	WATER	F
BE	D-F	**EVERY**	D-F	**HOW**	D-F	NOW	D-F	SLEEP	D-F	WAY	F
BECAUSE	D-F	EYES	F	HURT	D	O'CLOCK	F	**SMALL**	D-F	**WE**	D-F
BED	F	FACE	F	**I**	D-F	**OF**	D-F	**SO**	D-F	WELL	D
BEEN	D-F	FALL	D-F	**IF**	D-F	**OFF**	D-F	**SOME**	D-F	WENT	D
BEFORE	D-F	FAR	D-F	**IN**	D-F	OLD	D-F	SOON	D-F	**WERE**	D-F
BEST	D-F	FAST	D-F	**INTO**	D-F	**ON**	D-F	STAND	F	**WHAT**	D-F
BETTER	D-F	FAT	F	**IS**	D-F	**ONCE**	D-F	START	D-F	**WHEN**	D-F
BIG	D-F	FIND	D-F	**IT**	D-F	**ONE**	D-F	STOP	D-F	**WHERE**	D-F
BLACK	D-F	FINE	F	**ITS**	D	ONLY	D-F	**SUCH**	F	**WHICH**	D-F
BLUE	D	FIRE	F	JUMP	D-F	OPEN	D-F	SURE	F	**WHILE**	F
BOOK	F	**FIRST**	D-F	**JUST**	D-F	**OR**	D-F	TAKE	D-F	WHITE	F
BOTH	D-F	**FIVE**	D-F	KEEP	D-F	ORDER	F	TELL	D-F	**WHO**	D-F
BOX	F	FLY	D-F	KIND	D-F	**OTHER**	F	**TEN**	D-F	**WHY**	D-F
BOY	F	FOOD	F	KNOW	D-F	**OUR**	D-F	**THAN**	D-F	**WILL**	D-F
BRING	D-F	**FOR**	D-F	**LAST**	F	**OUT**	D-F	THANK	D-F	WISH	F
BROWN	D-F	FOUND	D-F	LAUGH	D	**OVER**	D-F	**THAT**	D-F	**WITH**	D-F
BUT	D-F	**FOUR**	D-F	LEAVE	F	OWN	D-F	**THE**	D-F	WOMAN	F
BUY	D-F	FRIEND	F	LEFT	F	PAIR	F	**THEIR**	D-F	WORK	D-F
BY	D-F	**FROM**	D-F	LET	F	PART	F	**THEM**	D-F	**WOULD**	D-F
CALL	D-F	FULL	D-F	LETTER	F	PEOPLE	F	THEN	D-F	WRITE	F
CAME	D-F	FUNNY	D-F	LIGHT	D	PICK	D	**THERE**	D-F	YEAR	F
CAN	D-F	GAVE	D-F	**LIKE**	D-F	PLAY	D-F	**THESE**	D-F	YELLOW	D-F
CAR	F	**GET**	D-F	LITTLE	D-F	PLEASE	D-F	**THEY**	D-F	YES	D-F
CARRY	D-F	GIRL	F	LIVE	D-F	PRESENT	F	THING	F	YESTERDAY	F
CLEAN	D-F	GIVE	D-F	LONG	D-F	PRETTY	D-F	THINK	D-F	**YOU**	D-F
CLOSE	F	GIVING	D	LONGER	F	PULL	D	**THIRD**	F	**YOUR**	D-F
CLOTHES	F	GO	D-F	LOOK	D-F	PUT	D-F	**THIS**	D-F		
COAT	F	GOES	D-F	LOVE	F	RAN	D-F	**THOSE**	D-F	314 Total Types	
COLD	D-F	GOOD	D-F	MADE	D-F	READ	D-F	THOUGH	F	217 Total Families	
COLOR	F	**GOT**	D-F	MAKE	D-F	RED	D-F	**THREE**	D-F		

Additional function words not in Dolch–Fry List (listed in frequency order as found in Children's Corpus)

THROUGH	YOU'RE	SEVERAL	BELOW	CERTAIN	UNLESS	DESPITE	THIRTEEN	SIXTEENTH
STILL	WOULDN'T	OTHERS	THEY'RE	MINE	TWICE	WHEREVER	FEWER	SEVENTEENTH
IT'S	EVERYTHING	BESIDE	THEMSELVES	WE'D	FIFTY	HERS	YOURSELVES	THIRTEENTH
SOMETHING	BETWEEN	TILL	SOMEBODY	YOURSELF	TWELVE	UNDERNEATH	SEVENTY	FUNCTION
I'M	HE'S	HERSELF	SHE'D	ANYBODY	FIFTEEN	WHOEVER	SEVENTH	FOURTEENTH
BEHIND	SINCE	HADN'T	ALTHOUGH	AREN'T	ASIDE	UNLIKE	TENTH	NINTH
ACROSS	WE'LL	SHE'S	WE'VE	BENEATH	HE'LL	FOURTEEN	TWELFTH	VIA
WASN'T	HE'D	ANYONE	BEYOND	ITSELF	FOURTH	SIXTEEN	ZERO	WHENCE
THAT'S	HALF	EXCEPT	THOUSAND	NONE	YOURS	EIGHTEEN	MINUS	AMONGST
I'LL	SOMEONE	EVERYONE	LESS	WHOSE	WHENEVER	HASN'T	NINETY	ELEVENTH
COULDN'T	ABOVE	DOESN'T	YOU'VE	NINE	THIRTY	PER	EIGHTY	THIRTIETH
FEW	I'D	EITHER	WEREN'T	TWENTY	SHOULDN'T	OURS	NINETEEN	HUNDREDTH
NOTHING	WE'RE	HUNDRED	YOU'D	NOR	FORTY	SIXTY	TOWARDS	MILLIONTH
AGAINST	ISN'T	YOU'LL	HOWEVER	HAVEN'T	WHOM	PLUS	WHEREAS	SHAN'T
HIMSELF	I'VE	NOBODY	BESIDES	FORTH	THROUGHOUT	SIXTH	EIGHTH	THOUSANDTH
ENOUGH	DURING	ONTO	THEY'D	GETS	SHE'LL	NINETEENTH	FIFTEENTH	THRICE
BEING	GETTING	AMONG	WHATEVER	MILLION	ELEVEN	SEVENTEEN	TWENTIETH	
WITHOUT	DOING	HAVING	OUGHT	NEITHER	OURSELVES	MUSTN'T	BILLION	
CAN'T	WON'T	EVERYBODY	WITHIN	THEY'LL	FIFTH	THEIRS	EIGHTEENTH	

Appendix B: Phrasal verb frequency counts of 20 highest frequency lexical verbs with 16 different particles

Verb	Out	Up	On	Back	Down	In	Off	Over	Round	About	Through	Around	Along	Under	By	Across	Grand Tot
GO	7,688	3,678	14,903	8,065	4,781	1,974	2,104	991	1,366	244	972	394	717	95	44	0	48,016
COME	5,022	5,523	4,830	8,029	3,305	4,814	518	1,004	1,107	741	567	139	1,270	2	7	0	36,878
TAKE	3,426	4,608	4,199	1,628	775	509	2,163	5,420	78	2	31	37	94	0	0	0	22,970
GET	3,545	3,936	2,696	4,552	1,538	1,127	1,086	293	365	102	533	241	163	3	42	1	20,223
SET	4,633	10,360	11	265	504	281	1,869	1	10	645	0	0	0	0	0	0	18,569
CARRY	10,798	36	3,869	172	84	32	170	131		29	127	107	52	0	0	0	15,617
TURN	4,284	2,710	292	1,373	1,051	149	594	975	1,146	38	1	423	0	4	0	0	13,040
BRING	1,425	2,507	390	2,200	1,022	2,505	31	129	105	2,083	11	18	88	0	0	0	12,514
LOOK	1,641	3,871	244	2,251	2,221	250	2	207	694	45	21	779	0	9	0	5	12,226
PUT	1,660	2,835	1,428	1,369	2,873	810	742	76	21	35	90	16	1	0	0	0	11,970
PICK	856	9,037	35	3	3	1	44	18	0	0	0	0	0	0	0	0	9,997
MAKE	1,105	5,469	25	270	65	16	277	75	16	0	40	2	8	0	0	0	7,368
POINT	6,984	104	0	7	56	0	6	2	0	0	0	0	0	1	0	0	7,159
SIT	191	1,158	118	834	4,478	145	1	3	34	18	4	126	1	0	0	0	7,112
FIND	6,619	33	9	128	34	57	4	5	3	3	10	29	0	0	0	0	6,934
GIVE	532	4,186	34	507	11	579	121	198	3	1	0	2	0	0	0	0	6,174
WORK	4,703	334	411	36	98	182	33	31	23	0	100	19	5	10	0	0	5,985
BREAK	996	1,286	3	4	2,199	220	549	2	0	0	169	0	0	0	0	0	5,428
HOLD	1,507	1,624	908	823	369	34	91	40	2	0	0	1	0	4	0	0	5,403
MOVE	573	477	1,419	566	306	790	242	201	19	178	2	340	84	0	0	0	5,197
Total	68,188	63,772	35,824	33,082	25,773	14,475	10,647	9,802	4,992	4,164	2,678	2,673	2,483	128	93	6	278,780
% of PV	13.1	12.3	6.9	6.4	5.0	2.8	2.1	1.9	1.0	0.8	0.5	0.5	0.5	0.0	0.0	0.0	53.7
Cum %	13.1	25.4	32.3	38.7	43.7	46.5	48.5	50.4	51.4	52.2	52.7	53.2	53.7	53.7	53.7	53.7	53.7

Source: Gardner and Davies, 2007, pp. 350–351.

Appendix C: New word lemmas (with counts) impacting American English between 2000 and 2008

Nouns	Verbs	Adjectives	Adverbs
e-mail 14,326	host 5,535	online 9,219	online 6,034
terrorism 10,360	click 4,094	terrorist 7,908	famously 1,173
terrorist 8,889	e-mail 2,139	Afghan 2,776	postoperatively 226
affiliation 8,713	download 1,851	Taliban 2,095	
adolescent 7,212	preheat 1,364	Shiite 2,052	offline 158
homeland 4,157	bully 916	Pakistani 1,967	wirelessly 141
website 3,909	makeover 853	same-sex 1,397	healthfully 72
Sunni 3,637	freak 649	sectarian 1,138	preemptively 66
wireless 3,492	partner 638	upscale 1,057	intraoperatively 58
prep 3,362	mentor 587	embryonic 1,036	triply 33
Taliban 3,006	morph 349	Islamist 929	day-ahead 30
insurgent 2,433	vaccinate 286	iconic 765	forensically 28
globalization 2,354	restart 258	faith-based 754	
SUV 2,068	reconnect 257	broadband 738	
RPG 1,970	sauté 251	handheld 734	
anthrax 1,954	hijack 245	pandemic 719	
steroid 1,898	co-write 236	web-based 711	
genome 1,867	ditch 183	nonstick 689	
blog 1,765	reference 148	steroid 655	
detainee 1,733	swipe 142	insurgent 586	
militant 1,610	outsource 141	avian 553	
ethanol 1,601	transition 136	dot-com 532	
insurgency 1,561	upload 127	Chechen 396	
yoga 1,533	refuel 126	old-school 360	
recount 1,491	profile 122	clueless 356	
cleric 1,466	encrypt 117	performance-enhancing 350	
coping 1,380	workout 117	high-stakes 337	
tsunami 1,310	prep 115	Al-Qaida 331	
cellphone 1,149	splurge 114	21st-century 331	
	snack 106	gated 326	

Source: adapted from Davies and Gardner, 2010, p. 150.

Appendix D: Common Core List from COCA and BNC

Key:	1 = GSL 1000	2 = GSL 2000	A = AWL (bolded)
	N = New (Italics)	Underlined = Dolch–Fry	

Core A function words (150)

A - 1	BESIDE - 1	FOUR - 1	NEXT - 1	SOME - 1	UP - 1
ABOUT - 1	BETWEEN - 1	FROM - 1	NINE - 1	STILL - 1	UPON - 1
ABOVE - 1	BEYOND - 1	GET - 1	NO - 1	SUCH - 1	VIA - A
ACROSS - 1	BILLION - 2	HALF - 1	NONE - 1	TEN - 1	WE - 1
AFTER - 1	BOTH - 1	HAVE - 1	NOR - 1	THAN - 1	WHAT - 1
AGAINST - 1	BUT - 1	HE - 1	NOT - 1	THAT - 1	WHEN - 1
ALBEIT - A	BY - 1	HOW - 1	NOTWITHSTANDING - A	THE - 1	WHENCE - N
ALL - 1	CAN - 1	HOWEVER - 1	OF - 1	THERE - 1	WHERE - 1
ALONG - 1	CERTAIN - 1	HUNDRED - 1	OFF - 1	THESE - 1	WHEREAS - A
ALTHOUGH - 1	COULD - 1	I - 1	ON - 1	THEY - 1	WHICH - 1
AMONG - 1	DESPITE - A	IF - 1	ONCE - 1	THIRTY - 1	WHILE - 1
AND - 1	DO - 1	IN - 1	ONE - 1	THIS - 1	WHITHER - N
ANOTHER - 1	DOWN - 1	INTO - 1	OR - 1	THOSE - 1	WHO - 1
ANY - 1	DURING - 2	IT - 1	OTHER - 1	THOUGH - 1	WHY - 1
AROUND - 1	EACH - 1	LAST - 1	OUGHT - 1	THOUSAND - 1	WILL - 1
AS - 1	EIGHT - 1	LESS - 1	OUT - 1	THREE - 1	WITH - 1
ASIDE - 2	EITHER - 1	MANY - 1	OVER - 1	THROUGH - 1	WITHIN - 1
AT - 1	ELEVEN - 1	MAY - 1	PLUS - A	TO - 1	WITHOUT - 1
AWAY - 1	ENOUGH - 1	MIGHT - 1	SECOND - 1	TOWARD - 1	WOULD - 1
BACK - 1	EVERY - 1	MILLION - 1	SEVEN - 1	TRILLION - N	YOU - 1
BE - 1	EXCEPT - 1	MORE - 1	SEVERAL - 1	TWELVE - 1	
BECAUSE - 1	FEW - 1	MOST - 1	SHALL - 1	TWENTY - 1	
BEFORE - 1	FIRST - 1	MUCH - 1	SHE - 1	TWO - 1	
BEHIND - 1	FIVE - 1	MUST - 1	SHOULD - 1	UNDER - 1	
BELOW - 1	FOR - 1	NEAR - 1	SINCE - 1	UNLESS - 1	
BENEATH - 1	FORTH - 1	NEITHER - 1	SIX - 1	UNTIL - 1	

Core A content words (999)

ABLE - 1	COMPANY - 1	FISH - 1	LITRE - 2	PRINT - 2	SQUARE - 1
ABSOLUTE - 2	COMPARE - 2	FIT - 1	LITTLE - 1	PRIVATE - 1	STAFF - 2
ACCEPT - 1	COMPLETE - 1	FLAT - 2	LIVE - 1	PROBABLE - 2	STAGE - 1
ACCORDING - N	COMPUTE - A	FLOOR - 1	LOAD - 2	PROBLEM - 1	STAIRS - 2
ACCOUNT - 1	CONCERN - 1	FLY - 1	LOCAL - 1	PROCEED - A	STAND - 1
ACHIEVE - A	CONDITION - 1	FOCUS - A	LOCK - 2	PROCESS - A	STANDARD - 1
ACT - 1	CONFER - A	FOLLOW - 1	LONG - 1	PRODUCE - 1	STAR - 1
ACTIVE - 1	CONSIDER - 1	FOOD - 1	LOOK - 1	PRODUCT - 1	START - 1
ACTUAL - 1	CONSULT - A	FOOT - 2	LORD - 1	PROFESSOR - N	STATE - 1
ADD - 1	CONTACT - A	FORCE - 1	LOSE - 1	PROGRAMME - 2	STATION - 1
ADDRESS - 1	CONTAIN - 1	FOREIGN - 1	LOSS - 1	PROJECT - A	STAY - 1
ADMINISTRATE - A	CONTINUE - 1	FORGET - 1	LOT - 2	PROPER - 1	STEP - 1
ADMIT - 1	CONTRACT - A	FORM - 1	LOVE - 1	PROPOSE - 1	STICK - 2
ADVERTISE - 2	CONTROL - 1	FORMER - 1	LOW - 1	PROTECT - 1	STOCK - 1
AFFECT - A	CONVERSE - A	FORTUNE - 1	LUCK - 2	PROVE - 1	STOP - 1
AFFORD - 2	COOK - 2	FORWARD - 2	LUNCH - 2	PROVIDE - 1	STORE - 1
AFTERNOON - 2	COPY - 2	FRANCE - N	MACHINE - 1	PUBLIC - 1	STORY - 1
AGAIN - 1	CORNER - 2	FREE - 1	MAIN - 1	PULL - 1	STRAIGHT - 2
AGE - 1	CORRECT - 2	FRIDAY - 1	MAINTAIN - A	PURPOSE - 1	STRATEGY - A
AGENT - 1	COST - 1	FRIEND - 1	MAJOR - A	PUSH - 2	STREET - 1

AGO - 1	COUNCIL - 1	FRONT - 1	MAKE - 1	PUT - 1	STRIKE - 1
AGREE - 1	COUNT - 1	FULL - 1	MAN - 1	Q - 1	STRONG - 1
AH - N	COUNTRY - 1	FUN - 2	MANAGE - 2	QUALITY - 1	**STRUCTURE - A**
AIR - 1	*COUNTY - N*	**FUNCTION - A**	MARCH - 1	QUART - 2	STUDENT - 1
ALLOW - 1	**COUPLE - A**	**FUND - A**	MARK - 1	QUARTER - 1	STUDY - 1
ALMOST - 1	COURSE - 1	FUTURE - 1	MARKET - 1	QUESTION - 1	STUFF - 2
ALREADY - 1	COURT - 1	G - 1	MARRY - 1	QUICK - 2	STUPID - 2
ALSO - 1	COVER - 1	GALLON - 2	MATCH - 2	QUIET - 2	**STYLE - A**
ALWAYS - 1	**CREATE - A**	GAME - 1	MATERIAL - 1	QUITE - 1	SUBJECT - 1
AMERICA - N	CRIME - 2	GARDEN - 1	MATTER - 1	R - 1	SUCCEED - 1
AMOUNT - 1	CROSS - 1	GAS - 1	MAYBE - 1	RACE - 1	SUDDEN - 2
ANALYSE - A	**CULTURE - A**	GENERAL - 1	MEAN - 1	RADIO - 2	SUGGEST - 1
ANIMAL - 1	CUP - 2	*GERMANY - N*	*MEANING - N*	RAIL - 2	SUIT - 2
ANSWER - 1	CURRENT - 1	GIRL - 1	MEASURE - 1	RAISE - 1	SUMMER - 1
APART - 2	CUT - 1	GIVE - 1	**MEDIA - A**	**RANGE - A**	SUN - 1
APPARENT - A	*DAD - N*	GLASS - 1	**MEDICAL - A**	RATE - 1	SUNDAY - 1
APPEAR - 1	DANGER - 1	GO - 1	MEET - 1	RATHER - 1	SUPPLY - 1
APPLY - 1	**DATA - A**	**GOAL - A**	MEMBER - 1	REACH - 1	SUPPORT - 1
APPOINT - 1	DATE - 1	GOD - 1	MEMORY - 1	READ - 1	SUPPOSE - 1
APPROACH - A	DAUGHTER - 1	GOOD - 1	MENTION - 1	READY - 1	SURE - 1
APPROPRIATE - A	DAY - 1	GOVERN - 2	MESSAGE - 2	REAL - 1	SURPRISE - 1
APRIL - 1	DEAD - 1	GRAM - 2	MIDDLE - 1	REALISE - 1	*SWITCH - N*
AREA - A	DEAL - 1	GRAND - 2	MILE - 1	REALLY - 1	SYSTEM - 1
ARGUE - 2	DEAR - 1	**GRANT - A**	**MILITARY - A**	REASON - 1	TABLE - 1
ARM - 1	*DEATH - N*	GREAT - 1	MILK - 1	RECEIVE - 1	*TABLESPOON - N*
ARMY - 1	**DEBATE - A**	GREEN - 1	MILLIMETRE - 2	RECENT - 1	TAKE - 1
ARRANGE - 2	**DECADE - A**	GROUND - 1	MIND - 1	RECOGNIZE - 1	TALK - 1
ARRIVE - 1	DECEMBER - 1	GROUP - 1	MINISTER - 1	RECOMMEND - 2	**TAPE - A**
ART - 1	DECIDE - 1	GROW - 1	MINUTE - 1	RECORD - 1	TAX - 1
ARTICLE - 1	*DECISION - N*	GUESS - 2	MISS - 1	RED - 1	TEA - 2
ASK - 1	DEEP - 1	GUN - 2	MODEL - 2	REDUCE - 1	TEACH - 1
ASSOCIATE - 1	*DEFENCE - N*	*GUY - N*	MOMENT - 1	REFER - 2	**TEAM - A**
ASSUME - A	**DEFINITE - A**	H - 1	MONDAY - 1	REGARD - 1	*TEASPOON - N*
ATTACK - 1	DEGREE - 1	*HA - N*	MONEY - 1	**REGION - A**	**TECHNOLOGY - A**
ATTEND - 2	*DEMOCRAT - N*	HAIR - 2	MONTH - 1	RELATION - 1	TELEPHONE - 2
AUGUST - 1	DEPARTMENT - 1	HALL - 2	MORNING - 1	*RELIGIOUS - N*	*TELEVISION - N*
AUTHOR - A	DEPEND - 1	HAND - 1	MOTHER - 1	REMAIN - 1	TELL - 1
AUTHORITY - A	DESCRIBE - 1	HANG - 1	MOTION - 2	REMEMBER - 1	TEND - 2
AVAILABLE - A	**DESIGN - A**	HAPPEN - 1	MOUNTAIN - 1	**REMOVE - A**	TERM - 1
AVOID - 2	DETAIL - 1	HAPPY - 1	MOVE - 1	REPORT - 1	TERRIBLE - 2
AW - N	DETERMINE - 1	HARD - 1	*MOVIE - N*	REPRESENT - 1	TEST - 1
AWARE - A	DEVELOP - 1	HATE - 1	MR - 1	REPUBLIC - 1	THANK - 2
AWFUL - N	DIE - 1	HEAD - 1	MRS - 1	**REQUIRE - A**	THEN - 1
B - 1	DIFFERENCE - 1	HEALTH - 2	*MUSEUM - N*	**RESEARCH - A**	**THEORY - A**
BABY - 2	DIFFICULT - 1	HEAR - 1	MUSIC - 1	**RESOURCE - A**	THEREFORE - 1
BAD - 1	DINNER - 2	HEART - 1	N - 1	RESPECT - 1	THING - 1
BAG - 2	DIRECT - 1	HEAT - 1	NAME - 1	**RESPOND - A**	THINK - 1
BALANCE - 2	*DIRECTION - N*	HEAVY - 1	NATION - 1	*RESPONSE - N*	THROW - 1
BALL - 1	DISCOVER - 1	*HELL - N*	NATURE - 1	RESPONSIBLE - 2	THURSDAY - 1
BANK - 1	DISCUSS - 2	HELP - 1	NECESSARY - 1	REST - 1	THUS - 1
BAR - 1	DISEASE - 2	HERE - 1	NEED - 1	RESULT - 1	TIE - 2
BASE - 1	DISTRICT - 1	HIGH - 1	**NETWORK - A**	RETURN - 1	TIME - 1
BASIS - N	DIVIDE - 1	HISTORY - 1	NEVER - 1	**REVEAL - A**	TODAY - 1
BEAR - 1	DOCTOR - 1	HIT - 2	NEW - 1	RID - 2	TOGETHER - 1
BEAT - 2	**DOCUMENT - A**	HOLD - 1	NEWS - 1	RIGHT - 1	TOMORROW - 2
BEAUTY - 1	DOG - 1	HOLIDAY - 2	NICE - 2	RING - 1	TONIGHT - 2
BECOME - 1	DOLLAR - 1	HOME - 1	NIGHT - 1	RISE - 1	TOO - 1
BED - 1	DOOR - 1	HONEST - 2	**NORMAL - A**	RISK - 2	TOP - 1
BEGIN - 1	DOUBLE - 2	HOPE - 1	NORTH - 1	RIVER - 1	TOTAL - 1
BEHAVIOUR - 2	DOUBT - 1	HORSE - 1	NOTE - 1	ROAD - 1	TOUCH - 1
BELIEVE - 1	DRAW - 1	HOSPITAL - 2	NOTICE - 1	ROCK - 1	TOWN - 1

BENEFIT - A	DRESS - 1	HOT - 1	NOVEMBER - 1	**ROLE - A**	TRADE - 1
BEST - 1	DRINK - 1	HOUR - 1	NOW - 1	ROLL - 1	**TRADITION - A**
BET - N	DRIVE - 1	HOUSE - 1	NUMBER - 1	ROOM - 1	*TRAFFIC - N*
BIG - 1	DROP - 1	*HUGE - N*	O - 1	ROUND - 1	TRAIN - 1
BIRTH - 2	*DRUG - N*	HULLO - 2	**OBVIOUS - A**	RULE - 1	**TRANSPORT - A**
BIT - 2	DRY - 1	HUMAN - 1	OCCASION - 1	RUN - 1	TRAVEL - 1
BLACK - 1	DUE - 1	HUSBAND - 1	**OCCUR - A**	SAFE - 1	TREAT - 2
BLOOD - 1	E - 1	IDEA - 1	OCTOBER - 1	SALE - 1	TREE - 1
BLOW - 1	EARLY - 1	**IDENTIFY - A**	**ODD - A**	SAME - 1	*TRIAL - N*
BLUE - 1	EARTH - 1	**IMAGE - A**	OFFER - 1	SATURDAY - 1	TRIP - 2
BOARD - 1	EAST - 1	IMAGINE - 2	OFFICE - 1	SAVE - 1	TROUBLE - 1
BOAT - 1	EASY - 1	**IMPACT - A**	OFFICIAL - 1	SAY - 1	TRUE - 1
BODY - 1	EAT - 1	IMPORTANT - 1	OFTEN - 1	SCENE - 1	TRUST - 1
BOOK - 1	**ECONOMY - A**	IMPROVE - 2	OH - 1	**SCHEME - A**	TRY - 1
BOTHER - N	EDGE - 2	INCLUDE - 1	OIL - 1	SCHOOL - 1	TUESDAY - 1
BOTTLE - 2	EDUCATE - 2	**INCOME - A**	*OKAY - N*	SCIENCE - 1	TURN - 1
BOTTOM - 2	EFFECT - 1	INCREASE - 1	OLD - 1	*SCORE - N*	TYPE - 1
BOX - 1	EFFORT - 1	INDEED - 1	ONLY - 1	SEASON - 1	U - 1
BOY - 1	EGG - 1	**INDICATE - A**	OPEN - 1	SEAT - 1	UNDERSTAND - 1
BREAK - 1	ELECT - 1	**INDIVIDUAL - A**	OPERATE - 1	SECRETARY - 1	UNION - 1
BRIEF - A	ELECTRIC - 2	INDUSTRY - 1	OPPORTUNITY - 1	**SECTION - A**	*UNIT - N*
BRILLIANT - N	ELSE - 1	INFORM - 2	OPPOSE - 2	**SECURE - A**	UNITE - 1
BRING - 1	EMPLOY - 1	INSIDE - 2	ORDER - 1	SEE - 1	UNIVERSITY - 1
BRITAIN - N	ENCOURAGE - 2	INSTEAD - 1	ORGANIZE - 1	**SEEK - A**	USE - 1
BROTHER - 1	END - 1	INSURE - 2	*ORIGINAL - N*	SEEM - 1	USUAL - 1
BUDGET - N	**ENERGY - A**	INTEREST - 1	OTHERWISE - 1	SELF - 2	V - 1
BUILD - 1	ENGINE - 2	INTERNATIONAL - 2	*OUNCE - N*	SELL - 1	VALUE - 1
BUS - 2	ENGLISH - 1	*INTERVIEW - N*	OWN - 1	SEND - 1	VARIOUS - 1
BUSINESS - 1	ENJOY - 1	INTRODUCE - 1	P - 1	SENSE - 1	VERY - 1
BUSY - 2	ENTER - 1	**INVEST - A**	PACK - 2	SEPARATE - 1	*VIDEO - N*
BUY - 1	ENTIRE - 2	**INVOLVE - A**	PAGE - 1	SEPTEMBER - 1	VIEW - 1
C - 1	**ENVIRONMENT - A**	ISLAND - 2	PAIN - 2	**SERIES - A**	VILLAGE - 1
CAKE - 2	EQUAL - 1	**ISSUE - A**	PAINT - 1	SERIOUS - 1	VISIT - 1
CALL - 1	ESPECIAL - 2	**ITEM - A**	PAIR - 2	SERVE - 1	VOICE - 1
CAMPAIGN - N	**ESTABLISH - A**	J - 1	PAPER - 1	SERVICE - 1	VOTE - 1
CANDIDATE - N	*EUROPE - N*	JANUARY - 1	PARENT - 2	SET - 1	W - 1
CAR - 1	EVEN - 1	**JOB - A**	PARK - 2	SETTLE - 1	WAGE - 1
CARD - 2	EVENING - 1	JOIN - 1	PART - 1	**SEX - A**	WAIT - 1
CARE - 1	EVENT - 1	JUDGE - 1	PARTICULAR - 1	SHAKE - 1	WALK - 1
CAREER - N	EVER - 1	JULY - 1	PARTY - 1	SHARE - 1	WALL - 1
CARRY - 1	*EVIDENCE - N*	JUMP - 2	PASS - 1	SHEET - 2	WANT - 1
CASE - 1	EXACT - 2	JUNE - 1	PAST - 1	SHOE - 2	WAR - 1
CAT - 2	EXAMPLE - 1	JUST - 1	PATIENT - 2	SHOOT - 1	WARM - 2
CATCH - 1	EXCUSE - 2	JUSTICE - 1	PAY - 1	SHOP - 2	WASH - 2
CAUSE - 1	*EXECUTIVE - N*	K - 1	PEACE - 1	SHORT - 1	WASTE - 2
CELL - N	EXERCISE - 1	KEEP - 1	*PENSION - N*	SHOW - 1	WATCH - 1
CENTIMETRE - 2	EXIST - 1	KEY - 2	PEOPLE - 1	SHUT - 2	WATER - 1
CENTRE - 1	EXPECT - 1	*KID - N*	**PERCENT - A**	SICK - 2	WAY - 1
CENTURY - 2	EXPENSE - 1	KILL - 1	PERFECT - 2	SIDE - 1	WEAPON - 2
CHAIR - 2	EXPERIENCE - 1	KILOGRAM - 2	PERFORM - 2	SIGN - 1	WEAR - 1
CHAIRMAN - N	**EXPERT - A**	KILOMETRE - 2	PERHAPS - 1	**SIGNIFICANT - A**	WEDNESDAY - 1
CHANCE - 1	EXPLAIN - 1	KIND - 1	**PERIOD - A**	**SIMILAR - A**	WEEK - 1
CHANGE - 1	EXPRESS - 1	KING - 1	PERSON - 1	SIMPLE - 1	WEIGH - 2
CHARACTER - 1	EXTRA - 2	KITCHEN - 2	PHOTOGRAPH - 2	SING - 1	WELCOME - 1
CHARGE - 1	EYE - 1	KNOCK - 2	**PHYSICAL - A**	SINGLE - 1	WELL - 1
CHEAP - 2	F - 1	KNOW - 1	PICK - 2	SIR - 1	WEST - 1
CHECK - 2	FACE - 1	*KNOWLEDGE - N*	PICTURE - 1	SISTER - 1	WHETHER - 1
CHILD - 1	FACT - 1	L - 1	PIECE - 1	SIT - 1	WHITE - 1
CHOICE - N	**FACTOR - A**	**LABOUR - A**	PINT - 2	**SITE - A**	WHOLE - 1
CHOOSE - 1	FAIL - 1	LADY - 1	PLACE - 1	SITUATE - 1	WIDE - 1
CHRIST - N	FAIR - 1	LAND - 1	PLAN - 1	SIZE - 1	WIFE - 1

CHRISTMAS - 2
CHURCH - 1
CITY - 1
CLAIM - 1
CLASS - 1
CLEAN - 2
CLEAR - 1
CLIENT - N
CLOCK - 2
CLOSE - 1
CLOSES - N
CLOTHE - N
CLUB - 2
COFFEE - 2
COLD - 1
COLLEAGUE - A
COLLECT - 2
COLLEGE - 1
COLOUR - 1
COME - 1
COMMENT - A
COMMIT - A
COMMITTEE - 1
COMMON - 1
COMMUNITY - A

FALL - 1
FAMILY - 1
FAR - 1
FARM - 1
FAST - 1
FATHER - 1
FAVOUR - 1
FEBRUARY - 1
FEDERAL - A
FEE - A
FEED - N
FEEL - 1
FIELD - 1
FIGHT - 1
FIGURE - 1
FILE - A
FILL - 1
FILM - 2
FINAL - A
FINANCE - A
FIND - 1
FINE - 1
FINISH - 1
FIRE - 1
FIRM - 2

LANGUAGE - 1
LARGE - 1
LATE - 1
LAUGH - 1
LAW - 1
LAY - 1
LEAD - 1
LEARN - 1
LEAVE - 1
LEFT - 1
LEG - 2
LEGAL - A
LET - 1
LETTER - 1
LEVEL - 1
LIE - 1
LIFE - 1
LIGHT - 1
LIKE - 1
LIKELY - 1
LIMIT - 1
LINE - 1
LINK - A
LIST - 2
LISTEN - 1

PLANT - 1
PLAY - 1
PLEASE - 1
POINT - 1
POLICE - 2
POLICY - A
POLITIC - 1
POOR - 1
POPULAR - 1
POPULATION - 1
POSITION - 1
POSITIVE - A
POSSIBLE - 1
POST - 1
POUND - 1
POWER - 1
PRACTISE - 2
PREPARE - 1
PRESENT - 1
PRESIDENT - 1
PRESS - 1
PRESSURE - 1
PRETTY - 1
PREVIOUS - A
PRICE - 1

SKILL - 2
SLEEP - 1
SLIGHT - 2
SLOW - 2
SMALL - 1
SMOKE - 2
SO - 1
SOCIAL - 1
SOCIETY - 1
SON - 1
SONG - N
SOON - 1
SORRY - 2
SORT - 1
SOUND - 1
SOURCE - A
SOUTH - 1
SPACE - 1
SPEAK - 1
SPECIAL - 1
SPECIFIC - A
SPEED - 1
SPEND - 1
SPORT - 2
SPRING - 1

WIN - 1
WIND - 1
WINDOW - 1
WISH - 1
WOMAN - 1
WONDER - 1
WOOD - 1
WORD - 1
WORK - 1
WORLD - 1
WORRY - 2
WORTH - 1
WRITE - 1
WRONG - 1
X - N
Y - 1
YEAR - 1
YES - 1
YESTERDAY - 1
YET - 1
YOUNG - 1
Z - N

Key: 1 = GSL 1000   2 = GSL 2000   A = AWL (bolded)
        N = New (Italics)   Underlined = Dolch–Fry

Core B content words (821)

ABUSE - N	*CITIZEN - N*	*ETC - N*	JOURNEY - 2	POCKET - 2	SOFT - 1
ACADEMY - A	**CIVIL - A**	**ETHNIC - A**	JOY - 1	POEM - 2	*SOFTWARE - N*
ACCESS - A	CLERK - 2	**EVENTUAL - A**	JUICE - 2	*POLL - N*	SOIL - 2
ACCIDENT - 2	CLIMB - 2	**EVOLVE - A**	*JURY - N*	POOL - 2	SOLDIER - 1
ACCOMMODATE - A	CLOUD - 1	EXAMINE - 2	**JUSTIFY - A**	*POP - N*	SOLID - 2
ACCURATE - A	*CLUE - N*	EXCELLENT - 2	KICK - 2	POT - 2	*SOLUTION - N*
ACID - N	*COACH - N*	EXCHANGE - 1	KNEE - 2	*POTATO - N*	SOLVE - 2
ACKNOWLEDGE - A	COAL - 1	EXCITE - 2	KNIFE - 2	**POTENTIAL - A**	**SOMEWHAT - A**
ADEQUATE - A	COAST - 1	**EXCLUDE - A**	**LABEL - A**	POUR - 2	SOUL - 1
ADJUST - A	COAT - 2	**EXHIBIT - A**	LACK - 1	PRACTICAL - 2	*SOUTHERN - N*
ADOPT - 1	**CODE - A**	**EXPAND - A**	LAKE - 1	PRAY - 2	*SPAIN - N*
ADULT - A	COMBINE - 2	EXPERIMENT - 1	*LANDSCAPE - N*	**PRECISE - A**	*SPECIES - N*
ADVANCE - 1	COMFORT - 2	EXPLORE - 2	*LANE - N*	**PREDICT - A**	*SPEECH - N*
ADVANTAGE - 1	COMMAND - 1	EXTEND - 1	*LAUNCH - N*	PREFER - 2	SPIRIT - 1
ADVICE - 2	COMMERCE - 2	*EXTENSION - N*	LEAF - 2	*PREGNANT - N*	SPLIT - 2
ADVISE - N	**COMMISSION - A**	*EXTENT - N*	*LEAGUE - N*	*PRESENCE - N*	*SPONSOR - N*
AFFAIR - 2	**COMMUNICATE - A**	EXTREME - 2	LEAN - 2	PRETEND - 2	SPOT - 1
AFRAID - 2	**COMPENSATE - A**	**FACILITATE - A**	**LECTURE - A**	PREVENT - 1	SPREAD - 1
AFRICA - N	COMPETE - 2	FACTORY - 1	LEND - 2	**PRIMARY - A**	**STABLE - A**
AGENDA - N	COMPETITION - 2	*FAILURE - N*	LENGTH - 1	**PRIME - A**	*STARE - N*
AHEAD - 2	COMPLAIN - 2	FAITH - 1	LESSON - 2	**PRINCIPLE - A**	**STATUS - A**
AID - A	*COMPLAINTS - N*	FAMILIAR - 1	**LIBERAL - A**	**PRIORITY - A**	STEAL - 2
AIM - 2	**COMPLEX - A**	FAMOUS - 1	LIBRARY - 1	PRISON - 2	STEEL - 1
AIRCRAFT - N	COMPLICATE - 2	FAN - 2	**LICENCE - A**	PRIZE - 2	STONE - 1
AIRPORT - N	**COMPONENT - A**	FASHION - 2	LIFT - 1	**PROFESSIONAL - A**	STORM - 2
ALARM - N	**CONCENTRATE - A**	FAT - 2	LIP - 1	PROFIT - 1	STRANGE - 1
ALIVE - 2	**CONCEPT - A**	FAULT - 2	*LITERAL - N*	PROGRESS - 1	STRENGTH - 1
ALONE - 1	**CONCLUDE - A**	FEAR - 1	LITERATURE - 1	PROMISE - 1	**STRESS - A**
ALTER - A	*CONCLUSION - N*	**FEATURE - A**	LOAN - 2	**PROMOTE - A**	STRETCH - 2
ALTERNATIVE - A	**CONDUCT - A**	FELLOW - 1	**LOCATE - A**	PROPERTY - 1	STRIP - 2
ALTOGETHER - 2	CONFIDENCE - 2	FEMALE - 2	LOG - 2	**PROPORTION - A**	STRUGGLE - 1
AMAZE - N	**CONFIRM - A**	FENCE - 2	**LOGIC - A**	**PROSPECT - A**	*STUDIO - N*
ANCIENT - 1	**CONFLICT - A**	FINGER - 2	LOOSE - 2	PROUD - 2	*SUBSTANTIAL - N*
ANGLE - 2	CONFUSE - 2	FIX - 1	LOUD - 2	**PSYCHOLOGY - A**	*SUE - N*
ANGRY - N	CONNECT - 2	*FLIGHT - N*	MAD - 2	**PUBLISH - A**	SUFFER - 1
ANNOUNCE - N	CONSCIOUS - 2	FLOAT - 2	*MAGAZINE - N*	PUMP - 2	**SUFFICIENT - A**
ANNUAL - A	**CONSEQUENT - A**	FLOW - 1	MAIL - 2	**PURCHASE - A**	SUGAR - 2
APARTMENT - N	*CONSERVATIVE - N*	FLOWER - 1	MALE - 2	PURE - 2	**SUM - A**
APOLOGY - 2	**CONSIDERABLE - A**	*FOLK - N*	MANNER - 1	**PURSUE - A**	*SUPER - N*
APPEAL - N	*CONSISTENT - N*	FOREST - 1	MANUFACTURE - 1	QUALIFY - 2	*SUPREME - N*
APPLE - 2	**CONSTANT - A**	FORGIVE - 2	MAP - 2	QUEEN - 1	SURFACE - 1
APPRECIATE - A	**CONSTRUCT - A**	FORMAL - 2	**MARGIN - A**	**QUOTE - A**	*SURGERY - N*
APPROVE - 2	**CONSUME - A**	**FOUNDATION - A**	MASS - 1	RAIN - 2	SURROUND - 1
ASLEEP - 2	CONTENT - 1	FRAME - 2	*MASSIVE - N*	RARE - 2	**SURVEY - A**
ASPECT - A	**CONTEXT - A**	*FRANK - N*	MASTER - 1	**REACT - A**	**SURVIVE - A**
ASSEMBLE - A	**CONTRAST - A**	FREEZE - 2	*MATHEMATICS - N*	*RECALL - N*	SUSPECT - 2
ASSESS - A	**CONTRIBUTE - A**	FREQUENT - 2	**MAXIMISE - A**	*RECESSION - N*	SWEAR - 2
ASSIGN - A	**CONVENE - A**	FRESH - 1	*MAYOR - N*	**RECOVER - A**	SWEET - 1
ASSIST - A	**CONVINCE - A**	FRUIT - 2	MEAL - 2	*RECRUIT - N*	SWIM - 2
ASSURE - A	COOL - 2	*FUEL - N*	MEANWHILE - 2	REFLECT - 2	TAIL - 2
ATTACH - A	*COPE - N*	*FURNITURE - N*	MEAT - 2	*REFORM - N*	TALL - 2
ATTEMPT - 1	**CORE - A**	GAIN - 1	MEDICINE - 2	REFUSE - 1	*TANK - N*
ATTITUDE - A	**CORPORATE - A**	GAP - 2	**MENTAL - A**	**REGISTER - A**	TAP - 2
ATTRACT - 2	*COUNTER - N*	GARAGE - 2	MERE - 1	REGULAR - 2	**TARGET - A**

AUDIENCE - 2	COW - 2	GATE - 1	*MESS - N*	**REGULATE - A**	**TASK - A**
AUNT - 2	CRACK - 2	GATHER - 1	METAL - 1	**REJECT - A**	TASTE - 2
AVERAGE - 1	*CRAZY - N*	*GEAR - N*	METHOD - A	RELATIVE - 1	TEAR - 1
AWARD - N	CREAM - 2	**GENDER - A**	MILL - 2	**RELAX - A**	**TECHNICAL - A**
BACKGROUND - N	**CREDIT - A**	**GENERATE - A**	**MINIMUM - A**	**RELEASE - A**	**TECHNIQUE - A**
BAKE - 2	*CREW - N*	*GENTLEMAN - N*	**MINOR - A**	**RELEVANT - A**	TEMPERATURE - 2
BAND - 2	CRIMINAL - 2	GIFT - 1	*MIRROR - N*	*RELIEF - N*	**TEMPORARY - A**
BATH - 2	*CRISIS - N*	GLAD - 1	*MISSION - N*	RELIGION - 1	**TEXT - A**
BATHROOM - N	**CRITERIA - A**	*GLOBAL - N*	MISTAKE - 2	**RELY - A**	THEATRE - 2
BATTERY - N	CRITIC - 2	GOLD - 1	MIX - 2	REMARK - 1	**THEME - A**
BATTLE - 1	CROWD - 1	*GOLF - N*	MODERN - 1	REMIND - 2	THICK - 2
BEACH - N	CRY - 1	*GOODS - N*	**MONITOR - A**	RENT - 2	THIN - 2
BEAN - 2	CURTAIN - 2	*GRAB - N*	MOON - 1	REPAIR - 2	THREAT - 2
BEER - N	CUSTOMER - 2	**GRADE - A**	MORAL - 1	REPEAT - 2	TICKET - 2
BEG - 2	**CYCLE - A**	GRADUAL - 2	*MORTGAGE - N*	REPLACE - 2	TIGHT - 2
BELIEF - N	DAMAGE - 2	GRASS - 2	MOTOR - 1	REPLY - 1	*TINY - N*
BELL - 2	DANCE - 2	GRATEFUL - 2	MOUTH - 1	REQUEST - 2	TIP - 2
BELONG - 1	DARE - 2	GREY - 2	MURDER - 2	RESERVE - 1	TIRE - 2
BELT - 2	DARK - 1	**GUARANTEE - A**	*MUSCLE - N*	**RESIDE - A**	TITLE - 2
BEND - 2	DEBT - 2	GUARD - 2	NAIL - 2	RESIST - 2	TOOL - 2
BIKE - N	*DECENT - N*	GUEST - 2	NARROW - 2	*RESOLUTION - N*	TOOTH - 2
BIND - 2	DECLARE - 1	GUIDE - 2	NATIVE - 1	RESTAURANT - 2	**TOPIC - A**
BIRD - 1	DEFEND - 2	GUILTY - 2	NECK - 2	**RESTRICT - A**	TOUGH - 2
BITE - 2	**DEFINE - A**	HANDLE - 2	**NEGATE - A**	RETIRE - 2	TOUR - 2
BLAME - 2	DELAY - 2	HARDLY - 1	*NEGOTIATE - N*	**REVENUE - A**	TOWER - 2
BLIND - 2	DELIVER - 2	HARM - 2	NEIGHBOUR - 1	**REVERSE - A**	TOY - 2
BLOCK - 2	DEMAND - 1	HAT - 2	*NERVE - N*	REVIEW - 2	TRACK - 2
BOMB - N	**DEMONSTRATE - A**	HEAVEN - 1	NET - 2	**REVOLUTION - A**	*TRAIL - N*
BOND - A	**DENY - A**	*HERO - N*	**NEVERTHELESS - A**	RICH - 1	**TRANSFER - A**
BONE - 2	**DEPRESS - A**	HIDE - 2	NEWSPAPER - 1	RIDE - 1	*TREMENDOUS - N*
BOOT - N	*DEPUTY - N*	**HIGHLIGHT - A**	*NOD - N*	*ROME - N*	**TREND - A**
BORDER - 2	DESIRE - 1	HILL - 1	NOISE - 2	ROOF - 2	TRICK - 2
BORROW - 2	DESK - 2	HIRE - 2	*NORTHERN - N*	ROOT - 2	*TROOP - N*
BOSS - N	*DESPERATE - N*	HOLE - 2	NOSE - 2	ROUGH - 1	*TRUCK - N*
BOUNDARY - 2	DESTROY - 1	HOLY - 2	**NOTION - A**	**ROUTE - A**	TUNE - 2
BOWL - 2	**DETECT - A**	HONOUR - 1	*NOVEL - N*	ROW - 2	TYPICAL - 2
BRAIN - 2	**DEVICE - A**	HOOK - 2	**NUCLEAR - A**	ROYAL - 1	**ULTIMATE - A**
BRANCH - 1	*DIET - N*	*HORRIBLE - N*	NURSE - 2	RUB - 2	**UNIQUE - A**
BREAD - 1	DIG - 2	HOST - 2	OBJECT - 1	RUSH - 2	UPPER - 2
BREAKFAST - 2	DIRTY - 2	HOTEL - 2	*OBLIGE - N*	*RUSSIA - N*	UPSET - 2
BREAST - N	*DISABLED - N*	*HOUSEHOLD - N*	OBSERVE - 1	SAD - 2	*URBAN - N*
BREATH - 2	*DISAPPEAR - N*	HUNGER - 2	**OBTAIN - A**	SALARY - 2	VALLEY - 1
BRICK - 2	DISAPPOINT - 2	HUNT - 2	**CCUPY - A**	SALT - 1	*VAN - N*
BRIDGE - 1	*DISASTER - N*	HURRY - 2	OCEAN - 2	SAMPLE - 2	VARIETY - 1
BRIGHT - 1	DISH - 2	HURT - 2	*OFFENCE - N*	SAND - 2	**VARY - A**
BROAD - 1	**DISPLAY - A**	ICE - 2	OPINION - 1	*SANDWICH - N*	*VAST - N*
BROWN - 2	DISTANCE - 1	IDEAL - 2	OPPOSITE - 2	SATISFY - 2	*VEGETABLE - N*
BRUSH - 2	**DISTINCT - A**	**IGNORANT - A**	**OPTION - A**	SCALE - 2	**VEHICLE - A**
BURN - 1	**DISTRIBUTE - A**	ILL - 1	ORANGE - 2	*SCARE - N*	**VERSION - A**
BUTTER - 2	**DOMESTIC - A**	IMMEDIATE - 2	ORDINARY - 1	**SCHEDULE - A**	*VICE - N*
BUTTON - 2	DOZEN - 2	**IMPLICATE - A**	**OUTCOME - A**	SCREEN - 2	*VICTIM - N*
CABINET - N	**DRAFT - A**	*IMPORTANCE - N*	**OVERALL - A**	SEA - 1	VICTORY - 1
CALCULATE - 2	DRAG - 2	**IMPOSE - A**	OWE - 1	SEARCH - 2	VIOLENT - 2
CAMERA - 2	**DRAMA - A**	*IMPRESS - N*	PAD - 2	SECRET - 1	**VIRTUAL - A**
CAMP - 2	DREAM - 1	**INCIDENCE - A**	**PANEL - A**	**SELECT - A**	**VISION - A**
CANCEL - N	DUCK - 2	*INCREDIBLE - N*	*PARLIAMENT - N*	*SENIOR - N*	**VOLUME - A**
CANCER - N	*DUMP - N*	INDEPENDENT - 1	*PARTICIPANT - N*	SENTENCE - 2	**VOLUNTARY - A**
CAPABLE - A	DUST - 2	*INDIA - N*	**PARTICIPATE - A**	*SESSION - N*	WAKE - 2
CAPACITY - A	DUTY - 1	INFLUENCE - 1	**PARTNER - A**	SEVERE - 2	WARN - 2
CAPITAL - 1	EAR - 1	**INITIAL - A**	*PATCH - N*	SHADOW - 1	WAVE - 1
CAPTURE - N	EARN - 2	**INITIATE - A**	PATH - 2	SHAME - 2	WEAK - 2
CASH - N	*EASTERN - N*	**INJURE - A**	PATTERN - 2	SHAPE - 2	WEATHER - 2
CAST - N	**EDIT - A**	*INSIST - N*	PEN - 2	SHARP - 2	*WEB - N*
CATEGORY - A	EFFICIENT - 1	**INSPECT - A**	*PERCEPTION - N*	**SHIFT - A**	*WED - N*
CATHOLIC - N	ELDER - 2	**INSTANCE - A**	PERMANENT - 2	SHIP - 1	*WEIRD - N*

CELEBRATE - N

CHAIN - 2

CHALLENGE - A

CHANNEL - A

CHAPTER - A

CHARITY - N

CHASE - N

CHEESE - 2

CHEMICAL - A

CHEST - 2

CHICKEN - 2

CHIEF - 1

CHINA - N

CHIP - N

CHOCOLATE - N

CIGARETTE - N

CIRCLE - 1

CIRCUMSTANCE - A

ELEMENT - A

EMERGENCY - N

EMOTION - N

EMPHASIS - A

EMPTY - 2

ENABLE - A

ENEMY - 1

ENGAGE - N

ENORMOUS - A

ENSURE - A

ENTERTAIN - 2

ENTITLE - N

EQUIP - A

ERA - N

ESCAPE - 1

ESSENTIAL - 2

ESTATE - A

ESTIMATE - A

INSTITUTE - A

INSTRUCT - A

INSTRUMENT - 2

INTELLIGENCE - A

INTEND - 2

INTENT - N

INTERNAL - A

INTERPRET - A

INVESTIGATE - A

INVITE - 2

IRISH - N

IRON - 1

ITALY - N

JACKET - N

JAPAN - N

JEW - N

JOINT - 1

JOKE - 2

PERMIT - 1

PERSPECTIVE - A

PERSUADE - 2

PIE - N

PIG - 2

PILE - 2

PILOT - N

PINK - 2

PIPE - 2

PIT - N

PITCH - N

PLAIN - 1

PLANE - 2

PLANET - N

PLASTIC - N

PLATE - 2

PLEASURE - N

PLENTY - 2

SHIRT - 2

SHOCK - 2

SHOULDER - 1

SHOUT - 2

SHOWER - 2

SIGHT - 1

SIGNAL - 2

SILENCE - 1

SIN - N

SINK - 2

SKIN - 2

SKY - 1

SLIDE - 2

SLIP - 2

SMART - N

SMELL - 2

SMILE - 1

SNOW - 1

WELFARE - A

WESTERN - 1

WET - 2

WHEEL - 2

WILD - 1

WINE - 2

WING - 2

WINTER - 1

WIPE - 2

WIRE - 2

WISE - 1

WITHDRAW - N

WITNESS - 2

WRAP - 2

YELLOW - 2

YOUTH - 1

ZONE - N

Key: 1 = GSL 1000   2 = GSL 2000   A = AWL (bolded)
        N = New (Italics)   Underlined = Dolch–Fry

Core C content words (887)

ABANDON - A	*COLUMN - N*	*EPISODE - N*	**INTERMEDIATE - A**	*PHRASE - N*	**SIMULATE - A**
ABORT - N	*COMEDY - N*	**EQUATE - A**	*INTERNET - N*	*PHYSICIAN - N*	*SIMULTANEOUS - N*
ABROAD - 2	**COMMENCE - A**	**EQUIVALENT - A**	INTERRUPT - 2	*PIANO - N*	SKIRT - 2
ABSENCE - 2	**COMMODITY - A**	**ERODE - A**	**INTERVAL - A**	*PILL - N*	*SLAM - N*
ABSORB - N	*COMMUNIST - N*	**ERROR - A**	**INTERVENE - A**	PIN - 2	SLAVE - 2
ABSTRACT - A	**COMPATIBLE - A**	*ESSAY - N*	**INTRINSIC - A**	*PL - N*	*SLICE - N*
ACCENT - N	**COMPILE - A**	ESSENCE - 2	*INVASION - N*	*PLATFORM - N*	SLOPE - 2
ACCOMPANY - A	**COMPLEMENT - A**	**ETHIC - A**	INVENT - 2	*PLEAD - N*	SMOOTH - 2
ACCOMPLISH - N	COMPOSE - 2	**EVALUATE - A**	**INVOKE - A**	*PLOT - N*	*SNAP - N*
ACCUMULATE - A	**COMPOUND - A**	**EVIDENT - A**	*IRAQ - N*	*PM - N*	**SO-CALLED - A**
ACCUSE - 2	**COMPREHENSIVE - A**	EVIL - 2	*ISLAM - N*	*POET - N*	SOCK - 2
ACQUIRE - A	**COMPRISE - A**	*EXAM - N*	**ISOLATE - A**	*POLE - N*	**SOLE - A**
ACRE - N	*COMPROMISE - N*	**EXCEED - A**	*ISRAEL - N*	POLISH - 2	*SOPHISTICATED - N*
ADAPT - A	**CONCEIVE - A**	EXCESS - 2	*JAIL - N*	*POLLUTE - N*	SOUP - 2
ADJACENT - A	*CONCERT - N*	*EXIT - N*	*JEANS - N*	*POND - N*	*SOVIET - N*
ADMINISTRATOR - N	*CONCRETE - N*	*EXPANSION - N*	*JET - N*	*PORCH - N*	SPARE - 2
ADMIRE - 2	**CONCURRENT - A**	**EXPLICIT - A**	**JOURNAL - A**	*PORT - N*	**SPECIFY - A**
ADVENTURE - 1	CONFESS - 2	EXPLODE - 2	*JOURNALIST - N*	**PORTION - A**	*SPECTRUM - N*
ADVOCATE - A	**CONFINE - A**	**EXPLOIT - A**	*JUNIOR - N*	*PORTRAIT - N*	SPELL - 2
AFFILIATE - N	**CONFORM - A**	*EXPLOSION - N*	*KISS - N*	*PORTRAY - N*	**SPHERE - A**
AGGREGATE - A	*CONFRONT - N*	**EXPORT - A**	*LABORATORY - N*	**POSE - A**	SPILL - 2
AGGRESSIVE - N	*CONGRESS - N*	**EXPOSE - A**	LAMP - 2	POSSESS - 1	SPIN - 2
AIRLINE - N	**CONSENT - A**	**EXTERNAL - A**	*LAP - N*	POVERTY - 1	*SPOKESMAN - N*
ALBUM - N	**CONSIST - A**	**EXTRACT - A**	*LATIN - N*	POWDER - 2	*SQUEEZE - N*
ALCOHOL - N	**CONSTITUTE - A**	EXTRAORDINARY - 2	LATTER - 1	**PRACTITIONER - A**	*STADIUM - N*
ALLEGE - N	*CONSTITUTION - N*	*FABRIC - N*	*LAWN - N*	PRAISE - 2	*STAKE - N*
ALLIANCE - N	**CONSTRAIN - A**	*FACULTY - N*	*LAWSUIT - N*	**PRECEDE - A**	STAMP - 2
ALLOCATE - A	**CONTEMPORARY - A**	FADE - 2	**LAYER - A**	**PREDOMINANT - A**	**STATISTIC - A**
ALLY - N	*CONTEST - N*	FALSE - 2	*LEAP - N*	**PRELIMINARY - A**	STEADY - 2
AMBIGUOUS - A	**CONTRADICT - A**	*FAME - N*	LEATHER - 2	*PRESCRIPTION - N*	STEM - 2
AMEND - A	**CONTRARY - A**	FANCY - 2	**LEGISLATE - A**	PRESERVE - 2	STIR - 2
ANALOGY - A	**CONTROVERSY - A**	FATE - 2	*LEGITIMATE - N*	**PRESUME - A**	STOMACH - 2
ANGEL - N	**CONVERT - A**	*FESTIVAL - N*	*LEMON - N*	PRIDE - 2	**STRAIGHTFORWARD - A**
ANGER - 2	*CONVEY - N*	*FIBRE - N*	**LEVY - A**	PRIEST - 2	**STRAIN - N**
ANKLE - N	*CONVICT - N*	*FICTION - N*	LIBERTY - 2	*PRINCE - N*	STREAM - 1
ANNIVERSARY - N	**COOPERATE - A**	**FINITE - A**	*LIFESTYLE - N*	*PRINCESS - N*	STRICT - 2
ANNOY - 2	**COORDINATE - A**	*FIST - N*	**LIKEWISE - A**	**PRINCIPAL - A**	STRING - 2
ANTICIPATE - A	*COP - N*	FLAG - 2	*LION - N*	**PRIOR - A**	*STROKE - N*
ANXIETY - 2	CORN - 1	FLAME - 2	*LITERARY - N*	*PRIVACY - N*	**SUBMIT - A**
ANXIOUS - N	**CORRESPOND - A**	FLASH - 2	*LOBBY - N*	*PRIVILEGE - N*	**SUBORDINATE - A**
APPEND - A	*CORRESPONDENT - N*	FLAVOUR - 2	*LONG-TERM - N*	*PRO - N*	**SUBSEQUENT - A**
APPROXIMATE - A	*CORRIDOR - N*	*FLEE - N*	LUMP - 2	PROFESSION - 2	**SUBSIDY - A**
ARAB - N	*CORRUPT - N*	FLESH - 2	LUNG - 2	*PROFILE - N*	SUBSTANCE - 1
ARBITRARY - A	COTTAGE - 2	**FLEXIBLE - A**	*MAGIC - N*	**PROHIBIT - A**	**SUBSTITUTE - A**
ARCHITECT - N	COTTON - 1	FLOOD - 2	**MANIPULATE - A**	*PROMINENT - N*	**SUBTLE - N**
ARCHITECTURE - N	COUGH - 2	FLOUR - 2	**MANUAL - A**	PROMPT - 2	SUCCESSOR - A
ARISE - 1	*COUNSEL - N*	**FLUCTUATE - A**	*MARINE - N*	PROOF - 1	SUCK - 2
ARREST - 2	COURAGE - 2	*FLUID - N*	*MASK - N*	*PROSECUTE - N*	*SUICIDE - N*
ASIA - N	COUSIN - 1	FOLD - 2	*MATE - N*	*PROTEIN - N*	*SUITE - N*
ASSAULT - N	*COWBOY - N*	FOOL - 2	**MATURE - A**	*PROTEST - N*	**SUMMARY - A**
ASSERT - N	*CRAFT - N*	*FOREVER - N*	**MECHANISM - A**	**PROTOCOL - A**	*SUPERIOR - N*
ASSET - N	CRASH - 2	**FORMAT - A**	*MEDAL - N*	*PROVINCE - N*	*SUPERVISE - N*

ATHLETE - N	CRAWL - N	**FORMULA - A**	**MEDIATE - A**	PROVISION - 1	**SUPPLEMENT - A**
ATMOSPHERE - N	CREATURE - 2	**FORTHCOMING - A**	*MEDICATION - N*	**PUBLICATION - A**	*SURGEON - N*
ATTAIN - A	*CREEK - N*	**FOUNDED - A**	**MEDIUM - A**	PUNISH - 2	**SUSPEND - A**
ATTORNEY - N	CRITICISE - N	*FRACTION - N*	MELT - 2	PUPIL - 2	SUSTAIN - A
ATTRIBUTE - A	CRITICISM - N	**FRAMEWORK - A**	MENU - N	PURPLE - 2	SWALLOW - 2
AUTOMATE - A	CROP - 2	*FRAUD - N*	*MEXICO - N*	PURSUIT - N	SWEAT - 2
AUTOMATIC - N	CROWN - 1	FRIGHT - 2	**MIGRATE - A**	**QUALITATIVE - A**	SWEEP - 2
AUTOMOBILE - N	**CRUCIAL - A**	*FRUSTRATE - N*	MILD - 2	QUESTIONNAIRE - N	SWING - 2
AVENUE - 2	*CRUISE - N*	**FUNDAMENTAL - A**	MINER - 1	*QUIT - N*	**SYMBOL - A**
AWKWARD - 2	*CRYSTAL - N*	FUNERAL - 2	**MINIMAL - A**	*RACIAL - N*	*SYMPTOM - N*
BAN - N	CUPBOARD - 2	**FURTHERMORE - A**	**MINIMISE - A**	*RACIST - N*	*TACKLE - N*
BARE - N	CURIOUS - 2	*GALLERY - N*	**MINISTRY - A**	**RADICAL - A**	*TALE - N*
BARREL - 2	**CURRENCY - A**	*GANG - N*	*MIRACLE - N*	*RAGE - N*	*TALENT - N*
BARRIER - N	*CURRICULUM - N*	GAY - 2	*MISSILE - N*	**RANDOM - A**	*TEEN - N*
BASEBALL - N	CURVE - 2	*GAZE - N*	*MIXTURE - N*	RANK - 1	*TEENAGE - N*
BASEMENT - N	CUSTOM - 2	*GENE - N*	**MODE - A**	*RAPE - N*	TEMPLE - 1
BASKET - 2	DAMN - N	**GENERATION - A**	MODEST - 2	RAPID - 2	*TENNIS - N*
BASKETBALL - N	DATABASE - N	GENEROUS - 2	**MODIFY - A**	RAT - 2	**TENSE - A**
BAT - N	DECK - N	*GENETIC - N*	MONSTER - N	**RATIO - A**	TENT - 2
BEAM - 2	**DECLINE - A**	GENTLE - 1	*MOOD - N*	**RATIONAL - A**	**TERMINATE - A**
BEEF - N	DECORATE - N	*GENUINE - N*	MOREOVER - 1	RAW - 2	*TERRITORY - N*
BEHALF - A	DEDICATE - N	*GESTURE - N*	**MOTIVE - A**	RAY - 2	*TERROR - N*
BEHAVE - 2	**DEDUCE - A**	GHOST - N	MOUNT - N	*REBEL - N*	*TESTIFY - N*
BENCH - N	DEFEAT - 1	*GIANT - N*	MOUSE - 2	*RECEIVER - N*	*TESTIMONY - N*
BIAS - A	DEFICIT - N	*GIRLFRIEND - N*	MUD - 2	*RECIPE - N*	*THERAPY - N*
BIBLE - N	DELICATE - 2	*GLANCE - N*	*MULTIPLE - N*	**REFINE - A**	**THEREBY - A**
BID - N	DELIGHT - 2	**GLOBE - A**	MULTIPLY - 2	*REFRIGERATE - N*	**THESIS - A**
BILL - 1	*DEMOCRACY - N*	*GLOVE - N*	*MUSLIM - N*	*REFUGE - N*	THROAT - 2
BIOLOGICAL - N	**DENOTE - A**	GRACE - 1	**MUTUAL - A**	**REGIME - A**	THUMB - 2
BISHOP - N	**DERIVE - A**	*GRADUATE - N*	MYSTERY - 2	**REINFORCE - A**	TIDY - 2
BITTER - 2	DESERT - 1	GRAIN - 2	*NAKED - N*	RELIEVE - 2	*TILE - N*
BLADE - 2	DESERVE - 2	*GRAPH - N*	*NASTY - N*	**RELUCTANCE - A**	TIN - 2
BLANK - N	**DEVIATE - A**	GRAVE - 2	*NAVY - N*	*REMOTE - N*	*TISSUE - N*
BLANKET - N	DEVIL - 2	GREET - 2	NECESSITY - 1	REPUTATION - 2	TOBACCO - 2
BLESS - 2	**DEVOTE - A**	*GRIP - N*	NEEDLE - N	RESCUE - 2	*TOILET - N*
BOIL - 2	*DIAGRAM - N*	*GROCERY - N*	*NERVOUS - N*	RESIGN - 2	*TOMATO - N*
BOLD - 2	*DIALOGUE - N*	**GUIDELINE - A**	**NEUTRAL - A**	**RESOLVE - A**	*TONE - N*
BONUS - N	DIAMOND - 2	*GULF - N*	*NIGHTMARE - N*	*RESORT - N*	TONGUE - 2
BOOM - N	*DIARY - N*	HABIT - 2	*NOMINATE - N*	*RESPECTIVE - N*	*TOSS - N*
BOOST - N	DICTIONARY - 2	HANDSOME - N	**NONETHELESS - A**	**RESTORE - A**	*TOURNAMENT - N*
BORING - N	DIFFER - N	HARBOR - 2	**NORM - A**	**RESTRAIN - A**	TOWEL - 2
BOUNCE - N	**DIFFERENTIATE - A**	*HARSH - N*	NUMEROUS - 1	*RESUME - N*	**TRACE - A**
BOYFRIEND - N	*DIGITAL - N*	*HEADLINE - N*	NUT - 2	*RETAIL - N*	*TRAGEDY - N*
BRAND - N	**DIMENSION - A**	*HEADQUARTERS - N*	OAK - N	**RETAIN - A**	*TRANSACT - N*
BREATHE - 2	**DIMINISH - A**	*HEEL - N*	OBJECTED - N	**REVISE - A**	**TRANSFORM - A**
BROADCAST - 2	*DINE - N*	*HEIGHT - N*	**OBJECTIVE - A**	REWARD - N	**TRANSIT - A**
BUCK - N	DISC - N	*HELICOPTER - N*	OCCUPATION - N	*RHYTHM - N*	*TRANSITION - N*
BULK - A	DISCIPLINE - 2	**HENCE - A**	OFFSET - A	RICE - 2	TRANSLATE - 2
BULL - N	DISCOUNT - N	*HERB - N*	*OLYMPIC - N*	*RIDICULOUS - N*	**TRANSMIT - A**
BULLET - N	**DISCRETE - A**	*HERITAGE - N*	**ONGOING - A**	**RIGID - A**	TRAP - 2
BUNCH - 2	**DISCRIMINATE - A**	HESITATE - 2	*ONION - N*	*RIP - N*	TREASURE - 2
BURDEN - N	DISGUST - 2	**HIERARCHY - A**	*ONLINE - N*	ROB - 2	*TREATY - N*
BUREAU - N	DISMISS - 2	*HINT - N*	*OPERA - N*	*ROCKET - N*	**TRIGGER - A**
BURST - 2	*DISORDER - N*	*HIP - N*	OPPONENT - N	ROD - 2	TRUNK - 2
BURY - 2	**DISPLACE - A**	*HOMEWORK - N*	ORGAN - 2	ROPE - 2	TUBE - 2
CABLE - N	**DISPOSE - A**	*HONEY - N*	**ORIENT - A**	*ROUTINE - N*	*TUCK - N*
CALM - 2	*DISPUTE - N*	*HORN - N*	ORIGIN - 2	RUBBISH - 2	*TUNNEL - N*
CAMPUS - N	DISTINGUISH - 1	*HORROR - N*	**OUTPUT - A**	*RUMOUR - N*	*TWIN - N*
CANADA - N	**DISTORT - A**	*HUMOUR - N*	*OVEN - N*	*RURAL - N*	*TWIST - N*
CANDLE - N	**DIVERSE - A**	*HURRICANE - N*	OVERCOME - 2	*SACK - N*	UGLY - 2
CAP - 2	*DIVORCE - N*	**HYPOTHESIS - A**	**OVERLAP - A**	SACRED - 2	UNCLE - 2

CAPTAIN - 1	*DOLL - N*	**IDENTICAL - A**	*OVERLOOK - N*	SAIL - 1	**UNDERGO - A**
CARBON - N	**DOMAIN - A**	**IDEOLOGY - A**	**OVERSEAS - A**	SAKE - 2	**UNDERLIE - A**
CARVE - N	**DOMINATE - A**	**ILLUSTRATE - A**	*OXYGEN - N*	*SALAD - N*	*UNDERMINE - N*
CATTLE - 2	*DOORWAY - N*	*IMMIGRANT - N*	*PACE - N*	*SALMON - N*	**UNDERTAKE - A**
CAVE - 2	*DOSE - N*	**IMMIGRATE - A**	*PALACE - N*	*SATELLITE - N*	**UNIFORM - A**
CEASE - A	DOT - 2	**IMPLEMENT - A**	PALE - 2	SAUCE - 2	**UNIFY - A**
CEILING - N	*DRAIN - N*	**IMPLICIT - A**	*PALESTINE - N*	*SCANDAL - N*	UNIVERSE - 2
CENT - 2	DRAWER - 2	**IMPLY - A**	PAN - 2	SCATTER - 2	*UPDATE - N*
CEREMONY - 2	*DRIFT - N*	**INCENTIVE - A**	*PANTS - N*	**SCENARIO - A**	URGE - 2
CHAMBER - N	**DURATION - A**	**INCLINE - A**	*PARADE - N*	*SCHOLAR - N*	**UTILIZE - A**
CHAMPION - N	**DYNAMIC - A**	**INCORPORATE - A**	**PARADIGM - A**	**SCOPE - A**	*VACATION - N*
CHAOS - N	EAGER - 2	**INDEX - A**	**PARAGRAPH - A**	*SCOUT - N*	**VALID - A**
CHART - A	*EAGLE - N*	**INDUCE - A**	**PARALLEL - A**	*SCREAM - N*	*VENTURE - N*
CHEEK - N	EASE - 2	**INEVITABLE - A**	**PARAMETER - A**	SCREW - 2	VERSE - 2
CHEER - 2	*ECHO - N*	*INFANT - N*	PARDON - 2	*SCRIPT - N*	*VERSUS - N*
CHEF - N	*ELBOW - N*	*INFECT - N*	PASSAGE - 2	**SECTOR - A**	*VETERAN - N*
CHEQUE - 2	*ELECTRONIC - N*	**INFER - A**	PASSENGER - 2	SEED - 2	**VIOLATE - A**
CHOP - N	*ELEGANT - N*	*INFLATE - N*	*PASSION - N*	*SEGMENT - N*	*VIRUS - N*
CHRONIC - N	*ELEMENTARY - N*	**INFRASTRUCTURE - A**	**PASSIVE - A**	*SENATE - N*	*VISIBLE - A*
CIRCUIT - N	*ELEVATE - N*	*INGREDIENT - N*	*PAT - N*	*SENATOR - N*	**VISUAL - A**
CITE - A	**ELIMINATE - A**	**INHERENT - A**	PAUSE - 2	SENSITIVE - 1	*VITAL - N*
CIVILISE - 2	*ELITE - N*	**INHIBIT - A**	*PEAK - N*	**SEQUENCE - A**	*VULNERABLE - N*
CLARIFY - A	*E-MAIL - N*	*INNOCENT - N*	*PEER - N*	SHADE - 2	WANDER - 2
CLASSIC - A	*EMBARRASS - N*	**INNOVATE - A**	*PENALTY - N*	*SHED - N*	WEALTH - 1
CLAUSE - A	*EMBRACE - N*	**INPUT - A**	PENCIL - 2	SHEEP - 2	**WHEREBY - A**
CLAY - 2	**EMERGE - A**	**INSERT - A**	PENNY - 2	SHELF - 2	WHISPER - 2
CLEVER - 2	EMPIRE - 1	**INSIGHT - A**	*PEPPER - N*	SHELL - 2	**WIDESPREAD - A**
CLIMATE - N	**EMPIRICAL - A**	*INSPIRE - N*	**PERCEIVE - A**	SHELTER - 2	*WILDLIFE - N*
CLINIC - N	**ENCOUNTER - A**	*INSTALL - N*	**PERSIST - A**	SHINE - 1	*WOLF - N*
CLOTH - 2	**ENFORCE - A**	**INTEGRAL - A**	*PERSONALITY - N*	*SHIT - N*	*WORKSHOP - N*
COALITION - N	**ENHANCE - A**	**INTEGRATE - A**	*PERSONNEL - N*	SHORE - 1	WORSE - 2
COHERENT - A	*ENTERPRISE - N*	**INTEGRITY - A**	PET - 2	*SIGH - N*	WOUND - 1
COINCIDE - A	*ENTHUSIASM - N*	*INTELLECTUAL - N*	**PHASE - A**	*SIGNATURE - N*	WRIST - 2
COLLAPSE - A	**ENTITY - A**	**INTENSE - A**	**PHENOMENON - A**	*SILLY - N*	*YELL - N*
COLONY - 1	ENVELOPE - 2	**INTERACT - A**	**PHILOSOPHY - A**	SILVER - 1	YIELD - 1

Appendix E: Online resources for learning high frequency vocabulary

Dolch and Fry word lists

URL	Description	Rating
http://quizlet.com/subject/dolch	Many *Quizlet* flashcard sets of Dolch words. *Quizlet* is a very robust flashcard program (free), with the possibility of written and spoken word presentations in multiple languages. Teachers can choose from a variety of existing Dolch word sets, or create their own.	*****
http://quizlet.com/subject/fry	Many *Quizlet* flashcard sets of Fry words. Quizlet is a very robust flashcard program (free), with the possibility of written and spoken word presentations in multiple languages. Teachers can choose from a variety of existing Fry word sets, or create their own.	*****
www.k12reader.com	Instruction for how to teach Dolch and Fry word lists. Activities and worksheets.	****
www.readingresource.net/sightwords.html www.readingresource.net/vocabulary/activities.html	Fun activities for practicing sight words and other vocabulary activities, and links to other websites with vocabulary games.	****
http://w4.nkcsd.k12.mo.us/~kcofer/fry_words_pg.htm	Fry word activities (spelling, gap-fill, etc.).	****
www.spellingcity.com/dolch-words.html	Gives Dolch lists of words (K–3) and creates a number of activities for them. Some other classifications of the words (K–12): words that have multiple meaning, compound words, etc. They all have activities.	****
www.mrsperkins.com	List of Dolch words and phrases and activities for Dolch list. Teachers can create different worksheets using the selected list of Dolch phrases.	****
www.uniqueteachingresources.com/Fry-1000-Instant-Words.html	Dolch and Fry Lists of words with flashcards.	****
www.abcteach.com/interactive_home.php	Games and other activities for some groups of words, including Dolch List.	**

Appendix E: (cont.) Online resources for learning high frequency vocabulary

URL	Description	Rating
http://quizlet.com	Many *Quizlet* flashcard sets of high frequency words. *Quizlet* is a very robust flashcard program (free), with the possibility of written and spoken word presentations in multiple languages. Teachers can choose from a variety of existing word sets, or create their own.	*****
www.lextutor.ca	Several vocabulary applications, with a focus on academic and high frequency vocabulary. Programs for analyzing, teaching, learning, and testing of vocabulary.	*****
http://innovativocab.wikispaces.com/Itinerary	Many resources for teaching. It is based on *Building Academic Vocabulary* by Marzano. Provides a number of instructive techniques for students and teachers.	****
http://jc-schools.net/tutorials/vocab/strategies.html	Good resource for teaching vocabulary; provides some activities and games for the classroom.	****
www.visualthesaurus.com/vocabgrabber	Program that analyzes a text, generating lists of the most useful vocabulary words and showing how those words are used in context. Users copy a text from a document and paste it into the box. Program automatically creates a list of vocabulary from the text, which can be sorted, filtered, and saved.	****
www.spellingcity.com	Creates a number of activities from the user's own word lists. Students can also write a paragraph using the words and save it in a PDF format. Can be used for any list of words.	****
http://www2.elc.polyu.edu.hk/CILL/sitemap.htm	Hong Kong Polytechnic University vocabulary and other resources, with references to other materials. Concordances for AWL and GSL. Activities, lists, and worksheets.	****
http://oald8.oxfordlearnersdictionaries.com	Lists of general and academic high frequency words with several tools for working with them, including British and North American pronunciations, definitions, example sentences, synonyms, etc.	****
http://pbskids.org/games/vocabulary.html	Engaging vocabulary games.	****
www.toolsforeducators.com	Templates that allow the teacher to make handouts for students with both images and text. Words are separated thematically. Teacher can make the following: bingo games, word search games, crossword puzzles, board games, writing and spelling worksheets, and others.	****
www.eslgamesworld.com/members/games/vocabulary/index.html	Many vocabulary games.	****

Academic high frequency words

URL	Description	Rating
www.superkids.com/aweb/tools/words/scramble	Teacher can create scramble worksheet for various words.	****
www.manythings.org	Word lists and a number of activities with these lists, including matching quizzes, crossword puzzles, anagrams, picture games, etc.	****
www.tv411.org/vocabulary	Instructions on how to use dictionaries, thesaurus, root words, and affixes. Includes different activities. Good for teaching morphology (for AWL also).	****
www.vocabulary.co.il	A variety of engaging vocabulary games (different levels). Also has vocabulary learning strategies, and tips for TOEFL, GRE, SAT, etc.	****
www.learninggamesforkids.com/vocabulary-games	Vocabulary games.	****
www.englishmedialab.com/vocabulary.html	A variety of vocabulary games (memory games, cloze, puzzle, match etc.), activities, and video lesson plans.	****
www.englishvocabularyexercises.com/vocab-categories.htm	Over 500 gap-fill exercises to learn and review 1,500+ items of general vocabulary in English. Online format of the exercises allows students to get immediate feedback on their answers.	***
www.learnamericanenglishonline.com/Vocabulary.html	Picture dictionary.	***
http://web2.uvcs.uvic.ca/elc/studyzone/200/vocab	Exercises for thematic beginning vocabulary.	***
www.esl-lab.com/vocab/index.htm	Mini lessons based on vocabulary lists by topic. Includes audio file, quiz, and activities.	***
www.esl-lab.com/quizzes.htm	Vocabulary quizzes separated by topic.	***
www.superkids.com/aweb/tools/words	Vocabulary builder games.	***
www.wordcount.org/main.php	Interactive presentation of the 86,800 most frequently used English words (based on the BNC).	**
www.ecenglish.com/learnenglish/subject/Vocabulary	Features a variety of vocabulary exercises submitted by ESL teachers. Topics of vocabulary are mixed together. Takes some time to find what you need.	**
http://a4esl.org/q/h/vocabulary.html	Self-study quizzes. Resources are submitted by teachers.	**
http://jbauman.com/gsl.html	Link to GSL.	**
www.robwaring.org/vocab/wordlists/lemma.html	2000 most common English words taken from the BNC lemma list.	**

Appendix E: (cont.) Online resources for learning high frequency vocabulary

URL	Description	Rating
http://quizlet.com/subject/awl/	Many *Quizlet* flashcard sets of AWL words. *Quizlet* is a very robust flashcard program (free), with the possibility of written and spoken word presentations in multiple languages. Teachers can choose from a variety of existing AWL word sets, or create their own.	*****
www.lextutor.ca	Several vocabulary applications, with a focus on academic and high frequency vocabulary. Programs for analyzing, teaching, learning, and testing of vocabulary.	*****
www.uefap.com/vocab/vocfram.htm	Includes AWL, GSL, and a list of less frequent words, exercises and information on vocabulary-building skills. AWL is used in academic contexts. Students can test their acquisition of AWL words through various exercises.	****
www.visualthesaurus.com	Program creates semantic maps of words, provides audio support. Color-coded meanings indicate parts of speech. Multiple definitions included for each word.	****
www.nottingham.ac.uk/~alzsh3/acvocab/index.htm	Several applications for learning and identifying AWL words. Users can enter their own texts for many applications.	****
http://www4.caes.hku.hk/vocabulary/tutorial/index1.asp	Features words (some AWL) that frequently occur in business and financial texts, legal documents, social work papers, and engineering reports. Words are presented in context with their meaning and pronunciation available to the user.	****
www.bergen.edu/pages1/Pages/4019.aspx	Academic vocabulary podcasts. Each word has a simple definition and a dialogue. The definitions for these examples reflect common uses of the words.	****
www.wordsift.com	Program highlights the frequent words from any text inserted by the user. Words can be sorted by lists: GSL, AWL, Science, Math, Languages, Social Studies, and others. Teachers and learners can check the lexical density of texts, and see how many words from the AWL and other lists are used in a particular text.	****
www.spellingcity.com	Creates a number of activities from the user's own word lists. Students can also write a paragraph using the words and save it in a PDF format. Can be used for any list of words.	****

URL	Description	Rating
http://www2.elc.polyu.edu.hk/CILL/sitemap.htm	Hong Kong Polytechnic University vocabulary and other resources, with references to other materials. Concordances for AWL and GSL. Activities, lists, and worksheets.	****
http://oald8.oxfordlearnersdictionaries.com/	List of academic words with several tools for working with them, including British and North American pronunciations, definitions, example sentences, synonyms, etc.	****
www.englishvocabularyexercises.com/AWL	Gap-fill exercises to learn and review 570 AWL words (10- sublists). Online format of exercises allows students to get immediate feedback on their answers.	****
www.myvocabulary.com	Activities for numerous themed word lists in education, with focus on Greek and Latin roots.	****
https://www.msu.edu/~defores1/gre/gre.htm	Activities for academic words, with focus on Greek and Latin roots in preparation for verbal sections of GRE, MCAT, GMAT, and LSAT.	****
www.dcielts.com/ielts-vocabulary/awl-exercises	Gap-fill exercises for AWL sublist 1 and incomplete sublist 2.	**
www.pbs.plymouth.ac.uk/academicwordlistatuop/index.htm	Designed for students. List of suggestions of how to learn vocabulary, and exercises for selective lists of the AWL.	**
www.englishdaily626.com/tfvocab.php	Multiple-choice quizzes for TOEFL vocabulary.	**
www.flashcardmachine.com/my-flashcards/set.cgi	Program for creating and sharing online flashcards.	**
http://springerexemplar.com	Concordancer for scientific terminology.	**
http://lexfiles.info/index.html	Many Latin and Greek prefixes, roots, and suffixes with their meanings (alphabetically).	**

Appendix F: Sample compound words (1,126) (repurposed from firstschoolyears.com)

afterbirth	bathroom	crossbones	drainpipe	farmhouse	football	freshwater	greyhound
airbrush	bedridden	crossroad	drawback	farmyard	footbridge	frogman	groundwork
aircraft	bedspread	crossword	drawbridge	farseeing	footfall	frostbite	guardhouse
airfield	bedtime	cutback	driveway	fatherhood	foothill	gangway	guardsman
airline	billboard	daredevil	dropout	featherbed	foothold	gaslight	guesswork
airman	blacklist	darkroom	drumstick	featherweight	footpath	gatecrasher	guidebook
airport	blackmail	dashboard	dustpan	feedback	footprint	gatekeeper	guideline
airship	brainstorm	daybreak	earache	fellowship	footrest	gateway	gunfire
anybody	brainwash	daydream	eardrum	figurehead	footstool	gearbox	gunman
anyhow	breakfast	daylight	earphone	fingernail	footwear	gearshift	gunpowder
anyway	briefcase	daytime	earring	fingerprint	forearm	gemstone	gunshot
anywhere	broadcast	deadline	earthquake	firearm	forecast	gingerbread	hacksaw
armchair	bulldog	dishwasher	earthworm	fireball	foreclose	globetrotter	hailstone
armpit	bulldozer	doorknob	elsewhere	firecracker	forefinger	glowworm	hairbrush
backdrop	bullfrog	doorman	endless	firefly	forego	goalkeeper	haircut
backfire	buttercup	doormat	evermore	fireproof	forehand	goldfish	hairdo
background	butterfingers	doorway	eyeball	firework	foreman	grandchild	hairdresser
backhand	chairman	doughnut	eyebrow	fishbowl	foresight	granddaughter	hairline
backlash	championship	downcast	eyeglass	fisherman	foretell	grandfather	hairpin
backlog	clockwise	downfall	eyepiece	flagpole	forewarn	grandmother	halfway
backside	clockwork	downhearted	eyesight	flagship	foreword	grandparent	handbag
backstroke	copycat	downhill	eyesore	flashback	fortnight	grandson	handball
backtrack	corkscrew	downpour	eyestrain	flashlight	foursome	grandstand	handmade
backward	countdown	downright	eyewitness	floodgate	framework	grasshopper	handout
bagpipes	courtyard	downstairs	fairway	floodlight	freehand	grassland	handpick
ballroom	cowboy	downstream	fallout	foghorn	freehold	gravestone	handshake
bankroll	crackdown	downtown	fanfare	folklore	freestanding	graveyard	handwriting
barnyard	crossbar	downwind	farewell	foolproof	freeway	greenhouse	handyman

hangman	heartbeat	homemade	infold	kindhearted	limestone	markup	neighbourhood
hangnail	heartbreak	homesick	inhale	kingfisher	linesman	mastermind	network
hangover	heartburn	homework	inkblot	kneecap	lipstick	masterpiece	nevermore
hardheaded	heavyset	honeybee	inkwell	knockout	litterbug	matchbook	newborn
hardship	heavyweight	honeycomb	inland	landfall	livestock	matchmaker	newcomer
hardware	hedgehog	honeydew	inmate	landlocked	lockout	maybe	newsboy
hardwood	heirloom	hookup	inpatient	landlord	longhand	mealtime	newscast
harebrained	henceforth	horseback	inroad	landmark	lookout	meantime	newsletter
harelip	hereafter	horsehair	inset	landslide	loophole	meanwhile	newspaper
haycock	hereby	horseman	inside	laughingstock	lopsided	merrymaking	newsprint
hayfork	herein	horseplay	insole	layman	lordship	middleman	newsreel
hayloft	hereof	hourglass	install	layoff	loudmouth	milestone	newsstand
haystack	hereon	houseboat	instep	layout	lovesick	milkmaid	nightcap
headache	hereto	household	invoice	leapfrog	lowdown	milkman	nightclothes
headband	hereunto	housekeeper	ironclad	leasehold	lowland	millstone	nightclub
headfirst	hereupon	housewarming	itself	leftovers	lukewarm	millstream	nightdress
headlight	herewith	housewife	jackpot	letterhead	lumberjack	mockup	nightfall
headline	herself	housework	jailbird	levelheaded	madhouse	molehill	nightgown
headlock	hideaway	hovercraft	jawbone	lifeblood	mainland	moonlight	nightshade
headlong	highland	however	jellyfish	lifeboat	mainstay	moonshine	nightshirt
headmaster	highlight	humankind	jigsaw	lifeguard	mainstream	moreover	nighttime
headmistress	highroad	hummingbird	keepsake	lifelong	makeshift	motherland	nobody
headphones	highway	humpback	keyboard	lifetime	manhandle	motorboat	noontime
headquarters	hillside	hunchback	keyhole	liftoff	manhole	motorcar	notebook
headrest	hilltop	huntsman	keynote	lightheaded	manhood	motorcycle	noteworthy
headset	hindmost	iceberg	keystone	lighthearted	manhunt	mouthpiece	nothing
headstrong	hindquarter	icebound	kickback	lighthouse	mankind	mudguard	nowadays
headway	hindsight	icebreaker	kickoff	lightweight	manpower	namesake	nowhere
hearsay	holdup	income	kidnap	likewise	marketplace	necktie	nutshell
heartache	homecoming	indoors	killjoy	limelight	marksman	needlework	oarsman

Appendix F: (cont.) Sample compound words (1,126) (repurposed from firstschoolyears.com)

oatmeal	outdated	outset	overheat	piggyback	pothole	riverside	schoolmistress
offbeat	outdo	outshine	overlap	pigheaded	potluck	roadside	schoolroom
offhand	outdoor	outside	overlay	pigpen	powerboat	roadway	schoolteacher
offset	outdoors	outskirts	overlook	pigsty	powerhouse	roommate	scrapbook
offshoot	outermost	outsmart	overpower	pigtail	pullover	roughneck	screenplay
offshore	outfield	outspoken	oversee	pillowcase	pushover	roundabout	screwdriver
offspring	outfox	outstanding	oversight	pincushion	quicksand	roundup	seaboard
oncoming	outgo	outstay	oversleep	pineapple	quickstep	rowboat	seacoast
oneself	outgoing	outwear	overthrow	pinhole	racecourse	runaway	seafarer
ongoing	outgrow	overact	overturn	pinpoint	racehorse	runway	seafood
onlooker	outhouse	overactive	overview	pinprick	racetrack	safeguard	seagoing
onrush	outlast	overarm	pacemaker	pinup	ragtime	safekeeping	seaman
onset	outlaw	overboard	painkiller	pipeline	railroad	sailboat	seaplane
openhanded	outlay	overcast	pancake	pitchfork	railway	saltshaker	seaport
otherwise	outline	overcoat	paperback	pitfall	rainbow	saltwater	searchlight
otherworldly	outlive	overcome	paperweight	playground	raincoat	sandstone	seashell
ourselves	outlook	overcook	paperwork	playmate	rainfall	sandstorm	seashore
outbid	outlying	overdo	passport	playpen	rainstorm	saucepan	seasickness
outboard	outnumber	overdose	password	plaything	rainwater	sawdust	seaside
outbound	outpatient	overdrive	patchwork	pocketbook	rattlesnake	sawmill	seaweed
outbreak	outplay	overdue	pathway	pocketknife	rearmost	scarecrow	seaworthy
outbuilding	outpost	overflow	payload	pointblank	redhead	scatterbrain	secondhand
outburst	output	overfull	payoff	policeman	redskin	schoolboy	sendoff
outcast	outrage	overgrown	payroll	policewoman	redwood	schoolchild	setback
outclass	outreach	overhang	peacemaker	popcorn	ringleader	schoolgirl	shakedown
outcome	outright	overhaul	peacetime	popeyed	ringside	schoolhouse	shakeup
outcrop	outrun	overhead	penknife	porthole	ringworm	schoolmaster	shamefaced
outcry	outsell	overhear	pickpocket	potbelly	riverbed	schoolmate	shareholder

sharpshooter
shellfish
shipbuilding
shipmate
shipshape
shipwreck
shipyard
shoehorn
shoelace
shoemaker
shopkeeper
shoplifter
shoreline
shortcake
shortchange
shortcoming
shorthand
shortsighted
shotgun
showcase
showdown
showman
showoff
shutdown
shuteye
sickbay
sickbed
sideboard
sideburns
sidecar

sidekick
sideline
sidelong
sidesaddle
sidestep
sidestroke
sidetrack
sidewalk
sideways
sightseeing
signpost
silkworm
singsong
skullcap
skylight
skyline
skyrocket
skyscraper
skywriting
slaughterhouse
sledgehammer
sleepwalking
sleepyhead
slingshot
snowball
snowplow
snowshoe
snowstorm
softball
somebody

someday
somehow
someone
someplace
something
sometime
sometimes
someway
somewhat
somewhere
songbird
soundproof
soundtrack
southeast
southwest
spacecraft
spaceman
spaceship
speakeasy
speedway
spellbind
spellbound
sportsman
sportswear
spotlight
springboard
springtime
spyglass
stagecoach
staircase

stairway
stalemate
standby
standstill
starfish
starlight
stateroom
stateside
statesman
steadfast
steamboat
steamroller
steamship
steeplechase
steeplejack
stepbrother
stepchild
stepdaughter
stepfather
stepladder
stepmother
stepparent
steppingstone
stepsister
stepson
stillbirth
stockbroker
stockholder
stockpile
stockyard

stopgap
stopwatch
storehouse
storekeeper
storeroom
stouthearted
stowaway
straightedge
straightforward
strawberry
streamlined
streetcar
strikeout
stronghold
suitcase
summertime
sunburn
sunday
sundial
sundown
sunflower
sunglasses
sunlight
sunlit
sunrise
sunset
sunshine
sunspot
sunstroke
sunup

superhighway
superhuman
supermarket
surfboard
sweepstakes
sweetbread
sweetheart
switchboard
swordfish
swordplay
swordsman
tablecloth
tablespoon
tableware
taillight
takeoff
teammate
teardrop
teaspoon
telltale
textbook
thanksgiving
themselves
thereabouts
thereafter
thereat
thereby
therefore
therein
thereunto

thereupon
thickset
thighbone
thoroughfare
threadbare
threesome
throughout
throwback
thumbnail
thunderbolt
thundercloud
thunderhead
thundershower
thunderstorm
thunderstruck
tidewater
tightfisted
tightlipped
tightrope
timekeeper
timepiece
timetable
tinfoil
toenail
tollgate
tombstone
toothpaste
toothpick
topcoat
topflight

topmost
topsoil
touchdown
townspeople
trademark
tradesman
treadmill
tribesman
troublemaker
truckload
trustworthy
tryout
turnabout
turnout
turnover
turnstile
turntable
twosome
typeface
typewriter
underachieve
underact
underarm
underbelly
underbid
undercarriage
undercharge
underclothes
undercoat
undercook

Appendix F: (cont.) Sample compound words (1,126) (repurposed from firstschoolyears.com)

undercover	underpay	underweight	upstage	wartime	weatherman	wholesale	woodcraft
undercurrent	underpowered	underworld	upstairs	washboard	weatherproof	wholesome	woodcutter
undercut	underrate	underwrite	upstanding	washcloth	weekday	whomever	woodland
underdeveloped	undersea	upbeat	upstart	washout	weekend	widespread	woodpecker
underdog	undersell	upbringing	upstate	washroom	weightlifting	wildcat	woodwork
underdone	undershirt	upcoming	upstream	washtub	whalebone	wildfire	workbench
undereducated	undershorts	upcountry	upsurge	wasteland	whatever	windfall	workbook
underestimate	underside	update	upswing	watchdog	wheelbarrow	windmill	workday
underfed	undersigned	updraft	uptake	watchman	wheelchair	windowpane	workhorse
underfoot	undersized	upend	uptown	watchword	whereabouts	windowsill	workhouse
undergarment	underskirt	upgrade	upturn	waterfall	whereas	windshield	workman
undergo	underspend	uphill	viewpoint	waterfowl	whereat	windsock	workmanlike
undergraduate	understaffed	uphold	vineyard	waterfront	whereby	windstorm	workout
underground	understand	upkeep	volleyball	watermark	wherefore	windswept	workroom
undergrowth	understate	uplift	waistcoat	watermelon	wherefrom	wingspan	workshop
underhand	understood	upon	waistline	waterproof	wherein	wintertime	worktable
underhanded	understudy	uppercut	walkout	watershed	whereof	wisecrack	worldwide
underlayer	undersupply	uppermost	wallflower	waterspout	whereto	wishbone	worthwhile
underlie	undersurface	upraise	wallpaper	watertight	whereupon	witchcraft	wrongdoer
underline	undertake	upright	warehouse	waterway	wherewith	withdraw	yachtsman
underlying	undertaker	uprising	warfare	waterworks	whichever	withhold	yardstick
undermine	undertrained	uproar	warhead	waveform	whirlpool	within	yearbook
undernourished	undervalue	uproot	warlord	wavelength	whirlwind	without	yourself
underpants	underwater	upset	warpath	waxworks	whitewash	withstand	
underpass	underwear	upshot	warship	wayside	wholehearted	wonderland	

Appendix G: Frequent hyphenated words

Top 100 hyphenated words in the *British National Corpus* (BNC) (retrieved from http://corpus.byu.edu/bnc)

long-term	day-to-day	one-day	sitting-room
co-operation	south-west	up-to-date	attorney-general
so-called	twenty-four	MS-DOS	Jean-Claude
full-time	five-year	long-standing	built-in
part-time	secretary-general	co-ordinated	self-employed
no-one	one-third	set-up	wide-ranging
working-class	pre-tax	two-year	line-up
short-term	would-be	back-up	semi-finals
north-east	co-ordination	twenty-one	Sally-Anne
post-war	left-wing	short-lived	world-wide
well-known	eighteenth-century	co-ordinate	co-ordinating
decision-making	semi-final	second-hand	half-way
middle-class	first-class	twentieth-century	self-esteem
make-up	well-being	three-dimensional	twenty-two
south-east	in-house	half-time	far-reaching
old-fashioned	middle-aged	pre-war	inner-city
twenty-five	three-year	one-off	by-election
two-thirds	co-operate	build-up	forty-five
large-scale	t-shirt	sub-committee	break-up
co-operative	follow-up	object-oriented	co-op
vice-president	x-ray	in-service	non-existent
Hewlett-Packard	right-hand	co-ordinator	small-scale
nineteenth-century	three-quarters	policy-making	time-consuming
north-west	Anglo-Saxon	dining-room	present-day
right-wing	socio-economic	left-hand	drawing-room

Highest frequency (4,052) lowest frequency (380).

Appendix G: (cont.) Frequent hyphenated words

Top 100 hyphenated words in the *Corpus of Contemporary American English (COCA)* (retrieved from http://corpus.byu.edu/coca)

voice-over	twenty-five	high-profile	twenty-four	long-standing
e-mail	uh-huh	all-time	brand-new	one-time
long-term	co-host	day-to-day	half-hour	thirty-five
mm-hmm	health-care	high-speed	cease-fire	one-year
so-called	wal-mart	hip-hop	medium-high	three-quarters
African-American	all-star	pre-formatted	long-distance	10-year
full-time	decision-making	on-line	president-elect	open-ended
self-esteem	large-scale	high-quality	fund-raising	first-time
unidentified-male	low-income	would-be	self-efficacy	in-depth
follow-up	African-Americans	three-year	3-D	19th-century
short-term	unidentified-female	good-bye	face-to-face	half-dozen
high-tech	two-year	re-election	Coca-Cola	cross-country
well-being	e-mails	same-sex	working-class	24-hour
well-known	five-year	year-round	all-purpose	three-dimensional
t-shirt	x-ray	Al-Qaeda	best-selling	on-site
two-thirds	hands-on	real-life	self-determination	award-winning
old-fashioned	middle-aged	nineteenth-century	high-end	last-minute
one-third	four-year	low-fat	low-cost	at-risk
middle-class	t-shirts	right-wing	high-risk	inner-city
part-time	built-in	black-and-white	high-level	long-range

Highest frequency (54,196) lowest frequency (1,985).

Appendix H: Screenshot from COCA (collocate queries)

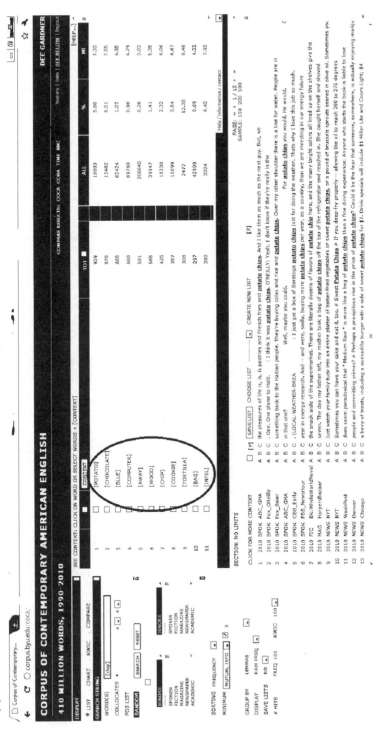

Glossary

affixes
cover term for both prefixes and suffixes.

allomorphs
different forms of the same morpheme (same meaning), varying either by sound (e.g. head*ed*, bak*ed*, shav*ed*), spelling (e.g. flex*ible*, drink*able*), or both (e.g. *il*logical, *im*possible, *in*direct, *ir*responsible, *un*forgettable).

balanced corpus
a corpus that covers a range of different registers, each with approximately the same number of running words (tokens).

beginner's paradox
term to address the fact that beginning English language learners often need to read in order to gain new vocabulary, but they also need sufficient vocabulary in order to read in the first place.

BICS
Basic Interpersonal Communicative Skills are basic language skills acquired by English Language Learners through everyday communication in social situations, such as on the playground, school bus, and sports field. BICS is non-specialized, context-embedded language that is not cognitively challenging. ELLs usually acquire BICS in six months to two years. (Compare with **CALP**.)

bilingual dictionary
a dictionary in which entries consist of words or phrases in a target language (e.g. English) and their translations in another language (e.g. Spanish).

bilingualized dictionary
a dictionary in which entries consist of (a) words or phrases in a target language (e.g. English) and their translations in another language (e.g. Spanish), and (b) a definition and example sentence in the target language (e.g. English).

CALP
Cognitive Academic Language Proficiency is language ability necessary to function well in academic settings. It is knowledge of the specialized language of school that is context-reduced and cognitively challenging. Some ELLs may acquire CALP in five to seven years, but others may never acquire it at levels needed to be successful in school. (Compare with **BICS**.)

cognates
words in one language that have similar forms to words in another language, and also similar meanings (e.g. English = *family*; Spanish = *familia*).

collocates (noun, singular *collocate*)
words that consistently co-occur with a target (node) word (e.g. common collocates of the target noun *cream* include *sour*, *whipped*, *heavy*, *fresh*, and *white*). Collocates are also referred to in some cases as *collocations*.

collocation
the condition that exists when two or more words consistently co-occur (beyond chance) within a certain distance of each other in actual linguistic contexts. Collocation exists in two major ways: *fixed collocations*, in which words co-occur in multiword expressions (e.g. *kicked the bucket, pop the question, chew out, break up, in order to, carbon dioxide*), and *thematic collocations*, in which words are closely related by a common theme or concept (e.g. *mummy* and *pharaoh*; *whip* and *cream*; *crime* and *investigate*).

complex discourse markers
discourse markers composed of more than one word (e.g. *in addition to, on the other hand, as a result of, for example, in contrast*). See also *discourse markers*.

compounds
lexical items composed of more than one word. Open compounds are separated by a space between words (e.g. *post office, science fiction, school bus*), whereas closed compounds have no space between words (e.g. *greenhouse, keyboard, notebook*).

concordancer
electronic tool that allows users to bring together multiple sentences containing the same word or phrase from a text or corpus.

context
the parts of a text or situation that work together to convey meaning.

context-free meaning
term used to describe the condition when a word has primarily one meaning, regardless of the various contexts in which it may occur (e.g. *photosynthesis*, *mitosis*, and *carbonation*).

corpus
a collection of materials (written or spoken) compiled for the purpose of linguistic investigation.

cotext
windows of actual text immediately surrounding a specific target (node) word.

deep orthography
a writing system in which words may not have clear symbol-to-sound correspondences (e.g. English, French). (See **shallow orthography** and **orthographic depth hypothesis**.)

derivation
morphological change (adding prefixes or suffixes) to a word that alter its meaning (e.g. logical → illogical), or change its part of speech (e.g. eat → eater).

discourse markers
lexical items that signal discourse-level relationships within a text (*however, moreover, therefore, in addition, for example, in contrast, furthermore*, etc.).

extensive reading
the reading of large quantities of material that is not too difficult for the reader.

false cognates
also known as *false friends*, are words in one language that have similar forms to words in another language, but their meanings are actually different (e.g. *bald* in German means *soon*, not *hairless*).

fixed collocations
collocations that have become frozen over time through constant usage. They tend to be lexical items in their own right (e.g. idioms, phrasal verbs, compound nouns) or combinations of words with strong co-occurring patterns (e.g. *dry eyes, sunny days*).

fourth-grade slump
also known as the *intermediate slump*, is a documented phenomenon that occurs at about the fourth grade, when nine- and ten-year-old children find it difficult to transition from reading easy materials, such as narrative fiction, to reading more difficult expository materials, such as textbooks and other school materials that convey complex information and concepts.

free roots
morphological parts of words (morphemes) that also function as words in their own right (e.g. the *hook* in *unhook*; the *play* in *player*; the *thought* in *thoughtless*).

front-loading
the practice of pre-teaching the unknown vocabulary in a text or task that learners are expected to negotiate.

gloss
the translation equivalent of a word or phrase.

graded readers
books that provide repetitive encounters with high frequency words in carefully designed contexts, such as simplified classics or original books written with both vocabulary presentation and interesting content in mind (e.g. *Oxford Bookworms Library*, 2011). The books are "graded" by difficulty level, determined mainly by the total number of different words used in the books.

grammaticalized lexis
the view that lexis (vocabulary) is primary in the language and grammar is secondary or supportive. (Compare with **lexicalized grammar**.)

heterographs
words with the same pronunciation, different spellings, and different meanings (e.g. *to, two too*).

heterophones
words that are spelled the same, but have different pronunciations and different meanings (e.g. *bow* – bending the body to show respect vs. *bow* – a weapon with a string).

homographs
words with the same spelling, but different meanings (e.g. *potato chip, computer chip*). Note that heterophones and some homophones are homographs in their written forms.

homonyms
superordinate term for all groups of words sharing the same written (homographs) or spoken forms (homophones).

homophones
words with (a) the same pronunciations, same spellings, but different meanings (e.g. *roll* – a document for keeping attendance vs. *roll* – a small rounded piece of bread), or (b) the same pronunciation, but different spellings, and different meanings (e.g. *two, too, to*).

idiom principle
the principle which highlights the fact that much of the language is comprised of pre-structured (pre-fabricated) word combinations. (Compare with **open-choice principle**.)

idioms
multiword items with figurative meanings established through common usage. The meanings of idioms are generally not understandable through analysis of the meanings of their component word parts (e.g. *dyed in the wool, dead as a doornail, up in the night, kick the bucket*).

inflection
morphological changes (primarily adding suffixes) to a word that alter its grammatical function, but not its primary meaning (e.g. *jump → jumps, jumping, jumped*).

integrated skills
a curricular approach that emphasizes all four major modes of communication: listening, speaking, reading, and writing.

labels
a specialized term emphasizing the forms of words (either spoken or written), as opposed to the meanings of words.

lemma
a set of words sharing the same base form and part of speech, but containing different inflectional suffixes (e.g. the verbs *climb, climbs, climbing, climbed*).

leveled readers
reading materials that have been judged to be appropriate for specific language proficiency levels. Criteria for judging reading difficulty levels include lexical complexity, sentence complexity, presence or absence of useful visual aids (photos, diagrams, etc.), and so forth.

lexemes
lemmas with unique senses (e.g. *roll* and *rolls* – noun lemma meaning "small round piece/s of bread" vs. *roll* and *rolls* – noun lemma meaning "document/s for taking attendance").

lexical density
a measure determined by calculating the number of different words (types) divided by the number of total words (tokens).

lexical item
a word or phrase.

lexicalized grammar
the view that grammar is primary in the language and that lexis (vocabulary) is secondary or supportive. (Compare with **grammaticalized lexis**.)

lexicon
the store of words in an entire language, or the store of words in an individual mind.

lexis
vocabulary (words).

monitor corpus
a corpus that is added to on a regular basis so that changes in language usage can be seen over time.

monolingual dictionary
a dictionary in which word entries consist of definitions and example sentences in one language only.

morphemes
word parts that convey either lexical (content) meaning (e.g. the *play* in *playing*) or grammatical meaning (e.g. the *ing* in *playing*).

morphological awareness
the ability to recognize words parts and word segments that convey either lexical (content) or grammatical meaning.

multiword items
combinations of words that function as one lexical unit – e.g. idioms (*kick the bucket, pop the question*, etc.), phrasal verbs (*break down, chew out*, etc.), stock phrases (*good morning, excuse me*, etc.), prefabrications (*the point is, the fact that*, etc.), and so forth.

off-list words
words that are not on traditional high frequency lists. They tend to be either specialized to a particular content area (discipline) or low frequency in general usage.

opaque orthography
writing systems like English and French containing many words that do not sound the way they are spelled (e.g. *through, enough, psychology, comb, philosophy*).

open-choice principle
the principle which highlights the fact that some of the language is composed of unique word combinations, constructed on a word-by-word basis. (Compare with **idiom principle**.)

open compounds
two or more words separated by spaces, but expressing one combined meaning (e.g. *United Kingdom, world war, interest rates, exchange rate mechanism, carbon dioxide emissions*).

open corpus
a corpus that can be added to.

orthographic depth hypothesis
hypothesis which states that word recognition processes are easier in languages with clear symbol–sound correspondences (**shallow orthographies**) than in languages with opaque symbol–sound correspondences (**deep orthographies**).

polysemes
words that have different, but related senses (e.g. *He broke his leg; The cup broke; She broke his heart*).

range
a calculation which indicates the number of different texts or registers that a word or phrase appears in.

reading hypothesis
the claim that the reading of large amounts of high-interest, authentic books (not made for school) will produce the vocabulary knowledge necessary for ELLs to transition to more complex academic reading. Many espousing this hypothesis assume that vocabulary acquisition through reading happens subconsciously while readers are attending to general comprehension of a text.

register
a variety of the language that has unique linguistic characteristics.

shallow orthography
a writing system in which words have clear symbol-to-sound correspondences (e.g. Finnish, Italian, Spanish). (See **deep orthography** and **orthographic depth hypothesis**.)

sight words
traditionally, sight words have been defined as words without clear connections between their spelling and their pronunciation (e.g. *give, could*). Sight words have also been associated with high frequency words of English and beginning reading in English. The Dolch and Fry lists are two of the most cited lists of sight words. However, some confusion exists in the connection of these lists with the term *sight words*, because the lists contain many words that do have spellings that match their pronunciations (e.g. *him, had*).

task-based instruction
instruction in which learners acquire language while performing meaningful tasks.

thematic collocations
collocations that occur when two or more words co-occur frequently (beyond chance) as a result of their relationships to certain themes or concepts (e.g. *mummy, pharaoh, embalming*; *tree, branch, leaves*).

theme-based instruction
instruction organized around themes to improve the recycling and potential acquisition of theme-related language.

threshold hypothesis
hypothesis which states that first language reading skills do not transfer well to second-language reading until the reader acquires a critical mass of second-language knowledge (vocabulary, grammar, syntax, discourse pragmatics, etc.).

token
an occurrence (count) of a type, phrase, or other lexical item.

transparent orthography
writing systems like Finnish and Italian containing many words that sound the way they are spelled.

type
a distinct series of letters bordered by spaces or punctuation (e.g. *car cat chair mitosis lunar*).

word family
a set of words sharing the same base form, but containing different inflectional and derivational suffixes, and possibly coming from different parts of speech (e.g. *agree, agrees, agreeing, agreed, agreement, agreements, agreeable, disagree, disagrees, disagreeing, disagreed, disagreement, disagreements, disagreeable*).

Annotated further reading (books)

Aitchison, J. (2003). *Words in the Mind*, 3rd ed., Oxford: Blackwell.
A classic introductory text exploring psycholinguistic approaches to vocabulary.

Carter, R. (2012). *Vocabulary: Applied linguistic perspectives*, Routledge Classics Edition, Abingdon: Routledge.
A key survey of issues first published in 1987.

Cobb. T. (2012). *The Compleat Lexical Tutor*, online, available at: www.lextutor.ca.
A widely used resource that uses computer technology to help with the learning and teaching of vocabulary.

McCarthy, M. (1990). *Vocabulary*, Oxford: Oxford University Press.
A classic teachers' guide with a range of classroom-based tasks and activities.

Nation, I. S. P. (1990). *Teaching and Learning Vocabulary*, New York: Newbury House.
A foundational and influential text on second-language vocabulary pedagogy.

Nation, I. S. P. (2000). *Learning Vocabulary in Another Language*, Cambridge: Cambridge University Press.
A widely used and cited book on teaching and learning vocabulary that updates and extends Nation (1990).

Nattinger, J. and DeCarrico, J. (1992). *Lexical Phrases and Language Teaching*, Oxford: Oxford University Press.
A seminal book that was one of the first to draw attention to the importance of formulaic language and its implications for the language classroom.

Read, J. (2000). *Assessing Vocabulary*, Cambridge: Cambridge University Press.
A foundational text on the testing of vocabulary in second and foreign language learning.

Schmitt, N. (2000). *Vocabulary in Language Teaching*, Cambridge: Cambridge University Press.
An accessible and wide-ranging introduction to key issues.

Schmitt, N. (2010). *Researching Vocabulary*, Basingstoke: Palgrave/Macmillan.
   A lucid and comprehensive guide to lexical research aimed primarily at the research community.

Sinclair, J. (1992). *From Corpus to Collocation*, Oxford: Oxford University Press.
   A seminal text on the uses of corpora in the study of vocabulary.

Wray, A. (2002). *Formulaic Language and the Lexicon*, Cambridge: Cambridge University Press.
   A foundational theoretical study of lexical patterning.

References

Adolphs, S. and Schmitt, N. (2003). Lexical coverage of spoken discourse. *Applied Linguistics*, 24(4), 425–438.

Alderson, J. C. (1984). Reading in a foreign language: a reading problem or a language problem? In J. Charles Alderson and A. H. Urquhart (eds.), *Reading in a Foreign Language* (pp. 1–24). London: Longman.

Anderson, N. (2008). *Practical English Language Teaching: Reading*. New York: McGraw-Hill.

Anderson, R. C. (1996). Research foundations to support wide reading. In V. Greaney (ed.), *Promoting Reading in Developing Countries* (pp. 55–77). Newark, DE: International Reading Association.

Anderson, R. C. and Freebody, P. (1981). Vocabulary knowledge. In J. T. Guthrie (ed.), *Comprehension and Teaching: Research reviews* (pp. 77–117). Newark, DE: International Reading Association.

Anthony, L. (2011). *AntConc: A freeware concordance program for Windows, Macintosh OS X, and Linux*. Available at: www.antlab.sci.waseda.ac.jp/software.html.

Beck, I. L., McKeown, M. G. and Kucan, L. (2002). *Bringing Words to Life: Robust vocabulary instruction*. New York. The Guilford Press.

Beck, I. L., McKeown, M. G. and McCaslin, E. S. (1983). Vocabulary development: all contexts are not created equal. *The Elementary School Journal*, 83(3), 177–181.

Bellairs, J. (1983). *The Mummy, the Will, and the Crypt*. New York: Dial Books for Young Readers.

Biber, D. (1988). *Variation Across Speech and Writing*. New York: Cambridge University Press.

Biber, D., Johansson, S., Leech, G., Conrad, S. and Finegan, E. (1999). *Longman Grammar of Spoken and Written English*. London: Longman.

Biemiller, A. (1999). *Language and Reading Success*. Cambridge, MA: Brookline Books.

Biemiller, A. (2003). Oral comprehension sets the ceiling on reading comprehension. *American Educator*, Spring. Available at www.aft.org/newspubs/periodicals/ae/spring2003/hirschsboral.cfm.

Biemiller, A. (2005). Size and sequence in vocabulary development: implications for choosing words for primary grade vocabulary instruction. In E. H. Hiebert and M. L. Kamil (eds.), *Teaching and Learning Vocabulary: Bringing research to practice* (pp. 223–242). Mahwah, NJ: Lawrence Erlbaum.

Biemiller, A. (2009). Teaching vocabulary: early, direct, and sequential. In M. F. Graves (ed.), *Essential Readings on Vocabulary Instruction* (pp. 28–34). Newark, DE: International Reading Association.

Biemiller, A. (2010). *Words Worth Teaching: Closing the vocabulary gap*. Columbus, OH: McGraw-Hill.

Bisel, S. C. (1990). *The Secrets of Vesuvius*. New York: Scholastic.

Bossers, B. (1992). *Reading in Two Languages: A study of reading comprehension in Dutch as a second language and in Turkish as a first language*. Rotterdam: Drukkerij Van Driel.

Boulton, A. (2009). Data-driven learning: reasonable fears and rational reassurance. *Indian Journal of Applied Linguistics*, 35(1), 81–106.

Brainard, J., Gray-Wilson, N., Harwood, J., Karasov, C., Kraus, D. and Willan, J. (2011). *CK-12 Life Science: Honors for middle school*. Retrieved on March 8, 2011, from www.ck12.org/flexbook/book/731.

Brockett, S., Green, R., Greenberg, D., Kershaw, J., Mergerdichian, B. and O'Donnell, C. (2010). *CK-12 Middle School Math – Grade 6*. Retrieved on March 8, 2011, from www.ck12.org/flexbook/book/2832.

Cambridge Learner's Dictionary (4th ed.). (2012). Cambridge: Cambridge University Press.

Carter, R. (1998). *Vocabulary: Applied linguistic perspectives* (2nd ed.). London: Routledge.

Carver, R. P. (1994). Percentage of unknown vocabulary words in text as a function of the relative difficulty of the text: Implications and instruction. *Journal of Reading Behavior*, 26(4), 413–437.

Carver, R. P. and Leibert, R. W. (1995). The effect of reading library books at different levels of difficulty upon gain in reading ability. *Reading Research Quarterly*, 30(1), 26–28.

Chall, J. S. (1983). *Stages of Reading Development*. New York: McGraw-Hill.

Chall, J. S. (1996). *Stages of Reading Development* (2nd ed.). Fort Worth, TX: Harcourt Brace.

Chall, J. S. (2000). *The Academic Achievement Challenge: What really works in the classroom?* New York: Guilford Press.

Chall, J. S. and Jacobs, V. A. (2003). Poor children's fourth-grade slump: the cause, the cure. *American Educator*, 27(1), online, available at: www.aft.org/newspubs/periodicals/ae/spring2003/hirschsbclassic.cfm.

Chall, J. S., Jacobs, V. A. and Baldwin, L. E. (1990). *The Reading Crises: Why poor children fall behind*. Cambridge, MA: Harvard University Press.

Cho, K. and Krashen, S. D. (1994). Acquisition of vocabulary from the Sweet Valley Kids series: adult ESL acquisition. *Journal of Reading*, 37(8), 662–667.

Clarke, M. A. (1979). Reading in Spanish and English: evidence from adult ESL students. *Language Learning*, 29, 121–150.

Clarke, M. A. (1980). The short circuit hypothesis of ESL reading – or when language competence interferes with reading performance. *Modern Language Journal*, 64, 203–209.

Coady, J. (1993). Research on ESL/EFL vocabulary acquisition: putting it in context. In T. Huckin, M. Haynes and J. Coady (eds.), *Second Language Reading and Vocabulary Learning* (pp. 3–23). Norwood, NJ: Ablex.

Coady, J. (1997). L2 vocabulary acquisition: a synthesis of the research. In J. Coady and T. Huckin (eds.): *Second Language Vocabulary Acquisition* (pp. 272–290). Cambridge: Cambridge University Press.

Cobb, T. (1999). Breadth and depth of lexical acquisition with hands-on concordancing. *Computer Assisted Language Learning*, 12(4), 345–360.

Cobb, T. (2012). *The Compleat Lexical Tutor*. Available at www.lextutor.ca.

Cobuild Corpus (1980–). *Cobuild Corpus* (also known as *Bank of English*). London: Harper Collins.

Corson, D. (1997). The learning and use of academic English words. *Language Learning*, 47(4), 671–718.

Coté, N., Goldman, S. R., and Saul, E. U. (1998). Students making sense of informational text: relations between processing and representation. *Discourse Processes*, 25(1), 1–53.

Coxhead, A. (2000). A new academic word list. *TESOL Quarterly*, 34(2), 213–238.

Crystal, D. (1995). *The Cambridge Encyclopedia of the English Language*. New York: Cambridge University Press.

Cummins, J. (1979). Cognitive/academic language proficiency, linguistic interdependence, the optimum age question and some other matters. *Working Papers on Bilingualism*, 19, 121–129.

Cummins, J. (1981). The role of primary language development in promoting educational success for language minority students. In California State Department of Education (ed.), *Schooling and Language Minority Students: A theoretical framework*. Los Angeles, CA: Evaluation, Dissemination and Assessment Center, California State University.

Cunningham, P. M. (1998). The multisyllabic word dilemma: helping students build meaning, spell, and read "big" words. *Reading and Writing Quarterly: Overcoming Learning Difficulties*, 14, 189–218.

Davies, Mark. (2008–) *The Corpus of Contemporary American English* (COCA): 410+ million words, 1990–present. Available online at www.americancorpus.org.

Davies, Mark. (2010–) *The Corpus of Historical American English* (COHA): 400+ million words, 1810–2009. Available online at http://corpus.byu.edu/coha.

Davies, M. and Gardner, D. (2010). *A Frequency Dictionary of Contemporary American English: Word sketches, collocates, and thematic lists*. Abingdon: Routledge.

Day, R. R. and Bamford, J. (1998). *Extensive Reading in the Second Language Classroom*. Cambridge: Cambridge University Press.

Decoo, W. (2011). *Systemization in Foreign Language Teaching: Monitoring content progression*. Abingdon: Routledge.

Dolch, E. W. (1948). *Problems in Reading*. Champaign, IL: Garrard Press.

Dow, L. (1990). *Whales: Great creatures of the world*. New York: Weldon Owen Pty Limited.

Eldridge, J. (2008). No, there isn't an "academic vocabulary," but... A reader responds to K. Hyland and P. Tse's "Is there an 'academic vocabulary'?" *TESOL Quarterly*, 42, 109–113.

Elley, W. B. (1991). Acquiring literacy in a second language: the effect of book-based programs. *Language Learning*, 41(3), 375–411.

Engels, L. K. (1968). The fallacy of word counts. *International Review of Applied Linguistics in Language Teaching (IRAL)*, 6(1/4), 213–231.

Erman, B. and Warren, B. (2000). The idiom principle and the open choice principle. *Text*, 20(1), 29–62.

First School Years (2006). Online educational resource. Available online at http://firstschoolyears.com.

Firth, J. R. (1951). Modes of meaning. *Essays and Studies* (pp. 118–149). London: English Association.

Fletcher, W. H. (2010). *kfNgram: A free stand-alone Windows program for linguistic research*. Available at www.kwicfinder.com/kfNgram/kfNgramHelp.html.

Flowerdew, L. (2009). Applying corpus linguistics to pedagogy. *International Journal of Corpus Linguistics*, 14(3), 393–417.

Folse, K. S. (2004). *Vocabulary Myths: Applying second language research to classroom teaching*. Ann Arbor, MI: University of Michigan Press.

Fountas, I. C. and Pinnell, G. S. (2006). *Leveled Books (K-8): Matching texts to readers for effective reading*. Portsmouth, NH: Heinemann.

Fry, E. (1996). *1,000 Instant Words*. Lincolnwood, IL: NTC/Contemporary Publishing Co.

Gardner, D. (1994). The effects of preunderlining as a text signaling device to facilitate adult ESL readers' processing of contextualized idioms. Master's thesis. Brigham Young University.

Gardner, D. (1999). Vocabulary acquisition through reading: assessing the lexical composition of theme-based text collections in upper-elementary education. Doctoral dissertation. Northern Arizona University.

Gardner, D. (2004). Vocabulary input through extensive reading: a comparison of words found in Children's narrative and expository reading materials. *Applied Linguistics*, 25(1), 1–37.

Gardner, D. (2007a). Validating the construct of Word in applied corpus-based vocabulary research: a critical survey. *Applied Linguistics*, 28(2), 241–265.

Gardner, D. (2007b). Children's immediate understanding of vocabulary: contexts and dictionary definitions. *Reading Psychology*, 28(4), 331–373.

Gardner, D. (2008). Vocabulary recycling in children's authentic reading materials: a corpus-based investigation of narrow reading. *Reading in a Foreign Language*, 20(1), 92–122.

Gardner, D. and Davies, M. (2007). Pointing out frequent phrasal verbs: a corpus-based analysis. *TESOL Quarterly*, 41(2), 339–359.

Gardner, D. and Davies, M. (under review). A new academic vocabulary list.

Gardner, D. and Nance, G. (2001). *Bridge Books Series B (Chinese/English)*. 25 Bilingual Instructional Readers. Springville, UT: Language Literacy Links.

Gilner, L. (2011). A primer on the General Service List. *Reading in a Foreign Language*, 23(1), 65–83.

Goldenberg, C. (2008). Teaching English language learners: what the research does – and does not – say. *American Educator*, Summer, 8–44.

Grabe, W. (2002). Narrative and expository macro-genres. In A. M. Johns (ed.), *Genre in the Classroom: Multiple perspectives* (pp. 249–267). Mahwah, NJ: Lawrence Erlbaum.

Grabe, W. (2009). *Reading in a Second Language*. Cambridge: Cambridge University Press.

Graves, M. (2006). *The Vocabulary Book: Learning and instruction*. Newark, DE: International Reading Association.

Hakim, J. (1994). *A History of US: Liberty for all*. New York: Oxford University Press.

Hancioğlu, N., Neufeld, S., and Eldridge, J. (2008). Through the looking glass and into the land of lexico-grammar. *English for Specific Purposes*, 27, 459–479.

Hart, B. and Risley, T. R. (1995). *Meaningful Differences in the Everyday Experiences of Young American Children*. Baltimore, MD: P. H. Brookes.

Hart, B. and Risley, T. R. (2003). The early catastrophe: the 30 million word gap by age 3. *American Educator*, 27(1), 4–9.

Hatch, E. and Brown, C. (1995). *Vocabulary, Semantics, and Language Education*. Cambridge: Cambridge University Press.

Heatley, A., Nation, I. S. P., and Coxhead, A. (2002). RANGE and FREQUENCY programs. Available at www.victoria.ac.nz/lals/staff/paul-nation.aspx.

Hu, M. and Nation, I. S. P. (2000). Vocabulary density and reading comprehension. *Reading in a Foreign Language*, 13(1), 403–430.

Hulstijn, J. (2001). Intentional and incidental second language vocabulary learning: a reappraisal of elaboration, rehearsal and automaticity. In P. Robinson (ed.), *Cognition and Second Language instruction* (pp. 258–286). Cambridge: Cambridge University Press.

Hunston, S. (2002). *Corpora in Applied Linguistics*. Cambridge: Cambridge University Press.

Hwang, K. and Nation, I. S. P. (1995). Where should general service vocabulary stop and special purposes vocabulary begin? *System*, 23(1), 35–41.

Hyland, K. (2008). Academic clusters: text patterning in published and postgraduate writing. *International Journal of Applied Linguistics*, 18(1), 41–62.

Hyland, K. and Tse, P. (2007). Is there an "academic vocabulary"? *TESOL Quarterly*, 41(2), 235–253.

Jackendoff, R. (1995). The boundaries of the lexicon. In M. Everaert, E. van der Linden, A. Schenk and R. Schreuder (eds.), *Idioms: Structural and psychological perspectives* (pp. 133–166). Hillsdale NJ: Lawrence Erlbaum Associates.

Jackson, D. M. (1996). *The Bone Detectives*. Boston, MA: Little, Brown and Company.

Katz, L. and Frost, R. (1992). Reading in different orthographies: the orthographic depth hypothesis. In R. Frost and L. Katz (eds.), *Othography, Phonology, Morphology, and Meaning* (pp. 67–84). Amsterdam: New Holland.

Krashen, S. (1985). *The Input Hypothesis: Issues and implications*. New York: Longman.

Krashen, S. (1989). We acquire vocabulary and spelling by reading: additional evidence for the input hypothesis. *The Modern Language Journal*, 73(4), 440–464.

Krashen, S. (1993). *The Power of Reading: Insights from the research.* Englewood, CO: Libraries Unlimited.

Krashen, S. (2010). Academic language proficiency: acquired or learned? In Y.-N. Leung (ed.), *Proceedings from the 19th International Symposium on English Teaching, Taiwan* (pp. 34–43). Taipei, Taiwan.

L'Engle, M. (1962). *A Wrinkle in Time.* New York: Farrar, Straus, and Giroux.

Landes S., Leacock C., and Tengi, R. I. (1998) Building semantic concordances. In Fellbaum, C. (ed.), *WordNet: An Electronic Lexical Database* (pp. 199–216). Cambridge, MA: MIT Press.

Lauber, P. (1985). *Tales Mummies Tell.* New York: Thomas Y. Crowell.

Laufer, B. (1997). The lexical plight in second language reading: words you don't know, words you think you know, and words you can't guess. In J. Coady and T. Huckin (eds.), *Second Language Vocabulary Acquisition* (pp. 20–34). Cambridge: Cambridge University Press.

Laufer, B. and Hadar, L. (1997). Assessing the effectiveness of monolingual, bilingual, and "bilingualized" dictionaries in the comprehension and production of new words. *The Modern Language Journal,* 81(2), 189–196.

Laufer, B. and Nation, P. (1999). A vocabulary size test of controlled productive ability. *Language Testing,* 16(1), 33–51.

Liao, Y. and Fukuya, Y. J. (2004). Avoidance of phrasal verbs: the case of Chinese learners of English. *Language Learning,* 54(2), 193–226.

Liu, N. and Nation, I. S. P. (1985). Factors affecting guessing vocabulary in context. *RELC Journal,* 16(1), 33–42.

Longman Dictionary of Contemporary English, 5th ed. (2009). London: Longman.

McCarthy, M. (1999). What constitutes a basic vocabulary for spoken communication? *Studies in English Language and Literature,* 1, 233–249.

McCarthy, M. (2008). Accessing and interpreting corpus information in the teacher education context. *Language Teaching,* 41(4), 563–574.

McCarthy, M. and Carter, R. (1997). Written and spoken vocabulary. In N. Schmitt and M. McCarthy (eds.), *Vocabulary: Description, acquisition and pedagogy* (pp. 20–39). Cambridge: Cambridge University Press.

McCarthy, M. and Carter, R. (2001). Size isn't everything: spoken English, corpus, and the classroom. *TESOL Quarterly,* 35(2), 337–340.

McKeown, M. G. (1993). Creating effective definitions for young word learners. *Reading Research Quarterly,* 28, 17–31.

Mel'čuk, I. (1995). Phrasemes in language and phraseology in linguistics. In M. Everaert, E. van der Linden, A. Schenk and R. Schreuder (eds.), *Idioms: Structural and psychological perspectives* (pp. 167–232). Hillsdale, NJ: Lawrence Erlbaum Associates.

Morgan, J. and Rinvolucri, M. (2004) *Vocabulary* (2nd ed.), Oxford: Oxford University Press.

Nagy, W. (2007). Metalinguistic awareness and the vocabulary-comprehension connection. In R. K. Wagner, A. Muse and K. Tannenbaum (eds.), *Vocabulary Acquisition: Implications for reading comprehension* (pp. 52–77). New York: Guilford.

Nagy, W. and Townsend, D. (2012). Words as tools: learning academic vocabulary as language acquisition. *Reading Research Quarterly*, 47(1), 91–108.

Nagy, W. E., Anderson, R. C., and Herman, P. (1987). Learning word meanings from context during normal reading. *American Educational Research Journal*, 24, 237–270.

Nagy, W. E. and Herman, P. A. (1987). Breadth and depth of vocabulary knowledge: implications for acquisition and instruction. In M. G. McKeown and M. E. Curtis (eds.), *The Nature of Vocabulary Acquisition* (pp. 19–35). Hillsdale, NJ: Lawrence Erlbaum.

Nan, Y. and Mingfang, Z. (2009). Using VOA special English to improve advanced English learners' productive use of high frequency words. *English Teaching Forum*, 3, 26–37.

Nassaji, H. (2003). Higher-level and lower-level text processing skills in advanced ESL reading comprehension. *Modern Language Journal*, 87, 261–276.

Nation, I. S. P. (1993). Vocabulary size, growth, and use. In R. Schreuder and B. Weltens (eds.), *The Bilingual Lexicon* (pp. 115–134). Amsterdam: John Benjamins.

Nation, I. S. P. (2001). *Learning Vocabulary in Another Language*. Cambridge: Cambridge University Press.

Nation, I. S. P. (2004). A study of the most frequent word families in the British National Corpus. In P. Bogaards and B. Laufer (eds.), *Vocabulary in a Second Language: Selection, acquisition, and testing* (pp. 3–13). Philadelphia, PA: John Benjamins.

Nation, I. S. P. (2006). How large a vocabulary is needed for reading and listening? *The Canadian Modern Language Review*, 63(1), 59–82.

Nation, I. S. P. (2008). *Teaching Vocabulary: Strategies and techniques*. Boston, MA: Heinle, Cengage Learning.

Nation, P. and Waring, R. (1997). Vocabulary size, text coverage and word lists. In N. Schmitt and M. McCarthy (eds.), *Vocabulary: Description, acquisition and pedagogy* (pp. 6–19). Cambridge: Cambridge University Press.

National Reading Panel (2000). *Teaching Children to Read: An evidence-based assessment of the scientific research literature on reading and its implications for reading instruction: Reports of the subgroups*. Bethesda, MD: National Institute of Child and Human Development.

Nist, S. L. and Olejnik, S. (1995). The role of context and dictionary definitions on varying levels of word knowledge. *Reading Research Quarterly*, 30(2), 172–193.

Ogden, C. K. (1934). *The System of Basic English*. New York: Harcourt, Brace.

Ordóñez, C. L., Carlo, M. S., Snow, C. E. and McLaughlin, B. (2002). Depth and breadth of vocabulary in two languages: which vocabulary skills transfer? *Journal of Educational Psychology*, 94(4), 719–728.

Oxford Advanced Learner's Dictionary (8th ed.) (2012). Oxford: Oxford University Press.

Oxford Bookworms Library (2011). Oxford: Oxford University Press.

Pawley, A. and Syder, F. H. (1983). Two puzzles for linguistic theory: nativelike selection and nativelike fluency. In J. C. Richards and R. W. Schmidt (eds.), *Language and Communication* (pp. 191–225). London: Longman.

Quizlet (2011). Quizlet.com. Quizlet LLC.

Raskin, E. (1978). *The Westing Game*. New York: Viking Penguin.

Ravin, Y. and Leacock, C. (2000). Polysemy: an overview. In Y. Raven and C. Leacock (eds.), *Polysemy: Theoretical and computational approaches* (pp. 1–29). Oxford: Oxford University Press.

Read, J. (2000). *Assessing Vocabulary*. Cambridge: Cambridge University Press.

Read, J. (2004). Plumbing the depths: how should the construct of vocabulary knowledge be defined? In P. Bogaards and B. Laufer (eds.), *Vocabulary in a Second Language: Selection, acquisition, and testing* (pp. 209–227). Amsterdam: John Benjamins.

Richards, J. C. (1974). Word lists: problems and prospects. *RELC Journal*, 5(2), 69–84.

Richards, J. C., Platt, J., and Platt, H. (1992). *Longman Dictionary of Language Teaching and Applied Linguistics* (2nd ed.). Harlow: Longman Group UK Limited.

Ride, S. and Okie, S. (1986). *To Space and Back*. Orlando, FL: Harcourt Brace.

Sanacore, J. and Palumbo, A. (2009). Understanding the fourth-grade slump: our point of view. *The Educational Forum*, 73, 67–74.

Schoonen, R., Hulstijn, J., and Bossers, B. (1998). Metacognitive and language-specific knowledge of native and foreign language reading comprehension: an empirical study among Dutch students in grades 6, 8, and 10. *Language Learning*, 48, 71–106.

Sinclair, J. (1987). Collocation: a progress report. In R. Steele and T. Threadgold (eds.), *Language Topics: An international collection of papers by colleagues, students and admirers of Professor Michael Halliday to honour him on his retirement*. Vol. II: (pp. 319–331). Amsterdam: John Benjamins.

Sinclair, J. (1991). *Corpus, Concordance, Collocation*. Oxford: Oxford University Press.

Sinclair, J. (2004a). *Trust the Text: Language, corpus and discourse*. London: Routledge.

Sinclair, J. (ed.). (2004b). *How to Use Corpora in Language Teaching*. Amsterdam: John Benjamins.

Snow, C. E. and Kim, Y. (2007). Large problem spaces: the challenge of vocabulary for English language learners. In R. Wagner, A. E. Muse, and K. R. Tannenbaum (eds.), *Vocabulary Acquisition: Implications for reading comprehension* (pp. 123–139). New York: The Guilford Press.

Stahl, S. A. (2005). Four problems with teaching word meanings: and what to do to make vocabulary an integral part of instruction. In E. H. Heibert and M. L. Kamil (eds.), *Teaching and Learning Vocabulary: Bringing research to practice* (pp. 95–114). Mahwah, NJ: Lawrence Erlbaum Associates.

Stahl, S. A. and Nagy, W. (2006). *Teaching Word Meanings*. Mahwah, NJ: Erlbaum.

Stanovich, K. (2000). *Progress in Understanding Reading: Scientific foundations and new frontiers.* New York: The Guilford Press.

Stoller, F. L. and Grabe, W. (1997). A six-T's approach to content-based instruction. In M. A. Snow and D. M. Brinton (eds.), *The Content-Based Classroom: Perspectives on integrating language and content* (pp. 78–94). White Plains, NY: Addison Wesley Longman.

Stubbs, M. (2002). *Words and Phrases: Corpus studies of lexical semantics.* Oxford: Blackwell Publishing.

Swales, J. (1990). *Genre Analysis.* Cambridge: Cambridge University Press.

The American Heritage School Dictionary. (1977). Boston, MA: Houghton Mifflin Company.

Townsend, D. and Collins, P. (2009). Academic vocabulary and middle school English learners: An intervention study. *Reading and Writing*, 22(9), 993–1019.

Townsend, D., Filippini, A., Collins, P. and Biancarosa, G. (2012). Evidence for the importance of academic word knowledge for the academic achievement of diverse middle school students. *The Elementary School Journal*, 112(3), 497–518.

Verhoeven, L. (2000). Components of early second language reading and spelling. *Scientific Studies of Reading*, 4, 313–330.

Vermeer, A. (2001). Breadth and depth of vocabulary in relation to L1/L2 acquisition and frequency of input. *Applied Psycholinguistics*, 22, 217–234.

Voight, C. (1991). *The Vandemark Mummy.* New York: Fawcett Juniper.

Webster's New Elementary Dictionary. (1970). New York: American Book Company.

Wesche, M. and Paribakht, T. M. (1996). Assessing vocabulary: depth and breadth. *Canadian Modern Language Review*, 53, 13–40.

West, M. (1953). *A General Service List of English Words.* London: Longman, Green.

Wilcox, C. (1993). *Mummies and Their Mysteries.* Minneapolis, MN: Carolrhoda Books.

Wilder, L. I. (1971). *Little House on the Prairie* (rev. ed.). New York: Harper and Row.

WordNet (2010). Princeton University electronic lexical database (Version 3.0). Retrieved September 16, 2010, from http://wordnetweb.princeton.edu.

Zimmerman, C. B. (1997). Do reading and interactive vocabulary instruction make a difference? An empirical study. *TESOL Quarterly*, 31(1), 121–140.

Zimmerman, C. B. (2009). *Word Knowledge: A vocabulary teacher's handbook.* Oxford: Oxford University Press.

Index